Cover Your <u>Ass</u>ets

AND

Become Your Own Liability

Self-Serving Destroys From Within!

Gene N. Landrum, PhD

New York

Cover Your Assets & Become Your Own Liability
Self-Serving Destorys From Within

Softcover ISBN: 978-1-60037-657-3
Hardcover ISBN: 978-1-60037-658-0
Library of Congress Control Number: 2009929150

MORGAN · JAMES
THE ENTREPRENEURIAL PUBLISHER

Morgan James Publishing, LLC
1225 Franklin Ave., STE 325
Garden City, NY 11530-1693
Toll Free 800-485-4943
www.MorganJamesPublishing.com

In an effort to support local communities, raise awareness and funds, Morgan James Publishing donates one percent of all book sales for the life of each book to Habitat for Humanity. Get involved today, visit **www.HelpHabitatForHumanity.org.**

America has a C.Y.A. Affliction

How did America lose the consumer electronics industry?
Easy!
Hired-Hands didn't have the guts to bet Today on Tomorrow.

Visionaries do have the guts. Why? They aren't afflicted with the deadly mind malady called the "Hired-Hand Syndrome"--a *Take Care of Me Now* mindset.

Instant-Gratification is a Fatal Disease of the head and the heart for those with the Hired-Hand Syndrome.

What do these esoteric words mean?

America landed on the moon while Japan landed in American living rooms.

In 1960, America produced approximately 90% of the world's consumer electronics. By 2000, their share had dropped to under 10%. What happened? One nation focused on protecting what they had and self-serving short-term agendas. The other focused on long-term market share. Moral? We get what we focus on! Those with *take care of me now* mentalities are doomed to failure. Sacrifice today for tomorrow and there is no tomorrow.

By sacrificing the present for the future, you set yourself up for success, not failure. Self-serving American industrialists are seldom so inclined--they place quarterly bonuses and job security ahead of their people and their products. That has proven a death-knell for both jobs and profits. It ensured they would not have a piece of that particular future.

C.Y.A. delves deeply into the subtleties of how this happened. It is a Greek tragedy about the psycho-dynamics of two cultures--one protecting what they had, and the other willing to sacrifice to get what the other left unprotected.

What would you be if you didn't know what you are?

To Transform, go within, as you are the master of your DESTINY!

Table of Contents

Dedicated To:

My new granddaughter Sadie Grace;
a girl that will hopefully grow up in a world
no longer in mortal fear of being different
and thus capable of altering personal paradigms!

Acknowledgements

To Hodges University for granting me the opportunity to research my work within the confines of their student base and my fellow professors to find some epistemological solace in why America can be so incredibly innovative and so miserably naïve of today's shrinking world order.

Chapter 1

A CYA Game – What Makes You, Can Break You

Transformation correlates well with mental states – good and bad.

"Innovation is the most important factor in determining a company's success in the 21st Century."
U.S. Council on Competitiveness

"Managers who work in stable environments tend to be Adaptive; those that work in turbulent environments tend to be innovative."
Michael Kirton, psychologist on Innovation Inventory

Covering your backside has been endemic in society for many millenniums. It becomes most dangerous when you are on top of an organization and attempting to keep your job. Not rocking the boat can be safe but is surely not innovative. Such a scenario is enacted daily in executive suites throughout the world. Few ever think that becoming great can prove to be your undoing. The truth is you are "either part of the solution or part of the problem." If replaced by a machine, the resilient do not whine. The resilient learn to sell those machines, program them or service them. Their counterparts who believe the *Sky is Falling* become victims of their own pessimism. Few people realize that what makes you is what can break you and ironically what breaks you can actually make you. An example of this is that those with the skill to talk their way through tough doors often talk their way right back out. This is what this book is about – leaders trying to protect what they have and their decisions to do costing America millions of jobs and trillions of dollars.

Negative news, catastrophes, and tsunamis sell papers and increase viewership. The media loves crisis as it helps them sell their wares. It is a muckraking epidemic in the news media that screams foul when we lose a job to some other nation or political pundits pontificating on bringing lost jobs back. Those that buy-in are naïve and often become victims of the media apocalyptic spin. Sell fast before the typhoon or earthquake hits! This was never more evident than the nuclear scares after World War II. Thousands actually built underground refuges to retreat from the coming nuclear holocaust. In many respects, the most dangerous are those predicting a coming Armageddon. We become victims of such reporting. Those worried over losing their jobs cower and become "yes" men. If you think things will get worse, they do! The media has found that muckraking works for them. Unfortunately, they leave an insipid residue in their wake. Sounds trite, but everyone's reality ultimately is nothing but a function of their perceived reality. Buy into a media dooms-day mania and you will recoil, cut back, or do what GM did in the fall of 2008. They cancelled Tiger Woods's Buick promotional deal to save money despite the fact Buick was #1 in China for no other reason than "Tiger mania."

Freud told us, "Neuroses is the inability to tolerate ambiguity." The future is ambiguous - at best. When you bet everything on right now, you often forfeit future potential. That is why America lost all mass consumer markets to the East. We learned to play the game to the CYA tunes and instant-gratification chorus, and sure enough, it is breaking us. Since what breaks us can make us it is important to get the subtleties of this since it is your very strengths that may well become your Achilles Heal. It is what happened when America lost the mass consumer markets to Asia. What had made her the #1 purveyor of mass consumer products in the world was a dynamic spirit. What cost her that honor was going into other dynamic ventures and leaving the less provocative production part to others. They should have continuing dancing with the damsel that had taken her to the party.

Firms or nations that go into a protective mode lose site of what brought them success. As they build assets they start wanting to protect those assets instead of using them to build new ones. There are a myriad of stories of firms like AT&T and Kodak that opted to stay with their cash cows and that very strategy came back to haunt them. The damsel that had made them came back to bury them. It is a fact of life that firms and people spend more time trying to keep their assets safe when they have lots of them. As they age they do the same. Young tigers don't mess with lawyers. It is the older ones with something to lose that retain lawyers. As we age we do the same. There isn't as much time to make the bucks again so we opt for protecting our nest eggs. My research shows this is only true of the CYA types and not the rugged individualists or entrepreneurs. Men like Rupert Murdoch at age eight are still betting their fortunes every month.

Those that bet everything on the short-term, you have little upside in the long. In the beginning, America chased new opportunities with unfettered verve and passion. She lived on the edge and went faster and further than most nations dared go. America was willing to be different and go where the meek feared – an intrepid warrior on the path to nirvana. But as the title states: *What makes us can also break us.* Live by the quarterly report and you will perish by the quarterly report. It is coming to fruition. Most people have become so mired in protecting the past they don't have a viable future. After the dot.com debacle, the nation's legal beagles passed SOX, an SEC law to protect stockholders of public companies. Instead of protection, it became an inhibiting agent that made firms even more afraid to venture into unknown waters to compete in a multi-national world.

Principle of Comparative Advantage Prevails

Life is subject to limits. Short men should not be looking for a career in the NBA just as shore women are not likely to excel in modeling. And France should not be trying to export commodities. That is the way of the world. Comparative advantage is a principle that says no one is good at everything. All nations must abide by this principle if they are to remain competitive Those that bitch about bringing jobs back to America that are no longer in demand, or are no longer viable are lost in the past. For America to be building low cost, labor intensive Christmas tree ornaments is not smart. Darwinian economics prevails in a dynamic world. There are products that Indian and China should produce due to high labor content or for other production criteria. There are many arenas in which America once excelled but no longer have an edge so they should not being competing in these arenas. Political pundits like to recall the good 'ol days. But when it's over it's over. We move forward or move backward. That is the nature of a capricious world. If India is more efficient at writing computer code, they should be doing it and export their output to America. If China is better at making computer cables they should be exporting those products to America. This scenario tells us that American jobs are a direct function of their value in terms of worldwide supply and demand.

Looking at key economic factors China has a real edge over America from a long-term perspective. It appears she will pass America in GDP or GNP by 2020. The reason is that China has far more human resources, significantly more natural resources and the Bell Curve intelligence data shows Asians scoring an average of between 2% - 10% higher intelligence scores on standardized tests than Americans. All Asians are far more adept at math and science and their dietary habits leave them with far more energy than the typical American. With all of these factors working in their favor their plodding style and other negatives will not keep them down for very long.

President Obama told the press in 2009, "I know that the Japanese can design an affordable, well-designed hybrid, then doggone it the American people should be able to do the same." But the reality is that no individual or nation excels at everything. Comparative advantage says that each nation should opt for those arenas in which they excel and let others do what they do best. One nation buys what the other produces most efficiently and vice versa. This is not rocket science. One nation should export what they do well and import what they do not do well. Saying America should be producing cars when they are not as proficient at doing so is what I label mental masturbation.

Budgets as Bibles & Quarterly Report Disease

The Quarterly Report discloses the results of the previous quarter. They are important for executives to look good and increase stock prices. For some it becomes so important they "cook the books" – ala Enron who became so creative they capitalizing expenses. Budgets often become bibles for those trying to keep the troops in line. The irony is that when you do that you walk away from deals that could double sales or triple profits, but such is the price for controlling the herd. Akio Morita, the founder of Sony was interviewed by the *Wall Street Journal* on what he would do if he were made a Czar of America. Akio said, "The very first thing I would do is outlaw the Quarterly Report." Wow! The travesty is that he was not an American politician but a foreigner who loved America. Those from other places often have more lucid insight into what is transpiring than those in charge. It is why they put press boxes above the field of play in sports. Up there the vision is unobstructed and you have a holistic view of what is transpiring below. What did Morita see that the natives did not? American management was self-destructing by self-serving actions. The quarterly reports were motivating short-term decision-making to the detriment of long-term opportunities. Next year's products and profits were being sacrificed by a need to look good. The entrepreneur from Japan was right on the money.

Leaders have long been enamored with budgets as a means of controlling those under their command. They use them to insure some maverick doesn't do something inane. Guess what? The opposite often occurs. Anyone who has ever sold the GSA or other governmental agencies has witnessed some real bad decision-making. At the end of the budget year this author once received a $1 million order for a product they didn't need but bought them to use up the budget monies to insure their next year's budget didn't get cut by $1 million. Ugh? I wonder how many billions are wasted each year due to such decisions. This CYA or take care of me now mentality is a long-term disaster occurring to insure some short-term gratification.

The sad story here is that America pioneered in many different arenas and wasn't willing to do what it took to keep them as cash cows for their own benefit. America invented silicon chips and memoires along with transistors, TV, stereos, and printers. They are now made in other nations, most in the Far East. Others saw the benefit of taking the products and concepts and commercializing them or commoditizing them. American leaders were far more enamored with protecting today's profits than chasing tomorrow's opportunities. An example is AT&T's invention of the transistor and use of the vacuum tubes as cash cows. They didn't dare jeopardize their own profit centers so licensed them to others to make sure they looked good in order to keep their jobs and keep the stock price intact. American leaders weren't astute enough or didn't' care enough about the future. For them, keeping the quarterly earnings intact was most important.

Hired-Hands – Self-Serving to a Fault

Most of us have experienced being a Hired-Hand so it isn't antithetic to eminence. Entrepreneurs like Bill Gates, Larry Ellison and Steve Jobs once worked for others and soon learned they were not cut out to play the 'yes men' game. They split early to do their own thing. Those that learn to play the surety game become mired in such a mentality, often not even realizing they are playing the fear game to remain intact. After some time the CYA mentality becomes so ingrained those that make it play the game with great penance. The game has become synonymous with playing the executive in America. Many of the factors endemic to the affliction are shown below – the reason America's biggest firms seldom develop new innovative products. This game of corporate hired-hands versus the gung-ho entrepreneurial mentality was seen in the Sun Systems acquisition by Oracle in April of 2009. IBM had the deal sewn up until the hired-hands got cute and played the waiting game. Larry Ellison - founder and CEO of Oracle - walked in the door as IBM walked out leaving Larry to cut a deal for $7.3 billion. The suits at Big Blue were fighting with a guy who flies sorties in simulated jet fighters over the Pacific Ocean with his son. The fight with Big Blue was child's play in contrast. Larry played the "run and gun" game while his adversary played the "today" game where prudence is godly. The underlying reasons America's largest never bring radical new products to market are:

1. **Arrogance & Narcissism** – Ever worked for someone so arrogant they know it all and will never willingly admit of ignorance in a given area? Many times! They are the problem and interfere with the solution as we will see in a later chapter on whey planes crash only when the Captain is at the controls and never is when the least experienced in charge. The same thing happens in business with CEO's who are too haughty to admit they don't know and need help. Many leaders get that top job, and then stay in their inner sanctum office, suddenly above being able to hang with those in the trenches. Entrepreneurs are seldom guilty of such mental myopia, as was shown by the words of Kyocera Founder Kazuo Inamori who told *The Wall Street Journal* (April 20, 2009 p. 5B), "Top executives should manage their companies by earning reasonable profits through modesty, not arrogance." This simple quality seems to be lost on those seated in the ivory tower. Men like John

of Merrill-Lynch, who took government bailout monies in 2009 and put $1.2 million in his corner office.

2. **NIH – Not Invented Here Syndrome** – It is true that about 95% of all decisions by most executives are self-serving first. Those so inclined are not just in the trenches or at the bottom, but they are also found in those corner offices. If it is not in their best interest, it isn't going to be implemented. That is an absolute. That is why the NIH factor needs to be put out to pasture along with those that live in its wake. When the Eiffel Tower icon was built in 1889 the leaders in Paris tried to get it canceled saying, "The Eiffel Tower is without a doubt the dishonor of Paris. It is an odious column of bolted metal." Arthur C. Clark had laws on such self-serving, with law #1 saying, *"When a distinguished but elderly scientist states that something is possible, he is almost certainly right. When he states that something is impossible, he is very probably wrong."*

3. **MBA Myopia** – MBA's are implored to "just to it by the numbers." They are trained to become good at analysis but that often becomes analysis-paralysis. We have all heard those in power say, "You can't do it; it's not in the budget." When you hear those words run for cover. You are working for an ill-advised bumpkin from the old-school. What if you could triple sales or double profits? Then to hell with the budget! It's a tool - often a good tool - but only a tool, and not sacrosanct. Validity comes from Sony. Between 1955 and 1982 Sony launched 12 breakthrough innovations including the transistor radio (1955), 12" TV (1959), Walkman (1979), and 3.5" disk drives (1981). In 1981 the innovative founder, Akio Morita retired to politics. In the next 19 years, the firm introduced no new breakthrough products. What happened? They brought in numbers-crunching MBA's who refined but did not innovate.

4. **Quarterly Report Disease Permeates Corporate America** – When a whole organization is driven to make each quarter profitable at any cost, it is deadly. Why? The quarterly report is sacrosanct for those attempting to ensure stock price stability. And for many middle-executives, it ensures their personal quarterly bonuses. When Akio Morita recommended outlawing the Quarterly Report, some people should have listened since he saw the short-term motivation it had created within the ranks of the power elite. Self-serving pervades all positions, including the very top of any organization. Studies show that when an executive tells an employee "No" three times, they stop asking. After ten times, they are merely staying until they can afford to leave. To have viable futures, organizations must stop betting everything on the present.

5. **Short-Term Instant-Gratification - the Bane of Innovation** – Bureaucrats have a penchant for sacrificing tomorrow for today. It helps make them look good in the short term but without regard for the future. Their self-serving instant-gratification mentality is destructive in the long run but they are lost in short-term survival mode. Peter Senge spoke of his in *The Fifth Discipline* saying, "Seeing the forest as well as the trees is a fundamental problem that plagues all firms." But no one hit the nail as squarely as Albert Einstein - a numbers guy - who wrote, "If at first the idea is not absurd, there is no hope for it." During the 2009 financial debacle, *The Wall Street Journal* (Feb. 26, 2009) wrote, "Short-term thinking has become endemic to business and investment and has posed a grave threat to the U.S. economy." They spoke of American business leaders becoming focused on stock prices rather than the productivity labeling it "financial engineering." They said, "Institutional and individual investors have become preoccupied with quarterly earnings forecasts and short-term share price changes." Maximizing share-holder value was their mantra to the detriment of long-term success.

6. **Risk & Leadership are not Synonymous** – Those afraid to push the limits or push the window of opportunity are unlikely to ever alter paradigms. To have launched Amozon.com Jeff Bezos had to quit a $1 million a year job. How many hired hands are so inclined? Try almost none. Don't rock the boat is an anthem played under the radar at most firms. It is their death-knell. Jonas Salk - the polio maven - said, "Risk always pay off. No matter how they work out, they either teach you what to do or what not to do." Oscar Wilde had a way with words and waxed eloquent when he wrote, "An idea that is not dangerous is unworthy of being called an idea." Touché! In March of 2009, one share of "New York Times" stock sold for less than the Sunday paper. Not good!

Organizational cultures tend to see the world through a similar filter and thus make concepts like those listed above into a ritualistic system. Not many executives or worker bees have the temerity to oppose such rules or systems of shared meaning. They don their instinct hat and thus become the mother of originality whereas the traditionalists keep on marching to that surety drum of 'don't rock the boat.' These fathers of change tend to be intrepid warriors. The most famous example is Bill Gore. This maverick entrepreneur quit Dupont to start Gore-Tex, where he eliminated job titles, budgets, organization charts, policies, and procedures. Gore-Tex has become one of the most successful firms ever. In *Organizational Behavior* (2009), Stephen Robbins had a list of those things that "captured the essence of an organization's culture," and it is a testimonial to the Gore-Tex way: "*Innovation and risk taking* – the degree to which employees are encouraged to be innovative and take risks."

What We Know Can Prove Lethal

What we "*know*" can often be as bad as what we "*don't know*." It's okay to not know but it is not okay to not know and not care. Bill Joy, the Silicon Valley techie known as the Edison of the Internet was of such a persuasion. As a child Bill "wanted to know everything about everything way before he should've even known he wanted to know," wrote Gladwell. The eminent in the world have been far more inquisitive than the also-rans. Few people are aware that their greatest strength is also their greatest weakness and vice versa. Ever known someone so adept at talking their way through closed doors that they then talk their way right back out? Fear is often the fuel for their failure. When people lose their job, many take it as a personal rejection. These types look for some magic potion. They opt for drugs or start drinking. Fear can debilitate and it can motivate. What is the variable? The mind! The head contains useful mantras, and it also contains some contaminants. Many mental viruses were placed there years ago by well-meaning people – many of whom know too much for their own good. Listening to so-called experts is often the Achilles Heal to success. As I've written often, "An expert has such a psychological investment in what *is* they cannot see *what might be.*" This was never truer than in a New Zealand "Bad Writing Contest" in which the following was written:

The "Bad Writing Contest" had three English professors taking the top three places for bad writing. The winner - or was he the loser? - was Frederic Jameson, a professor of Comparative Literature at Duke University for his work, <u>Signatures of the Visible</u> (1997).

Why is this so often true? English professors know so much they have a propensity to let their prescient knowledge interfere with their ability to inform or entertain. Perfectionists are wired with what has been labeled a "Fixed Mindset." These types tend to be Concrete-Sequential Learners - people so enamored with "correct" they are seldom "creative." Not so for neophyte writers who tend to be "abstract" learners. One example is the queen of romance, Danielle Steel. This pragmatist understands the fantasy needs of her female fans. She never quite made it out of high school, and once admitted to a biographer that she didn't know the difference between a comma and a colon. But she knows a lot about how to take her fans beyond the real and through passionate invective into exotic places. Danielle Steel's ability to titillate lonely females has led to the sale of a half a billion books and many movies, and has left this dynamic fiction writer with a personal net worth of $300 million.

Breakdown - A Path to Breakthrough

No matter what we do to prevent it, or how good we are, bad stuff happens! That is the nature of the world. Those afflicted with problems need to stop fretting and adopt a *cest la vie* attitude. Armed with a free mind in the midst of chaos is what separates the eminent from the pack. The Russian biologist Ilya Prigogine won the Nobel Prize for validating that breakdown leads inextricably to breakthrough. Prigogine found the 2nd Law of Thermodynamics far too nihilistic in that it says, "all things end in a heat death." So he concocted a theory that proves that is not necessarily true. The American futurist Ray Kurzweil concocted a *Law of Increasing Entropy (1999)* that agreed with Prigogine. He wrote, "The order of life takes place amid great chaos." But Prigogine told us, "Many systems of breakdown are actually harbingers of breakthrough." In his validation of this principle, he wrote, "Psychological suffering, anxiety, and collapse lead to new emotional, intellectual, and spiritual strengths, confusion and death can lead to new scientific ideas" (Dr. Ilya Prigogine 1984 – "Order out of Chaos").

What does this have to do with recessions and losing a job? A lot! The past is prologue. In this author's dissertation, *The Innovator Personality* (1991), virtually every eminent individual had encountered a major life-threatening crisis prior to emerging on top. One such individual was Sol Price. Sol was fired from his merchandising CEO job at age sixty. While walking the streets of San Diego, he discovered a problem of inefficiency in small-retailer distribution. He asked the small retailers if they would opt for a drive outside town to buy their wares at lower prices but pay cash and do so in a concrete floor warehouse. They love the idea leading Sol to open the very first wholesale warehouse venture to serve as middleman to small retailers. In ten years his brilliant idea led to fame and fortune. Sol's prescient idea for eliminating the middleman in the distribution business would become what is now known as Costco and Sam's Club. Sam Walton once admitted to the media, "I've learned more from Sol Price than anyone else in the discounting business." Within ten years of launching his new idea, Sol was a billionaire. The moral learned? Had Sol not been fired, it wouldn't have happened.

A similar Horatio Alger story comes from Frank Lloyd Wright. As a young man, Wright was terminated from Chicago's largest architectural firm for moonlighting. Not deterred, he opened his own office down the street and would become one of the world's more revered architects. Walt Disney was fired as a cartoonist, his idyllic job, from a Kansas City daily newspaper. Not much later he filed for bankruptcy on his fledgling cartoon business. That debacle led Walt to Hollywood. As they say, *the rest is history*. An even more enlightening example of hitting bottom to find the top comes from the life of Buckminster Fuller. Bucky was in his twenties when his daughter died. Being an often absent father, he blamed himself. Not long after, he was fired from his job by his father-in-law. Then his mother told him he was a loser. It was more than he could handle, so he walked to the shores of Lake Michigan, intent on ending his life. Sitting on the edge of the frigid waters of Lake Michigan, Bucky began looking at his failed life. It inspired him when he saw that it wasn't him, it was them. The debacle led to an epiphany. Bucky would later write in *Critical Path*, "You do not have the right to eliminate yourself; you do not belong to you; you belong to the universe." Those were profound words by a man at his wit's end and contemplating ending his life. Bucky spent the next two years as a mute. He stormed home and told his long-suffering wife that he would not speak to her or any other human being for two years. Out of that stark world of meditative reflection emerged a transformed man of such introspective insights that he was arguably one of the most important innovators of the 20th century. Bucky left us with many great inventions, nearly 1,000 patents, and the world's domed stadiums. All this took place despite little formal education in the arenas of his greatest contributions. Bucky's theory labeled the *"tetrahedron"* is the building block of optimum strength. This triangulation formulates the genesis of the geodesic domes that now grace the world's sports stadiums. It now adorns the entrance to Epcot. It is but one of Fuller's many contributions to the world, and it would not have happened had he not been fired. Later he would tell the world, "Everyone is born a genius, but the process of living de-geniuses them."

The problem was Buckminster Fuller was a visionary, and due to innovative thinking – global orientation versus a short-term local orientation - he operated way out of the so-called box – that place where most traditionalists remain mired for eternity. Bucky had always been out of lockstep with traditionalists and a non-visionary society. It is a problem that afflicts all those in the world that dare see the big picture. They are questioned, ridiculed, and often despised by the traditionalist intent on keeping everything the same. The instant-gratification world prefers the safe to the possibilities. They will always opt for what is known rather than that which is labeled "opportunity." *Now* is pervasive in any competitive or capitalistic society, other than what is prevalent in places like Japan that have a culture of egalitarianism – teamwork of mutual rewards and lifetime employment. Bucky was quite introspective. It was apparent when he wrote, "Most of my advances were by mistake. You uncover what *is* when you get rid of what *isn't*. That was profound.

Mind Viruses Contaminate

Harvard's Howard Gardner - the father of the multiple personalities - also believes that the behavior within is the driving force of what we are and what we become. Gardner wrote, "Highly creative people are more likely to stand out in terms of personality rather than sheer intellectual power. They differ from their peers in *ambition, self-confidence,* and *passion about their work.*" (Gardner 1998). That is why my research has shown that visionaries look for reasons to chase new opportunities and traditionalists get mired in the safe old ways. Visionaries search for reasons to do the new while traditionalist are locked into a need to not change. To this end, psychology has discovered that "Happiness is not in acquiring things or hitting the lotto. It is closely tied to personality – attitude and lifestyle." ("Scientific American Mind," March 2007).

Most people so identify with their jobs that they go into shock or play the tranquilizer game when they hit bottom. Identifying with a job is not good since the job or firm does not identify with you. Identify with something worthwhile, like becoming self-employed, becoming a talk-show host, an inventor, or a world traveler. Why is this mental dialogue and philosophical repartee so important? We are all in need of mental reprogramming! We all walk around with past mental messages – unconscious imprints - put there by well-meaning parents, teachers, preachers, who were trying to keep us safe. Well, safe is not correlated at all with success. In fact, it correlates well with mediocrity. Psychology has told us for years that 95% of our decisions are unconscious. Those inner ideas of what we think of as *right* are what led to the New Coke debacle. We think our decisions are valid, but many studies show they are invalid. Gerald Zaltman of Harvard studied the cause of the New Coke fiasco that cost the company hundreds of millions. Zaltman discovered that people don't know why they like or dislike products:

> *"People can't tell you what they think because they don't know. Their deepest thoughts, the ones that account for their behavior in the marketplace, are unconscious."* - ZMET Harvard study by Zaltman

This same kind of miss-thinking occurs to us all. A parent tells their child, "Don't talk to strangers, honey." When you are twenty-eight and trying to launch a new business or find a new job, or opting for a new career, you had better be talking to a lot of strangers. I've heard mothers preach, "Just be normal, honey." Well, in the big picture, normal is but a synonym for inhibiting behavior. Dump the mental baggage of the past. Fill your brain with positive, new axioms. If you are thinking backward, you can't be thinking forward. New brain research shows that we can now alter how we think. Much of this pioneering work was done by University of California psychologist, Michael Merzenich, who wrote, "In order to keep the brain fit we must learn something new rather than simply replaying already-mastered skills. It causes the brain to grow and expand, while the obsessive ruts make us old before our time." In *Strangers to Ourselves* (2002), author Wilson wrote, "Our greatest illusion is to believe that we are what we think ourselves to be." Contrary to centuries of thinking, the brain is not hard-wired. It is highly malleable like a muscle. So just sit down and decide what you really want to do with the rest of your life and let nothing or nobody interfere with the trip. My anthem is, 'What would you be if you didn't know what you were.' Most of us are too grounded in what we know we are.

What Makes Us *Strong*, Makes Us *Weak*

Homer saw the truth in all this some 2,500 years ago. In his work, he depicted Prometheus as the Titan that brought light to mankind as the maestro of innovation. In Greek lore, Prometheus was a defiant visionary who chose to ignore his boss, Zeus, to seek out new opportunities. Just as it would be in today's world, that behavior got him into big trouble. Zeus would have him chained to a rock where his liver was torn asunder by birds of prey. It is no accident that psychologists have labeled the world's *Intuitive-Thinking* personality types as Prometheans. The name is now a metaphor for those who see the world globally and deal with their vision rationally. It is such individuals that have won the Nobel Prizes, Pulitzers and altered paradigms. Leonardo da Vinci was such a person as are those titans at the top of every discipline. Such individuals are defiant enough to ignore what the pack is doing to create new ways. They see the big picture and deal with their vision in a very rational manner.

In psychology, these individuals are labeled "change-masters." They represent a very small portion of any given cohort – typically less than ten percent. Writes have labeled Prometheus the "Forethought God – wisest of all the Titans." They dominate architecture and invention such as Frank Lloyd Wright and Thomas Edison. They are known as "architects of change," and it is in change that they thrive in contrast to the so-called normal population. The things that define them are typically:

✓ **They are highly inquisitive;**
✓ **analytical visionaries of the first order;**
✓ **always chase life's possibilities no matter the risk;**
✓ **have a global vision and don't suffer the little stuff or details;**
✓ **try new things to sate some raging inner passion to the chagrin of mates;**
✓ **and Master Builder Types who love to build new castles in the sky but seldom move in**

Such individuals have been labeled Prometheans by psychologies, people with a large picture view of things and the ability to deal with what they see very rationally. Prometheans are very different. They tend to be change masters chasing life's possibilities. They are ardently inquisitive and love to seek knowledge in all venues. They are often in places they are unfamiliar with but never lost. Such individuals appear to have been programmed with a temperament willing to ignore societal rules and to pursue a personal sense of adventure. They are imaginative and prone to be frivolously wild, according to psychologists. It is interesting that the Promethean female tends to refuse liaisons with inferior males while their male counterparts are prone to highly promiscuous behavior. There are a myriad of lurid examples from Howard Hughes infamous Hollywood trysts to Bill Clinton's liaisons.

When bad stuff happens, Prometheans tend to deal with it philosophically. Most understand that business is a game with the money the way to keep score. Winning and losing is part of the puzzle, and they write off losses as a philosophical action or some accident of fate. Crawling into a bottle or going into a self-deprecating tantrum is never a viable solution for the Promethean temperament. Prometheans are indoctrinated early to become masters of their fate. They are prone to see problems as temporary roadblocks that must be dealt with on the trek to the top. They have a very philosophical bent - change-masters trying to build new castles in the sky but often don't want to move in once they are built. Michelangelo was such a personality saying, "The greatest danger for most of us is not that our aim is too high and we miss it, but that it is too low and we reach it." This is so true. If your job is replaced by robots, you need to learn to fix those robots or move on to another arena that could be better than the one you just left. That is lost on the CYA's. They tend to be lost in their own reverie of sure and safe. Prometheans are of the opposite persuasion - willing to fail in order to win.

Be very careful what you do well, it may come back to haunt you. Those able to talk their way through doors due to verbal expertise are often the ones that talk their way right back out those doors. Fear can make us safe but more often than not keeps us from achieving at a high level. Rock star Elvis Presley is an example. Elvis was pathologically shy, so much so he never had a date for his senior prom. When the King of Rock first walked on a Memphis, TN stage to perform his legs were shaking due to fright. During that legendary performance the young girls in the audience were screaming. At the break Elvis asked the producer why they were so charged up. "Your leg is shaking provocatively," he told Elvis, "Don't stop." He didn't and made leg shaking the signature move that led to fame and fortune. America's rise to the pinnacle of power has a similar story. She was willing to tread in dangerous new start-up ventures and go where the more traditional nations would not. It paid huge dividends. When she got to the very top she stopped doing what got her there. Wake up America and start dancing again with dame fortune that brought you to the big dance!

Chapter 2
The POWER Game -
A HIRED-HAND Affliction

Visionaries are not prone to play politics – it is a no-win game.

"Giving money and power to government is like giving whiskey and car keys to teenage boys". – P.J. O'Rourke

"Chinese will soon be the most widely used language on the Internet." Alvin Toffler, *Revolutionary Wealth* (2006)

Mediocrity is a mental disease that I call a *Hired-Hand Syndrome* – a self-serving mind malady. It is called CYA in many organizations where the majority of the staff become 'Yes' men and women rather than do what is the right decision. It is a mental state that can have dire results for any business or political body. Instant-gratification is the culprit a need to sacrifice tomorrow for today. It has become one of the most destructive problems facing firms in the 21st century. It is a 'me game' with deleterious consequences far beyond what the individual perceives. A simplistic version is hiding behind answering machines that make it impossible to ever speak to a real live person at places like the IRS, Social Security or other government agencies. In such instances the person has placed their personal solitude above the best interest of the customer. It is a 'me game' that drives away clients. It is the consummate today versus tomorrow game that has dire consequences.

Self-serving led to using electronics to hide. The victims turn out to be a firm's investors and a government's clients and everyone's grandchildren. It is not questioned by those on top due to what I have labeled as a *Hired-Hand Syndrome*. This was never more apparent than in a study on global competitiveness by the nonpartisan think-tank *Information Technology and Innovation Foundation*. Of the 40 nations in this study, the United States was found to have made the least progress on improving international competitiveness and innovation since the millennium began. China and Singapore ranked #1 and #2 in having made the most progress. This validates why the power game is closely aligned to the *Hired-Hand* games. Ole-time entrepreneurial spirits would never have tolerated such self-serving ineptitude at any level of an organization. Do you think Henry Ford or Thomas Edison would have used their creations to hide from their customer base?

Judith Estrin - author of "Closing the Innovation Gap" and a former chief technology officer at Cisco Systems says the U.S. is reaping the benefits of seeds planted years and decades ago, but has not planted enough seeds to fuel innovation on the road ahead. "We have become increasingly short-sighted with our views about innovation," she said. "We have become more focused on incremental innovation. There's not enough of a focus on breakthrough, disruptive innovation." Touché! Power is a crucial agent for success. Winston Churchill wrote, "If you have ten thousand regulations, you destroy all respect for the law." Such power becomes a means for the power brokers to keep the pack in line with their view of what is right. The laws reduce freedom and become an agent of distress for the self-employed and entrepreneurs trying to fight the good old boy system of control.

Each of us have power, but very few are willing to defy the dudes at the top. Bureaucracy creates its own disciples by refusing to tolerate the renegade who sees the inefficiency and mediocrity of passing inane laws like the Sarbanes-Oxley to keep the bad ones in line. Just because you have the wrong people leading an organization, does not justify passing laws to mediocritize everyone. If you have the wrong horse on the course, change the horse, not the course. An example of the different approach in the East and West could be seen in the depth of the 2009 worldwide recession. John Thain of Merrill-Lynch opted to splurge on a $1.2 million office makeover. AIG's Richard Fuld gave himself a $22 million bonus while the president, Haruka Nishimatsu, of Japan Airlines, could be seen riding to work on the bus, eating in the company cafeteria and cutting his salary to save money.

Pragmatism Prevails in the Innovative Suites

The Japanese have been preeminent practitioners of taking minimal resources and maximizing them to the point they become powerful agents. It can be seen in the rise of the Japanese Yen. It has been the world's #1 currency for many decades. Why? Due to a continuing positive trade balance grounded in their total dominance of the consumer electronics industry. It began with the launch of the world's very first pocket transistor radio by Sony in the 1950s. The inventor of the transistor was a subsidiary of AT&T, Bell Labs. They told Akio Morita that a transistor radio wasn't feasible, but he ignored their sage advice. Within a few years, Sony wiped out the American radio industry. That success soon expanded to all facets of the electronic industry – TV's, stereo systems, and computers. The more other nations spent on Japanese products, the more valuable became the yen. What is intriguing about this scenario is how a small island nation with virtually no natural resources could have pulled off such a coup. The answer is complex. But it isn't so strange when looking at the indomitable will that dominates the Japanese mind that is transfixed with long-term versus short-term mindsets, intensive cost innovation, market share, an economy of scale production, and a will to win that comes armed with a kamikaze spirit. They focused on removing fractions of a penny from one part while America was more focused on short-term dollars. In essence, the Japanese had a very long-term attitude – try 100-year business plans, and a simplistic but impersonal work ethic. That contrasted with the Americans who were short-term oriented and armed with more of a self-serving attitude. They have what I label a "globalized," rather than "localized" vision for producing mass consumer products. America dominated virtually every mass consumer market after World War II exporting as much as 90% percent of all consumer electronics products. That dwindled to less than 10% by the millennium, with only the capital equipment items like heavy duty machinery, tractors, and aircrafts keeping America's production at about 20% of output for the world.

The Japanese showed the West their ability to elevate *will-power* to a kind of sacred or majestic role in the 2nd World War. When all was lost, they opted for what was known as a *kamikaze* approach - *divine wind* – to kill what they couldn't own. That translated into market share and market domination after the war. In World War II, their pilots were sent out on a death flight to destroy invading American warships. The *kamikaze* is a commitment of heart, body, and soul to do whatever it takes to conquer an adversary or a market. Japanese people saw young smiling pilots as they waved goodbye. In contrast, American soldiers viewed death and destruction when the pilots' planes exploded upon crashing into their ships. These very different points of view continue to influence Japanese and American perceptions of kamikaze pilots even today, not unlike the perceptions that differ today in conquering markets. The Japanese people - even today - believe that the brave young pilots suffered tragic deaths in defense of their homeland. The letters, poems, and diaries written by kamikaze pilots have had a significant influence on Japanese people's views. Such a *divine wind* can be seen in their eyes at American trade shows such as the Consumer Electronics Shows and Comdex.

A similar *do or die* mental set is seen in the religious fanaticism of Al-Qaeda today. It is laden in a kind of "no hope" of catching up, so they turn to destroying what they can't control. It is mired in a kind of xenophobia not unlike what happened with the Japanese kamikaze attacks. The 9/11 terrorist attacks on the World Trade Center towers in New York had their genesis in wanting to destroy what they couldn't have. Their rage emanated from what they saw as the West attacking their cultural and religious dogmas. The West had challenged their cherished values, and that made them an enemy worthy of bringing down. The threat came in the form of foreign music, fashion, literature, media, and progressive ideologies. It was seen as a cultural threat to all they valued. This was lost on the Bush administration when they invaded Iraq - a nation that had nothing to do with 9/11 - but it caused a *"fati compli"* cause throughout the Middle East. Washington - in a state of fear and revenge - created a holy World War, the kind that can never be won by either side. When one's cultural values are being attacked or threatened, suicide warfare is not unusual. In fact, it is an expected role by everyone in such a society. When the Al-Qaeda bought those flight tickets to their targets, it was to them a simple substitute for long-range weapons to fight an imperialist nation they did not understand and hated for invading their cultural homeland. Their ideas were deluded, but they had a cultural genesis for a nation with a loss of hope while trying to avenge their cultural values and credos.

In the waning days of World War II, McArthur set up a system known as *keiretsu* - a cartel or clan-like group of firms, suppliers, bankers, and MITI joined together like a fighting clan to dominate an industry or consumer market. Each participant in the clan owns stock in each other's ventures linking them together financially and economically. Instead of saving them, it is what turned out to make them more powerful than they were prior to being devastated by American bombs. The Japanese came equipped with an indomitable spirit. With that, as an intrinsic weapon and the keiretsu system they were unstoppable. Lifetime employment was a cultural nuance that also instilled a one-for-all and all-for-one mentality that led them to have a long-term perspective that is diametrically opposed to the West. In the West, there is a highly transient mentality at work. Studies show that about 80% of individuals do not believe the organization has their best interest at heart. That is not true in the East.

Nietzsche was never more profound when he said, "Power accedes to he who takes it." If you are in the middle of a jungle, it is not the General that has power. It is the Private that knows the way out and has the guts to say to the troops, "Follow me." Such power is often latent. Anthropologists have long known that the largest apes – Darwin's Alpha Males – have first call on food and females. When the beta or lesser male monkeys are beaten by an alpha male, they lose the color that attracts females. When an Alpha Male Walrus beats his adversary, they become impotent. In this animal world, it is proven that when the female is the largest in the pack, they have the power. They are then dominant in that they have first call on both food and mates. A baby that cries in the middle of the night has incredible power. It isn't physical, it's metaphysical. But money is often an incredibly potent source of power. This could be seen in the life of Howard Hughes. When he was in power as the richest man in the world and owner of Trans World Airlines, he always flew media giants Luella Parsons, Hedda Hopper, and Walter Winchell anywhere in the world without paying. Consequently, he owned them while he was alive, and there never was any bad publicity for a man that was a maverick and renegade and one of the world's most ardent womanizers. This was a titan who had learned from his father how to bribe to gain power. Hughes owned a number of Senators and even Presidents. This misogynist who was the richest man in the world never had bad publicity during his entire lifetime. It was after his death that the truth finally came out.

The Hired-Hand Syndrome is a Deadly Disease of the Mind

Hired-Hands are antithetic to little guy power. Why? It is endemic to the Yes Dudes and self-serving that comes with the territory. They tend to make decisions based on what is best - not for the firm or organization - but what is safest for them. Hired-hands do what they are told even when they know it is inane. This is true of governments or Fortune 500 firms. Just look at the 2009 AIG debacle where the head dudes gave themselves millions in bonuses despite the fact the firm was underwater and close to bankruptcy. This is the classic case of self-serving at the expense of all else. The Hired-Hand follows job descriptions to the letter even when they are stupid. And if something isn't on theirs, they refuse to take on that responsibility. Do you think that would ever happen with an owner or an entrepreneur? Never! This is what I have labeled in other works as a "clerk mentality." We have all suffered from this self-serving mindset. You call for help and the clerk says, "That's not my area of responsibility." Such thinking and action originates from how the leader programmed them. They are programmed to just do what they are told and nothing else. Pay for normal and you get normal. Pay for special and you often get special. That seems to be lost on the vast majority of leaders and virtually all bureaucrats. The Hired-Hand has a mental set that tells them that they work here and thus they are just doers - not innovators. They are not the owner, so they don't function like one. It is incumbent on great leaders to program their personnel to be part of the ownership team. That can be done with stock and stock options, but mostly through word-of-mouth. Treat the people like they are partners, not employees, like Sam Walton did at Wal-Mart. Sam told all his managers they were his partner. Consequently, they functioned as that with total autonomy and responsibility beyond the pale of an employee. This is subtle, but it makes a huge difference in how personnel function. When an employee sees themselves as Hired-Hands, they tend to take that middle road that leads to the following:

⚰ **No Bad Deals, thus no exceptional deals;**
⚰ **Self-Serving & CYA Behavior Dominates;**
⚰ **Now-Orientation in lieu of Future-Orientation;**
⚰ **Budgets are Never violated since #'s are sacrosanct;**
⚰ **and Controlled Operating Styles & Loss of Freedom within.**

Empowerment is More Surreal than Real

Empowerment is more metaphysical than grounded reality. It implies that we can rise above our station in life and actually do what we once only dreamed of being able to achieve. Asians - especially those with a Buddhist bent - are far more inclined to elevate above the reality. They use their Zen orientation to transform into a more surreal mode of operating. This is mostly due to their early life where they learn that the Buddha is the God within. This seems to arm them with a formidable power of self-transformation. Buddha means *Awakened One*, thus Buddhism can be taken to mean Awake-ism. It would therefore be natural to think that if you were looking to wake up, you are what Americans know as "having a positive attitude." Zen emphasizes experiential wisdom—particularly as realized in the form of meditation known as *zazen* - an awakening, or more succinctly, the path to enlightenment.

In the West, we have seen an awakening of sorts with brain experiments that show that enriched environments create brighter and more powerful rats for running a maze. Impoverished environments cause the loss of such power. Jonas Salk found, "Brain growth is 15% greater due to enriched environments than in impoverished environments." UCLA's Valerie Hunt in *Infinite Mind* (1996) wrote, "The greatest scientists of all time say their experimentation is guided by mystical, intuitive insights." Hunt went on to say, "When you believe strongly in what you say, people may argue with you, but they rarely ignore you. But when you are insecure about what you are saying, people simply accommodate you by ignoring you." (Hunt p. 186) When pushing the limits of the ordinary, we often find ourselves able to find the extraordinary. Napoleon was so inclined. In his memoirs he wrote, "Power is my mistress." Later, a man striving to gain a similar place in history adopted a similar strategy albeit far more self-serving and Machiavellian. Adolph Hitler wrote in *Mein Kampf,* "Right only exists through power and force." It had emanated from his adoration of Nietzsche's will-to-power thesis. One thing has been found to be true: We can empower others by giving them responsibility and authority. It shows that we respect them enough to allow them to succeed or fail and either is okay as long as they come to grips with the outcome. Charismatic leaders like Gandhi validate this principle. He told his disciples, "We must become the change we want to see." It was also in the lexicon of the world's wealthiest man, Bill Gates who said, "By empowering workers you'll make their jobs far more interesting, and they'll be able to work at a higher level than they would have without all that information just a few clicks away."

The West became lost in the reverie of their power and success. Once they made it to the top, they became a bit complacent and lost much of that which they had conquered. American leaders often refuse to delegate those things that could bury them to others, and consequently, they do not bring a wide range of powers to their defense. There is a strong power-base in Asian cultures, but everyone is more comfortable with subordinates doing what they are told. In Japan, the organization and they are "one," and are treated as such - not as an independent or adversarial body. In America, it is far more "me for me" and "you for you" kind of relationship than in Asia. It sounds counter-intuitive, but it is why in the spring of 2009 IBM sent 5,000 more software jobs to India. Foreign workers accounted for 71% of Big Blue's personnel. That was an increase from 65% three years earlier. What is the underlying motivation? Cut costs to meet the increasing global-perspective of the firm's future.

Power Comes in Various Forms

What is the derivation of power? Is it that of the jungle where the strongest prevails? Or is it those with the most bucks, or those with the power of a title? No! It is not these external powers, but the internal ones that are most important. Power emanating from within is seen in a new born. When a baby cries, everyone jumps. The baby has no muscles, money, or title. They exude power from within. Ram Dass spoke of this quite profoundly in *Be Here & Now,* "As soon as you give it all up you can have it all; as long as you want power, you can't have it. The minute you don't want power you'll have more than you ever dreamed possible." The Dass aphorism was never truer than the power latent in the life and work of Mahatma Gandhi. This man without shoes or a house defied the British power elite. They were bedazzled and befuddled by this little man with no shoes, no following, no money, no title, and no interest in anything material. The Brits were used to bribing or using money to get their way. That was how they got tea shipped from India to England, how they controlled Singapore and kept power in the Bahamas. Every one of their tried and true weapons of power was useless with the Indian maverick. They tried everything including the threat of death, but it didn't work. Brits tried to seduce Gandhi with money, female concubines, imprisonment, and titles. Gandhi met them, shook their hands, and kept on trekking down the dirt roads to his goal of an independent India. When they put him in prison, he went on a hunger strike, willing to die rather than capitulate. It worked! It was beyond anything the British ever had to deal with and it drove them crazy. After years of trying to deal with his form of power, they left India. Gandhi's *Satyagraha* – passive resistance through positive non-violence was the ultimate power for that time and that place.

Machiavelli had a way with words to convey power. In *The Prince* he told us, "It is much more secure to be feared than to be loved." Why is this true? Because people fear those in power more than those they see as lesser beings. That was the power that Napoleon and Hitler saw when they killed a man unremorsefully. The masses were afraid and cowered before them. "Keep acquiring more and more power, all the rest is chimerical," were his words written while in St. Helena. Such mental avarice led to him saying, "If I lose my throne I will bury the world beneath my ruins." He did! "Men are so simple of mind," wrote Machiavelli, "and so much dominated by their immediate needs, that a deceitful man will always find plenty who are ready to be deceived." Abraham Lincoln used far more positive rhetoric saying, "Nearly all men can stand adversity, but if you want to test a man's character, give him power." Touché! As Secretary of State, Henry Kissinger made the front page of the nation's newspapers when he said, "Power is the ultimate aphrodisiac." It drives some people and destroys some. Many like Napoleon and Adolph Hitler went to great lengths to feel powerful.

Remember, no matter how good you get in any endeavor, how many assets you acquire or how powerful you become there is always someone bigger, faster, stronger and with more money and more power. Show up as if you had none of your resources and wherewithal you will be far more inclined to maintain what you have. Most of us become enamored of our station in life and it is our undoing.

Diabolical Political Power Mavens

The Power Game can be a political pawn to gain votes and a constituency. The one thing Machiavelli said about this has proven true for centuries, "Change has no constituency." Today it is a buzzword, but used more to make people feel they will change their lives from needing more to having more. The objective of politicians is often self-gratification. They wrap their agendas to fit their own inner need for power. A 2009 article in *The Wall Street Journal* offers insight into what happens in American politics. This article linked poverty with a political party. The analysis was quite interesting, especially when American cities were ranked by their party affiliations and their degree of poverty. In reading it, my first thought was Einstein's profound aphorism, "The definition of insanity is doing the same thing over and over again and expecting different results."

Top Poverty Rated U.S. Cities are all Democratic
America's Top Ten Poverty Rated Cities

1. Detroit, MI - hasn't elected a Republican mayor since 1961

2. Buffalo, NY – hasn't elected a Republican mayor since 1954

3. Cincinnati, OH – hasn't elected a Republican mayor since 1984

4. Cleveland, OH – hasn't elected a Republican mayor since 1989

5. Miami, FL – has never elected a Republican mayor

6. St. Louis, MO – hasn't elected a Republican mayor since 1949

7. El Paso, TX – has never had a Republican mayor

8. Milwaukee, WI – hasn't elected a Republican mayor since 1908

9. Philadelphia, PA – hasn't elected a Republican mayor since 1952

10. Newark, NJ – hasn't elected a Republican mayor since 1907

The disadvantaged have habitually voted Democrat. Yet they almost always remain disadvantaged. Why? They feel those in power and with a liberal attitude will give them something for free. In the long run, the Democrats or Socialists or Communists will take care of them, so they keep on giving them power so they will take care of them. Ayn Rand must be turning over in her grave.

Government Laws & Their Impact on Growth
In early 2009, with America fighting to survive a Wall Street collapse and recession, *The Wall Street Journal* wrote, "Kill Sarbanes-Oxley or make it voluntary. Right now!" They went on to say:

"Entrepreneurs gave us everything – from Wal-Mart to iPhones, from microprocessors to Twitter. Without entrepreneurs, we will never get out of our current predicament. Entrepreneurs Can Lead Us Out of the Crisis. When the brilliant young companies can once again go public without the prospect of being stuck with a massive, expensive reporting infrastructure, they will do so – creating new wealth, important new corporations and reigniting venture capital investment."

Eric R. Smith (December 16, 2008) wrote in *Real Clear Markets* that "many regulations quickly passed following market crisis have later been determined to be detrimental to the capital markets and operating in those markets." Martin Seligman of the University of Pennsylvania told the Journal in 2007, "Optimists tend to do better in life than their talents alone might suggest, except lawyers." Why is this? Lawyers are trained to keep people safe, to say "no" in order to keep their clients out of court. That is integrally tied in to a very negative mindset. Entrepreneurship is correlated with taking high risks so the legal-beagles trying to say "no" is contra to their mission. In law, pessimism is considered prudence. They try to keep entrepreneurs safe when the nature of launching a new enterprise is not safe. When Mary Kay Ash lost her husband and decided to proceed with her cosmetic launch, her lawyer begged her not to go ahead as it was too dangerous. Good thing she didn't listen. "Nothing is predictable," Peter Drucker told us just prior to his passing, "except that today's profitable business will become tomorrow's white elephant."

Pass a Law – Lose a Freedom
Eons ago the leaders of the pack learned that if you frighten the herd with hell and promise them salvation, they will follow you any-

where, even to strange places. Cultists like Jim Jones and David Koresh learned this axiom well. They used such insidious logic to lead the disenfranchised and weak to strange places that resulted in their deaths. President George W. Bush did the same in his invasion of Iraq. He used the fear of terrorism attacks after 9/11 and promised the electorate that the war would ensure it would never happen again. Later, Bush would admit to a close associate that God told him to do it. It is a fact that more people have been killed in the name of religion than any political agenda in history. The Blackstone Ratio says, "We as a nation that would rather have the criminal justice system convict 10 innocent people than let one guilty person go free." In the *End of Faith*, Sam Harris wrote, "Our laws against vice have nothing to do with keeping people from physical or psychological harm and everything to do with not angering God – oral sex is a criminal offense in 13 states and consensual sodomy in 9 states." The Iraq war cost the American taxpayers a trillion dollars or so plus thousands of American lives and even more emotional causalities. Some day it will be written that it was all due to an inner need to sate a president's inner hatred of those that saw the world through a different filter. The Middle East worships differently, thinks differently, and treats their kids and women differently. That may not seem right to many, but it is not justification to spend taxpayer's money and cost American lives to sate one's own power needs.

Laws are often enacted to control what we fear. Some are good. Some are not so good. We need traffic laws to keep those living in highly populated cities safe. But we don't need laws to make weak people feel strong or to placate their need for power. That often happens. There are laws against smoking marijuana despite the fact studies have shown that it isn't as lethal or detrimental to one's health as alcohol. In fact, it is used to medicate terminal patients in many hospitals. It is a fact that more people die each year due to driving, flying, and hitting golf balls than smoking marijuana. *The Wall Street Journal* wrote an editorial saying, "Lets end drug prohibition, since compared to alcohol it is relatively harmless and not nearly as dangerous." Harvard economics professor Jeffrey Miron says, "Legalizing marijuana will save $7.7 billion on enforcement and generate $10 billion in taxes on $12 billion in revenues." Are there risks associated with making some drugs legal? Of course! But the vast majority of products have risks. You don't outlaw cars since you could hit and kill someone.

The Enron and World.com debacles caused a fracas in Washington that led to the Sarbanes-Oxley legislation in 2002. Fear governed logic and produced a law that would keep firms from capitalizing expenses or using company monies to advance their personal needs. Guess what? When you buy a truck, you capitalize the cost of that truck. If it costs $30,000, you depreciate that cost over its estimated life. That permits you to put the truck on your Balance Sheet as an asset. You remove its cost gradually. That is okay if the truck lasts five years - you deduct expenses of $6,000 each year. That is what Enron did. But they did it in the billions for other reasons, to make their profits look better than they were. What were they doing? They were capitalizing expenses for a short-term expediency! Politicians decided it as a political power-play and passed SOX. The cause was bad horses on the course, not the right to capitalize and depreciate, which was already a law in the IRS code. The new law cost businesses millions annually in order to remain in compliance. The fear of corporate crime led to laws that were in many ways worse than the crime. SOX included so much inane C.Y.A. paperwork that no firm can afford to be honest and comply. The *Economist* found that "20% of public firms are considering going private to avoid the cost of compliance with Sarbanes-Oxley." Within the first five years of enactment, Sox cost the U.S. economy over $1 trillion. One newspaper article wrote, "The attempt to avoid accounting fraud creates busywork that drains resources. All of this is really just paper-pushing. I haven't met one investor who thinks it's a good thing," says the CEO of Captaris.

In 1919 the United States ratified the 18th Amendment to the Constitution on Prohibition as The Noble Experiment. It was passed due to the power of the Women's Christian Temperance Union who wanted husbands to stop hanging out at the corner pub so he would come home to the family. The law passed Congress over President Woodrow Wilson's veto on October 28, 1919. The irony is that it led to the exact opposite that it was intended to stop. For the next fifteen years there was far more drinking, organized crime, and police corruption than any time in American history. Prohibition put legitimate brewers out of business and created an opening for the underworld and mafia to take over what was once a lawful business. It helped spawn the Al Capone era and place the mafia in power. The true irony of the law is that it led to young women hanging out in speakeasies, when before they would not have thought of entering a corner bar. It led young girls to smoking, carousing, and hanging out with nefarious characters they would not have spoken to prior to Prohibition.

Power & Independence Mantra

Harvard psychologist David McClelland wrote in *The Achieving Society*, "Men prefer acting powerfully; women traditionally show more interest in being strong." He went on to say something that is fundamental to eminence:

> *"Achievement motivated people are more likely*
> *to be developed in families in which parents hold*
> *different expectations from normal families. They*
> *expect their children to start showing independence*
> *between ages six and eight, making choices and*
> *doing things without help, such as knowing the*
> *way around the neighborhood and taking care of*
> *themselves around the house."*

Thus power is molded early and is what makes some people independent and powerful and others weak. Donald Trump is considered powerful. His power came from his father sending him out at age eight and nine with a rent-collector in New York City's Queens projects in order to learn what it was like on the street. When they knocked on the door the guy told Donald, "Now step back to avoid the gun shots that may come through that door." Did that mold "The Donald" early? Sure did.

American politicians try to gain power by appealing to blue collar voters. They pontificate endlessly on bringing jobs back to America, implying they have such power or that it is possible, which in most cases it is not. This makes the voters believe such politicians see the world like they do and they are on their side. Unfortunately, it works more often than not. Bringing back the good old days is good rhetoric, but Thomas Woolf was correct when he said so prophetically that you can never go back home. That good 'ol boy rhetoric is almost always incorrect and ill-advised, but the masses don't get it so they buy in to the promises. For someone running for office, the facts are never as important winning the election. Many would sell their mothers down the river to win. Saying they will bring back American jobs lost to Asia is pure nonsense. The world is changing. When a job is lost, there is a reason. The man or woman making shoes or jeans in this country who starts believing that it is possible to bring back those industries is either not very astute or merely a pawn being manipulated by an unscrupulous politician. The truth is what needs to be disseminated. If a person has been replaced by cheap labor in India or China, they need to see that the past is history. They need to learn a new craft, go back to school, or train in another arena. Many opportunities exist in electronic servicing. Not many computer firms offer the customer a Sunday afternoon fix of their PC. That could be a truly opportunistic business in many markets in America. The unemployed could start selling iPods or Blackberries. Let us not forget that China is now changing much like America did a century ago.

Astoundingly, 80% of the Chinese people were rural in 1980 and 75 % in India just a few decades ago. In 2004, China was down to 58% rural and India 72%. In the case of China, that is 1% of the population or three million people relocating to the cities and urban factories each year. Flat-panel TV screens were pioneered by RCA in America in the late 1960s. The $100 billion business is now dominated by Meta-National Networks with Japan's Sony and Korea's Samsung doing 43% of the business in Best Buy, Wal-Mart, and Target. A 42-inch LCD Plasma TV contains a panel from Korea, electronics from China, processors from U.S.A. and it is assembled in Mexico for American distribution. If you want to be international, one must act as if they are international and not provincial. What Americans refer to as "Six Sigma" – six standard deviations of perfection in products - the Japanese call *kaizen* for flawless Quality Control.

Those in power like to pass laws that make them look good. When they do, the laws become self-serving instruments to make that society or culture fit the mindset of the leader promulgating them. George Bernard Shaw told us, "A government which robs Peter to pay Paul, can always count on the support of Paul." History shows that people and nations become what they concentrate on the most. This is scary when considering the U.S. has one lawyer for every 320 people (1:320) while Japan has one for every 8,000 (1:8000). While America is graduating lawyers, Japan and China graduate engineers. China now has five times more engineers than America. And of course, once they are on the street, they must find work. An example for the traveler is that in Japan there is a vending machine on every city corner purveying sodas, cigarettes, and hard liquor. They would be illegal in the U.S. Ayn Rand, the mother of Objectivism said it quite well, "The only power any government has is the power to crack down on criminals. Well, when there aren't enough criminals, one makes them. One declares so many things to be a crime that it becomes impossible to live without breaking laws."

Unions Can Stifle Progress

American unions came into existence at a time they were direly needed to curb the abuse of tyrannical industrialists taking advantage of individuals that had no power. As in many things, the pendulum did not swing back to the middle. It flew past the middle to the others side that has left unions with such power a GM car has $2,200 of labor for people who have not worked at GM for many years. When Chrysler filed for Chapter 11 bankruptcy in spring 2009 there were workers were not commiserating since they by contract would be paid 80 percent of their wages. That causes a counter-incentive mentality to come into play. Those workers are not looking for new careers as they are now on the dole. More of a problem is that the UAW ends up owning a significant share of the company and that does not bode well for future growth.

There is no individualism in a union. The group decides your fate and the individual must follow or leave for greener pastures. Union members have given up their personal power for that of the group and must live by the rules of the group. That is why unionism has a recent history of stifling growth. Detroit can no longer, and has not been able to compete with Asian cars for many years, as shown above in the GM example. In Japan a person in a union does not stop working when on strike. They envision themselves and the firm as one and would not want to hurt the company in any way. That is a stark difference from what takes place in America. The Japanese worker carries signs and makes noise, but nothing that would be detrimental to a company they love. In Japan the firms are the people and they know that. Not so in America. The Detroit debacle that hit in 2008 and 2009 had been festering for many years, but did not show its ugly face until the gas crisis caused the problem to surface.

In 2009 the Wall Street Journal labeled General Motors as Government Motors. It offers prescient insight into what happens when weak management capitulates to unions for the sake of keeping their own jobs. You cannot operate like Detroit and remain in business for the long run. Paying people that haven't worked for the firm for many years is not competitive and is a program for disaster. Here are some of the problems created by a company dominated by the unions:

? GM takes 23 hours to build a car compared to Nissan's 18 hours

? GM has 7,500 workers in its Jobs Bank being paid despite not working for the firm - $2,200 Per each car built in 2008

? Every GM vehicle includes $1,500 in healthcare costs, more than cost of steel in the car. Japan has $450 of healthcare in each vehicle

? GM workers earn average wage that is 70% more than the average U.S .manufacturing wage - $70 per hour including fringe benefits

? GM supports three retirees (2 million of them) for every active worker

? Toyota, Honda, and Nissan generate $2,400 more profit per worker than the Detroit Big Three (GM, Ford, Chrysler)

The Wall Street Journal (March 10, 209 p. A4) wrote on the unions attempt to hijack American business - about the desperation rampant today in the auto industry. As we know, desperate people do desperate things. In this case, it was about legislation to assure a firm's survival but the government ended owning half of GM – shades of socialism. The reason for the union's desperation is their membership has been declining steadily since 1953 and is now at its lowest level in over fifty-five years. When the Working Life Organization started tracking union membership in 1948, the unions had over 14 million members or 31.8% of the workforce. It was 1953 when the union power in America peaked at 32.5% of the workforce. It has been on a steady decline ever since to the point they now only control 12.5% of the American workforce or less than 15.5 million workers. If this trend continues, the union membership will be cut in half in less than twenty years. If the trend of shipping manufacturing jobs overseas continues, the unions could be out of business in ten years.

Americans Should Learn *Keiretsu* (clanny) & *Kaizen* (flawless QC)

A *keiretsu* is a cartel or clan-like group of firms, suppliers, bankers, and MITI joined together like a fighting clan to dominate an industry or consumer market. Each participant in the clan owns stock in each other's ventures linking them together financially and economically. In Japan a firm like Sony would have board members that include their bankers, suppliers, government officials, maybe even someone from MITI (the Ministry of Industry and Trade), all present to ensure the firm's new products make it in the market and are very competitive. They all are in a cooperative venture to ensure the company and their products are able to dominate in world markets. It has worked eminently well in Japan to the point that this small island nation has been able to out-maneuver and out-produce much larger adversaries on the world stage. *Kaizen* is when everything comes out of the plant flawlessly.

Let's create an imaginary, new company that we have named Inno-Vision with a new product – the Magic Pen to demonstrate the concept of the *keiretsu*. This fantasy firm is located in a small island nation that we'll call UtopiaVille. In Utopia-Ville they have a culture that is out of the Four Musketeers legend: *All for one and one for all.* So Inno-Vision forms a committee to ensure their success in the launch of the Magic Pen that will be sold in the market place for $99.95. What does the Magic Pen do that other pens don't? It writes like any other pen with the exception it has a built-in microprocessor memory, speaker, camera, and incredible software that can interpret words written on paper and images. It comes packaged with a world map. So if you were in Paris and in a restaurant and wanted to order a beer, you could write beer in English, touch Paris on the map, and the pen will say, "Beer" in French. When you arrive in Rome, just touch Rome on the map and it will order your beer in Italian, and the same in Moscow, Shanghai, Rio, Mexico City, and so on. That is the unique product we have ready to take to the worldwide market.

The Inno-Vision board meets on this new venture. Included is the Managing Director, a head of the commerce department for Utopia-Ville, the director of the nation's largest bank, the head of an export shipping conglomerate, and the CEO of the largest chain of bookstores and educational retailers. The banker asks about the amount of money needed to make this a $100 million dollar enterprise within three years. The Managing Director says, "We need about $25 million, but we have raised equity from outside investors of $5 million, so we need to find another $20 million." The banker says, "I will get two of my investment banking buddies, and I think we can make that happen right away." The shipping magnate says, "But how are you going to get the orders when no one knows about this Magic Pen?" And the Managing Director says, "The product will appear on all of the top TV shows starting in the fall. My friend at the networks says he will make it happen for stock in the company." The educational sage looks at the head of the table and says, "Each of the universities have told me they would place an order for ten cases of the product to be ready when the TV spots hit the air. I already have a verbal order for 100,000 units – $5 million. I've checked with our banker friend here and he tells me there is a guaranteed terms package so that we have 60-days to pay for the order and from what I can tell, they will have moved off the shelves by then." The shipping magnate speaks up, "I have arranged for export of these to America and have worked with our bank here for the Letter of Credit for what looks to be another order for 100,000 units." Wow! That is power.

Let us look at the genesis of *keiretsu*. It began with the American occupation of Japan after World War II. General McArthur was given the task of rehabilitating a country that was blown asunder by American bombs. There were a few very large conglomerates known as *zaibatsu*. General McArthur tried to abolish them, but the nation had a clan-orientation and the 16 *zaibatsu* targeted for dissolution formed alliances between them. It is important to note that in Japan it was good to be in engineering, finance, or manufacturing. It was not so good to be in sales, and that led to the creation of the Japanese Trading company. These large internationally oriented firms did the selling and exporting. Within the new corporate cultures, keiretsu came to be known as the "new clan" or "alliance." It is a tight-knit alliance to work toward each other's mutual success. The *keiretsu* operates globally. They are integrated both vertically and horizontally and are organized around their trading company and company bank. Each is capable of controlling nearly every step of the economic process. The Japanese *horizontal keiretsu* included what has been labeled the "Big Six" - Mitsui, Mitsubishi, Sumitomo, Fuyo, Sanwa, and Dai-Ichi Kangyo Bank Groups. The *vertical keiretsu* are industrial groups, manufacturers and part suppliers, wholesalers, and retailers. These vertical *keiretsu* include car and electronics producers that turned out to be Toyota, Nissan, Honda--Matsushita, Hitachi, Toshiba, Sony, and their "captive" subcontractors. The major *keiretsu* is typically oriented around one bank that holds an equity position in the firm. Each bank had more control over a firm than what Western nations would want or could tolerate. One effect of this structure was to minimize the presence of any hostile takeover of the company. It was the old Golden Rule principle that those with the bucks would be making the rules.

Different Cultures Create Different Behaviors

Cultural studies find that the Asians are more tenacious due to the rigors of growing up in rice fields In solving puzzles American children lasted 9 – 47 minutes prior to giving up while the Japanese children struggled on 40% more time – 13 - 93 minutes. Other studies show that a 4-year old in China can count to 40 by the time they are four years old. American four year olds an only count to 15 and this leads to an edge in math for Asian children who on average score at the 98% level in math compared to the U.S., UK, France and Germany scoring between 26% and 36%.

Large firm want predictability and thus opt for control but it has failed badly simply because it's too structured. Aspen Institute labeled the new economic world as a Collective Intelligence. In such an Internet driven world, it is imperative for each nation to be far more competitive. That is difficult for men or nations that resist change. America has been for a century the most acquisitive society in the history of man. Yet it has a negative savings rate (2006 study) due to wanting "it" now. The Chinese have a savings rate of 50% with the European Union at about 20%. Both are passing America in economic clout. The world is 5% American with an inner presumption for the right to dictate socio-political & cultural ideas on the other 95%. Americans believe they have a right to tell China how to behave in societal situations or Europeans on teenage drinking or speed limits. It is tantamount to China saying, "Make it safe to walk at night in LA, Detroit, and Atlanta or we won't ship you shoes." The vast divide between the East and West can be seen in the differences between the ways the two cultures function professionally. One is egalitarian to a fault and the other autonomous or independent to a fault. Studies show that "how you do in life depends more on social place than almost any other individual difference you can measure." That includes money, IQ, and education. In Asia the social system pervades all else including individual. Dr. Gene's assessment:

Americans are Individualistic to a Fault	Asians are Egalitarian to a Fault
➤ Short-Term employment	Lifetime Employment
➤ Individual Decision-Making	Consensual Decision-making
➤ Personal Responsibility	Collective Responsibility
➤ Rapid Advancement &Promotions	Slow Advancement
➤ Explicit & Formal Control	Implicit & Informal Control
➤ Job Specialization	Non-Specific Career-Pathing
➤ CYA & Self-Serving rules	Team Spirit – Egalitarian rules
➤ Air condition plant 1st, offices last	Air condition office 1st, plant last
➤ Short-Term Strategies Dominate	Long-Term Strategies Dominate

The Enormous Educational Divide between the East & West

The U.S. ranks 24th out of 29 nations in applying math skills to real-world problems, according to a 2004 study by the *Organization for Economic Cooperation & Development*. Not good! In tests the American teenager ranks below: Finland, Korea, Japan, Netherlands, Canada, Belgium, Switzerland, and New Zealand. Many U.S. math classes teach analytical or theoretical thinking, not everyday math application. Peter Drucker put his finger on the pulse of what was happening in America saying, "Businessmen owe it to themselves and to society to hammer home that there is no such thing as "profit." There are only "costs" of doing business, costs of staying in business, and costs of labor and raw materials." Those are pretty profound words from the father of modern management.

"In Seoul, Korea no one drops out," says principal Yong of Weha Girls High School. "A student may transfer to another school, but no one just drops out. To drop out is a major disaster, a catastrophe." In South Korea 93 % graduate from high school on time, compared to just 75 % in the U. S. or 1.2 million each year. The U.S. is one of only two countries in the world, along with Estonia, where the percentage of high school graduates is lower among younger workers than among their parents. In the U.S. the percentage of 55-64 year-olds who eventually get a high school diploma or a GED is exactly the same as those in the 25-34 year old group – 87%. In contrast, 97% graduate in South Korea. That is up from 37% in the same time period ("USA Today," Nov. 19, 2008 B1). Since research shows that the lack of natural talent is no longer irrelevant to great success, it is all about education and learning to be great. "Fortune" wrote an article that talked about emphasizing the importance of reading, research, and studying. The U.S. and Estonia are the only two nations where the percentage of high school graduates are lower today than for their parent's generation. In America the percentage of 55-64 year-olds who eventually get a high school degree, including a GED, is exactly the same as those in the 25-34 year old group – 87%. In South Korea 93% of students graduate from high school on time compared to just 75% in America. Education for Asians is more important than for Americans.

In China Mao tse Tung once proclaimed, "Power is what comes out of the end of a gun." Russian writer Aleksandra Solzhenitsyn offered further insight saying, "You can have power over people as long as you don't take everything away from them. But when you've robbed a man of everything, he's no longer in your power." Power comes packaged in a wide variety of forms. Those with the most power take over organizations. Those with money make it in the country-club world. Those with charisma gain disciples and get themselves elected to public office. The really magnetic ones become Pope or President. In many nations it takes the right bloodline to become King. Carl Jung said, "Where love rules, there is no will to power; and where power predominates love is lacking. The one is the shadow of the other." This begs the most eloquent words of Lord Acton who wrote, "Power tends to corrupt, and absolute power corrupts absolutely. Great men are almost always bad men."

For Power Be a Philosopher King

In the beginning of Western thought, Plato encouraged all to don the role of a philosopher-king. He believed that otherwise, a man is unworthy of leading men to a new cause. Why? He will not have the global perspective demanded of a leader. In Plato's *Cave Allegory*, he offers insight into today's dilemma that can be seen as illusory and often self-imposed idiocy:

> **"There once was a people who lived their entire lives within a Cave of Illusions. They came to believe that their own shadows cast upon the walls were the substance of reality…Obsessed with the shadow play the people became accustomed to and imprisoned by their dark reality" - Plato's** *Allegory*

In the *Dialogues,* Plato went further in describing the need for a philosopher as leader saying, "There will be no end to the troubles of states, or of humanity itself, till philosophers become kings or till those we now call kings and rulers really and truly become philosophers, and political power and philosophy thus come into the same hands." Touché! Some of the great artisans saw themselves as more philosopher and poet than how the world perceived them. Picasso is a classic example. This surrealist painter told the media, "I have the revelation of the inner voice. There is not a painting of mine that does not exactly reproduce a vision of the world." His masterpiece *Guernica* portrayed his outrage as a monument to destruction after the barbaric bombing of the Spanish town during the Second World War. At 50, Pablo wrote his epitaph. These prophetic words offer insight into his power – a poet and philosopher putting his ideas on canvas - "Here lies a poet, philosopher and sometimes painter." When criticized for his Gertrude Stein portrait, he wrote, "Portraits should possess not physical, not spiritual, but psychological likeness. A picture lives only through the one who looks at it – what they see is the legend surrounding the picture."

Power comes in many forms. Machiavelli told us, "The ends justifying the means." In *The Prince* he wrote, "It is much more secure to be feared than to be loved." Machiavelli was telling the world that the relevance of morality in political affairs was not pertinent. For him, the only thing of merit was to be crafty and deceitful as a means of maintaining political power. In some cultures, Machiavellianism is a kind of "Get them before they get us." It is a philosophy of power that is still being practiced in business and politics. Such power emanates from within a person who sees a recession as a golden opportunity to steal market share from the competition. It is often a survival of the fittest mentality. When others cut back on marketing or give up on marginal markets, take them for yours. Winners are those that use havoc to strengthen themselves.

Chapter 3

The *BUCKS Game* – Chasing Money is an Entropic Trek

Those that chase the almighty dollar lose to those that don't

"Contrary to business school doctrine, maximizing *shareholder wealth or profit maximization was not the dominant force or primary objective* in the history of visionary companies." Collins & Porras (1999 p. 55) *Built to Last*

"Chasing money is entropic. You can make money or make sense. The two are mutually exclusive." Bucky Fuller, *Critical Path*

Chasing money can be a paradoxical adventure. The harder you strive for it, the less you end up with. Why? You make the wrong decisions to make much money. Without even being aware of it when you are after the almighty buck you body languages sends signals to those able to get you bucks. And even more important is that you will make the wrong decisions in your quest to grow big and gain market share no matter your discipline. This is a given and one that visionaries seem to get and the worker bees don't see. "I say that money does not bring virtue," said Socrates to his followers in Athens, "but rather that from being virtuous one can attain money." Thomas Edison wrote, "I don't care so much about making my fortune, as I do for getting ahead of the other fellows. I care more about how to change the world." Do you think Bill Gates ever made one decision based on some short-term expediency or money? No way! Biographer Ward Kimball wrote of the Disney success saying, "If you want to know the real secret of Disney's success, it's that he never tried to make money." The inventor of the geodesic dome was the poster child for this theory. In *Critical Path* he told us, "The drive to make money is entropic. You have to decide if you want to make money or make sense since the two are mutually exclusive." An example of this is the manner in which entrepreneurs operate compared to a hired-hand. Ted Turner was making a deal in New York City on the very first 24-hour cable news. Every network thought he was nuts as did such media mavens as the Washington Post and *The Wall Street Journal*. When he finally reached a deal with RCA's top executives, their legal beagles reached across the table and shook hands with the brash young Ted. This young tiger was betting $100 million - his total net worth - on something about which he had no clue. They looked at him quizzically and asked if he didn't want to take some time to consult with his financial advisors or legal department. Turner was equally as puzzled at the question, and he told them it was his money and his deal and he needed no other counsel other than his own. Later, he would admit he didn't have so much as a business plan on a deal that would make him a pauper if it tanked. Would a Hired-Hand do such a thing? No way! And that is the difference between those that are in charge and those working for others without the guts to dare what a Ted Turner would dare.

Money & Romance are Paradoxical Concepts

Much of what we experience in life is paradoxical. Victor Frankl accidentally hit on what he labeled "Paradoxical Intention" while treating impotent men. The harder his patients tried to get an erection the less chance they were capable. Only when they stopped trying did it pop up. The mind is the enemy in romance and in most other things we attempt, including blasting out of sand traps. Frankl validated his principle by studying children with a stuttering affliction. If the children tried not to stutter, they did. When they tried to stutter, they did not. Wow! Frankl also validated the principle with handwriting tests. Try to write your name very carefully just as you do without trying. It is not easy, and is usually impossible. Why? You aren't trying too hard. In *Search of Meaning* Frankl wrote, "Fear brings about that which one is afraid of and hyper-intention makes impossible what one wishes." Dr. Gene's Life Paradoxes are shown below:

- ✗ **Paradox of Fear:** Fear is vanquished when attacked. Fear flying? Take flying lessons. Fear the water? Then take scuba lessons and it will disappear. It is axiomatic that fear motivates and it also can debilitate since our ***Kryptonite*** is in the mind.

- ✗ **Paradox of Happiness:** Trying to be happy is contra to being happy. Why? Because happy is a side effect of doing what you love, being what you love and with whom you love.

- ✗ **Innovation Paradox:** Those needing to change are the least likely to change. Those not needing to are the ones always chasing new ideas – gym rats don't need to be there as much as the all-you-can eat buffet crowds need to be working out. Those needing to creatively destroy what they 'are' always found stuck as couch potatoes and unwilling to change

- ✗ **Pendulum Swing Paradox:** Pendulums seldom, if ever, swing back to a norm; people drink too much then become missionaries against all drinking. Religious zealots are those that once were without morals. Once sexual discrimination was rampant; now you can't compliment a lady at work for fear of a lawsuit.

- ✗ **Seductive Paradox:** An easy conquest always has a lower value than a difficult one; until you are willing to walk away, you will never command the same seductive power.

- ✗ **Paradox of Money:** "The drive to make money is entropic" Bucky Fuller wrote; since you seldom get what you chase too ardently, money should be low on your priority list.

- **Paradox of Following Rules:** Being too *Correct* is Contra to being *Creative*; inhibition leads people to follow stupid rules with stupid results; in contrast, iconoclasts refuse to listen to rules, and for this reason they are the one's most likely to alter paradigms.

- **Paradox of Risk-Taking:** Risk & Reward is a Zero-Sum game; Safe=Mediocrity; Risk = Rewards; this is why intrepid warriors invest in dotcoms; conservatives invest in bonds.

- **Paradox of Prudence:** Iconoclasts like Leonardo da Vinci and Picasso were raging renegades on a maniacal mission to the impossible; it can be seen in their outputs such as Mona Lisa and Cubism – non-traditional innovative creations.

- **Paradox of Selling:** Having to make a sale is contra to making one; trying too hard at anything has proven to be contra to getting it; a person emits an aura or energy that sends subliminal messages to buyers who become frightened by the needy - back off and you get orders.

- **Paradoxical Intention:** Impotence is self-induced. Victor Frankl found that the harder you try anything the less chance there is of achieving it – including an erection; Be hot and you get hot; try to be hot and you get cold. The mind is the enemy, not the body; watch the golfer on a par five hole - trying to hit the longest drive ever will usually result in the shortest one ever.

An incredible paradox can be found in planes that crash. Studies show that a troubled plane that is least likely to crash is the one without the Captain at the controls. The one most likely to crash is the one that has the Captain in charge. How could that be? It is what I have talked about earlier. Arrogance and mitigation of authority is present. Junior pilots are not afraid to ask for help, to listen to warnings from others or heed the advice of very junior individuals or flight control. Not so for the top dogs who must feel they are in charge and take a position of authority. Superiority reigns supreme. This is also found in large businesses like Fortune 1000 firms. The CEO's in charge are Hired Hands but see themselves as on the hot seat and make sure all those under them adhere to their position of power. These types are far less inclined to admit when they don't know or ask for help since it would appear as weakness if they dared ask for help from a junior executive. It helps them crash when in a new changing arena.

A paradox of progress can be seen in technological progress. The *telephone* enhanced our ability to communicate. The cost is privacy and a chance for intimate time alone without distractions. The *automobile* improved transportation. The cost is air pollution. *Tranquilizers* free us of anxiety. The cost is the loss of sensitivity. *Birth control pills* permitted couples to control their rights to birthing. The price has turned out to be unprecedented and rampant STD's - Sexually Transmitted Disease. We chase *correctness*. Studies show that it costs the chance for creativity. *Voice Mail* captures messages in our absence, but it has turned out to be a means of hiding from having to answer the phone. The *Internet* trumps snail-mail as a communications device, but the shy use it to avoid confrontation. Leaders must learn that what makes us can break us and it is one of life's ironic paradoxes.

Are You a Bucks Game Player?

Be careful of what you chase as it becomes more of a target and consequently distorts thinking. Money is the quintessential commodity validating the concept. Americans don't mind spending money to invent a new product, but are reticent to spend money to optimize market share of their inventions. Why is that so? They see inventions as a creative venture with high value. To commiserate over dollars or even pennies - to become a commodity maven - is not so high on the priority list in America. Instant-gratification rears its ugly head in this arena. The Japanese are far more inclined to be the task-masters in the minutia game and have raised it to an art. They are dedicated to cheapen the inventions that Americans create. That has led to them dominating world markets in the mass consumer markets. They make the American specialties into commodities.

Americans worry over next quarter's profit, what I have labeled the "buck's game" in another chapter. The Asians worry more over the long-term viability of dominating the market. Selling price is #1 in the American mind while cost is #1 in the Asian mind. One is a long-run perspective. The other is a short-run mentality – my quarterly or annual bonus or the price of the stock. This is a fundamental difference in strategy that always permeates the reasoning latent in any organization. It is where leaders spend their time and energy, and it is where they lead. We do get what we pay for ala the Enron debacle. They paid for their people to make quick profits no matter what game they had to play, and guess what? They got exactly what they were paying to get. Sir Richard Branson offered prescient insight into this when he demeaned money-based decisions versus pragmatic ones, "When starting a business listen to your heart, not your bankers."

In *The Innovator's Solution*, the authors found, "Innovation fails at large firms, Not because of some fatal technological flaw or because the market isn't ready. They fail due to inept management." That is so true. As discussed earlier, few hired hands make savvy decisions. Why? Because they are too caught up in looking good to keep their jobs, they optimize short-term profits to get a bonus, or their time is spent looking for a promotion. Isn't it ironic that when a supermarket has a sale, people can't wait to buy as much as they can afford? Christmas fire sales often cause a virtual riot in the store. Why doesn't the stock market get treated with the same enthusiasm when it drops precipitously as it did in 2009? Fear! Why don't the people who have bailed from the market buy homes selling at distressed prices? Fear! They have bought into the media recession spin, and that has negative energy flowing through their brains and effecting every decision they make. That is why the whole 2008/09 fiasco happened, only in reverse. The market was good, really good, and everyone was buying, thus few saw an end to an insatiable market demand where prices rose and never fell.

In the early years of Wal-Mart, Sam Walton could not get investment bankers to give him the time of day. What did he do? The intrepid one purchased an Arkansas bank, called a meeting, and told them, "We have found a viable new venture that needs money. Give it to them." Wow! Entrepreneurs like Walton, Rupert Murdoch, Ted Turner, or Richard Branson do well by using leverage. What is leverage? Using present assets to acquire new assets! All of the early growth by News Corp came from Murdoch's willingness to bet the future on what he already had. Ted Turner was the master of this art, acquiring the Atlanta Braves without a penny down. How? He pledged the Superstation and the team's assets and paid the asking price. When the seller is the banker you pay what they ask. When you have nothing at risk the risk isn't quite as large. In Turner's case it became a huge success once he made the Braves America's team by broadcasting virtually every game on his Superstation, WTBS. Branson repeatedly used his assets as collateral to go into new business ventures.

Chasing Money is Contra to Getting It!

Socrates said 2,450 years ago, "I say that money does not bring virtue, but rather that from being virtuous one can attain money." Peter Drucker preached, "Profitability is not the purpose, but a factor on business enterprise and activity." In *Built to Last*, the authors were looking for why some American institutions had prevailed through the ups and downs of the capitalist system while many, even more laudable firms were gone. They concluded, "Contrary to business school doctrine, maximizing shareholder wealth or profit maximization was not the dominant force or primary objective in the history of visionary companies." Chase the almighty buck and you get many things, but not success. Bucky Fuller saw this corporate self-serving affinity so well and so often he wrote of a fictional firm that he labeled, *Obnoxico*.

This fantasy corporation was a self-serving bureaucratic beast that worshipped at the altar of the almighty dollar to the detriment of what was right. Fuller constantly wrote on the money-grubbing self-serving mentality prevalent in corporate America. He found that most leaders were grounded in personal gratification and inhibited thinking writing in *Critical Path*, "Society tends to think statically, and fatally often fails to see great trends evolving."

There is an interesting parallel in money scams and religious connections. Scam artists and religious zealots seem to have a similar modus operandi. Many of the scams and frauds have a genesis in church, social gatherings, or ethnic arenas. Many of Bernie Madoff's victims were spiritually connected or friends he had met at the temple. In tiny Naples, Florida, a $100 million fraud was engineered in a Baptist Church where almost all of those taken had met the man that took their money. Another Ponzi scam artist is in prison for having cheated a high school buddy. The most glaring example is the Ponzi scheme of Bernie Madoff, a New York Jewish investment banker who had been the head of NASDAQ, thus beyond reproach. Those hardest hit in Madoff's $50 billion dollar Ponzi scheme were Hall of Fame pitcher Sandy Koufax, TV talk show host Larry King, film maker Stephen Spielberg, Jewish Nobel Prize laureates, and a number of top Israeli officials. French tycoon Rene-Theirry Magon killed himself over the debacle.

Speed Fuels Visionaries & Stifles Bureaucrats

C. Northcott Parkinson documented the eerie nature of success and bumbling with his findings in the British Admiralty in World War II. Unfortunately, Parkinson's Laws (1957) have been validated over and over in business. Parkinson wrote, "Work expands so as to fill the time available for its completion." This can be seen in every organization at every level. Give someone four hours of work and they will stretch it to fit their eight-hour day. Give them ten hours of work, and they'll complete it in the same eight hours or bitch and moan that they need overtime to finish it. Parkinson was never more astute than when he spoke of a board trying to decide between free coffee in a work environment on the same agenda as a new roof for the building or a new worldwide computer network. Three-fourths of the meeting is eaten up by the coffee problem because everyone gets it and is a bit of an expert. The roof project takes far less time and the computer puzzle is passed within minutes. What is going on here? One is complex and no one cares to appear stupid so they say nothing. The bicycle rack or free coffee gets lots of talk time since everyone knows about those things.

It is true that the world's preeminent entrepreneurs are afflicted with a kind of rushing sickness. They do not drink decaf and are unlikely to get caught up in a bureaucratic maze of self-aggrandizement. They do fit the traditional mold. They tend to be afflicted with very short attention spans with a long-term vision and are willing to sacrifice now for later. That was true of Henry Ford, considered the greatest entrepreneur of the 20th century. It was also the style of Coco Chanel, often named the most successful female in that century. Sir Richard Branson of Virgin fame told the media:

> **"I can honestly say, I have never gone into business to make money. I rely more on gut instinct than researching huge amounts of statistics. I make up my mind about a business proposal or new people I meet within 30 seconds."**

Sir Richard fits the speed and change initiative spoken of in this work, the quintessential entrepreneur billionaire with Bucks & Balls. Branson wrote in his memoir, "I have always thrived on havoc and adrenaline. I set myself huge unachievable goals and try to rise above them." Branson was intuitively right when he rejected the age-old tradition of placing profits #1, products #2. and people #3. He reversed the procedure and placed people first, products second, and profits third. His logic is without question right on the money since motivated people will make the products right and with that done the profits come. He is also an advocate of the Socialization 150 rule. When a Virgin company reaches 150 people Branson breaks it up. Why? If he doesn't know the people there, he isn't happy. The firm is too large to be effective or reactive.

Entrepreneur whiz-kid Michael Dell was on a fast track that left traditionalists in his wake. In his mid-30's the hyper one wrote in his memoir about his need for speed saying, "I'd rather be first than be late in making decisions; being first and wrong is better than 100% perfect but two years late." That is a bit different than the Washington politician who finds it too tough to show up much of the time. Michael went on to say, "In managing innovation, you are either quick or you are dead. A little too late is just too late... since component costs decline in value an average of ½ to 1% per week." Dell Computer buys all of their components and systems from offshore and they are doing just fine. You do not find them bitching and moaning about offshore competition. They beat IBM in the PC business. They went offshore while Big Blue insisted on manufacturing their own products. Consequently, they went the way of the dinosaur – too big and inflexible to stay alive while Dell thrived. The need for speed is not limited to business or entrepreneurship. Honore Balzac, the father of the modern novel and Mao Tse Tung, the modern miracle worker for China stopped bathing for fear it would slow them down. Romance queen Danielle Steel told a biographer, "If I'm working on a book I pretty much work around the clock. Every 20-22 hours I take a break. I seldom sleep more than four hours a night." Does it sound like any of these highly successful visionaries were doing it for the money? Hardly!

Mastery of any discipline takes time, ten years according to most studies. The myth of Wolfgang Mozart being an instant prodigy is without merit. No question he was very talented and at a very young age, but many of his early works were suspiciously written in the hand of his father, an accomplished composer in his own right. By 21 he started composing works that were his true legacy, but by then he had been working at his craft for 18 years. I charted the timeline of success for entrepreneurs in *Entrepreneurial Genius* (2003) and *Empowerment* (2006) and showed the timeline to success was about ten years and to eminence was about twenty years. Mozart fits that profile as does Tiger Woods, Michael Dell, and most people who reach the very pinnacle of success. Florida State professor Anders Ericsson says, "Expertise in any discipline from music, sports, chess, science and business management is about ten years or about 10,000 hours of persistent, focused training and experience."

Long-Term Mindsets

Fortune ran an article on the importance of cash, interviewing Bill Gross of Silicon Valley fame who said, "I'm convinced that too much money early on will insure failure later. If companies don't know that they can run out of money, they won't be thinking of ways not to run out of money." This was the way of Solomon Price, the quintessential master of managing money based on market demand, and not on costs. A hired-hand would never have operated like Sol. He took the long-term path in deciding the viability of a product at retail, not the short-term expediency path. Sol told the press, "My motto is, how can I sell this for less. If I get a special deal, I pass it on to the consumer." Such thinking never takes place at a firm like Sears or any other public chain in the merchandising business. Sol Price was the hierarchy at his firm and such decisions were never left to a hired-hand or even his sons. That is why he told the media, "The lower the price the more business you get. You should price products as though you were buying them right and then you'll find out if you can do the buying right." In other words, he was thinking long-term, not much different than how they think in Asia. If the right price is $19.95 and you price it at $30 and it doesn't sell, you haven't learned a thing other than believing the product was not viable. The price was not viable. Pricing it at $19.95

when you lose money at that price tells you whether it will sell or not. Then you can buy sufficient volume to get the cost low enough to sell at that price and if not you don't do it. That fundamental logic, strange as it may seem, is lost on the preponderance of retail executives.

President Harry Truman told the media, "If you can't stand the heat, get out of the kitchen." That is what American short-term thinkers should do – they got out of the kitchen and are now on the sidelines. Politicians say, "Bring back the jobs to America." They are lost in their own deluded reverie. You can't bring back jobs that have no productive viability or ones that you lost due to your own CYA - self-serving decision-making to insure you are not a casualty. If you've lost a job take it as a warning sign and change careers. If your industry is going down the tubes jump into one that is on a tear. That is what the millenary workers did decades ago when their products moved offshore. They used their brands and imported their wares from offshore. Stop worshipping at the altar of past places and ideas. Move on or it is inevitable that you will be contaminated by past thinking. The past is gone and the future is the only viable game to play.

Retirement - the #1 Wish of Most Americans

One American study revealed that the #1 wish of most working people is to retire. Why? The majority of workers hate what they do every day of their lives. Why would someone continue to torture themselves by doing what they hate? Fear of changing and living a life of pure survival. They have a xenophobic nature of remaining in places that are familiar and safe. That is a strong argument for never working for others and launching your own venture with you as boss. This study on "#1 Worker Wish" was expected to lead to not retiring but to reveal some inner craving such as becoming rich and famous, dating Britney Speers or Tom Cruise, or living forever. No! It was to retire. Were the subjects drunk or on drugs? They were merely revealing the underlying seething hate for showing up and working in some bureaucratically driven environment where the manta is "Don't rock the boat" or "Do it since the policy says we should." That is the personification of the CYA. mentality so prevalent in all large organizations. I once asked an executive, "Why are you doing...this certain thing?" He responded, "Because it is in the policy manual." Amazed, I stated, "But it is not the most efficient way to do it." He agreed, but was not willing to violate policy even though it was stupid.

Most people work to survive, to pay the mortgage, or to placate a mate or parent. Not the best reason for a career choice. This is a sad commentary. Do you think Leonardo de Vinci, Picasso, Thomas Edison, Irving Berlin, or Dr. Seuss ever did anything they disliked? And they were found working on Christmas Day and Easter Sunday when worker bees were resting. Did they ever consider the prospect of retirement? No chance! That is why they lived such long and productive lives. Theirs was a labor of love, not hate. Did they work hard every day? Yeah! Many were guilty of working 24/7 to the chagrin of mate and family. Edison kept a daily log of his work in the lab. At age 65, way past his life expectancy, Edison spent 122 hours per week in his lab for one whole year. Did he think of it as work? Of course not! For him it was fun and why he led such a rewarding and fulfilling life. Irving Berlin seldom went to bed before dawn. What was he doing? Writing songs on a piano he didn't even know how to play. He would have been fired in a job, but he died rich and famous doing what he loved.

Self-employed artisans and entrepreneurs are passionate to a fault. After Wright was terminated by Louis Sullivan - the inventor of the skyscraper - he went on to create magnificent edifices like Fallingwater and the Guggenheim Museum. After age 80 he did one-third of the total output of his life with the Guggenheim designed at age 90. And even Sullivan who told us "Form Follows Function" was a dilettante who knew that once the problem was analyzed, "We must heed the imperative voice of emotion." For such people, pleasure is their paycheck. Plato opened up The Academy in Athens when he was 40 years old, when he was already past his life expectancy age of 36. The philosopher king ran his Academy, the world's first university until age 80 with such students as Aristotle. Pursuing positive dreams usually leads to power and passion as well as a long and fulfilling life. Is money important to such people? Only as a means to a larger end! The whole concept of retirement does not fit the lexicon of those who chase their dreams and do what they love. Creative and powerful wunderkinds all admit they would work without pay. Money is merely the way we keep score and often those that chase passion end up with lots of bucks.

International Trade & Economic Impact

When the dollar declines relative to other world currencies, there is a hue and cry from Wall Street. That is not necessarily all bad. In fact, it can be good in the sense that American products become cheaper in Europe and Asia and exports rise. A cheap dollar increases the balance of trade more than a strong dollar. When the dollar rises, as it did for many decades in the 20th century, it causes foreign products to be cheaper for Americans to buy, thus imports rise. A strong dollar makes tennis shoes from China cheaper to buy and American cars less attractive in Paris. What makes us strong makes us weak. That dictates that we should become a bit more philosophical in times of change. That doesn't seem to resonate in the minds of those suffering or afraid. In such times politicians pontificate on "Buy American" when that often is not in the cards based on the economics. Many times such statements are inane if not ignorant. If we can buy a TV of our choice cheaper from Asia, assuming quality and all else is equal, we should be buying the best for less. A tariff aimed at keeping American products selling is like marching backwards in time as is protecting obsolete jobs or industries. Such laws are antithetic to progress. It is like leveling the playing field when things are not equal or level.

When the dollar declines relative to the Yen or Euro, it motivates people from those nations to invest in America. They buy American real estate, businesses, or properties. The unread and economic illiterate bitch about such things, but it is only due to their ignorance. When the dollar increases in value, it permits Americans to buy vacation homes in Paris or Monte Carlo. Xenophobia often reigns supreme with media outrage when foreigners start acquiring American property. Such purchases actually bring new money into the American economy. In the 1990s Japan bought 429 firms for $25.3 billion including California's historic golf haven at Pebble Beach, New York City's Rockefeller Center, and Hollywood's Columbia Pictures. In 2006 IBM's personal computer division was sold to China's Lenova. America was happy to get the bucks from the East, but it frightened many politicians who used the transactions to put fear in the minds of voters. When cash is infused into America, it leads to a balancing of cash flows and is positive for the nation's economic growth. In 2009 the most gold jewelry was bought from which nation? It was India where 470 tons of gold was bought. Number two was China at 327 tons, followed by the United States that sold 179 tons of gold.

China's 2007 GDP passed Germany's for #3 in the world. China's 1.3 billion people generate 25.7 trillion Yuan annually or $3.5 trillion in 2007 dollars. That compares to Germany's GDP of $3.3 trillion that equates to 2.4 trillion Euros. The United States is still #1 in GDP with $13.8 trillion. They are followed by Japan's $4.4 trillion at #2, but China is expected to pass Japan by 2013. Germany still ranks well ahead of China in standard of living as they have a GDP per person of $38,800. That compares to China's per capita income of $2,800. Chinese officials admitted in early 2009 that 100 other nations have a higher per capita income than they do. But China is more interested in long-term moves that will enhance the nation and people are the puppets to that end. Unlike in America, saving is a way of life for the Chinese who save about half what they make each month. A shopaholic mentality is alive and well in America. The average household income in China in 2006 was 24% of their disposable income (Wall St. Journal 3-19-09 p. 38). That compared to America's measly .7%. China's domestic savings were 49% of their economic output in 2007, compared to 14% in America. *The Wall Street Journal* did an analysis of Economic trade freedom in the world. They found that the top five nations were: Hong Kong, Singapore, Australia, America, and New Zealand. The bottom five were: North Korea, Cuba, Libya, Zimbabwe, and Burma. Progress and standard of living are closely tied to economic freedom. In a survey on ease of doing business in 2008, Singapore ranked #1.

The World is Shrinking – Alter Your Behavior to Fit the New Way

In 2007 forty billion people sent an e-mail each day with 100 billion worldwide. It shows the shrinking nature of the world in which we live and work. There is much political pandering over Chinese imports. But those products hitting American stores are a bit different than most people realize: Computer parts are #1 - 16% of the total; Household goods are #2 - 15%; Toys and Recreation goods come in #3 at 12%; Computers are #4 at 10%; and Textiles #5 at 8% of the total.

China has 30 million cars and light trucks to service 1.3 billion people. America has 240 million cars for 300 million people. In 2007 China's population growth was 8 million people - the size of New York City - and its monthly growth was 667,000 – the size of Memphis. The nations that are on a roll are what the World Bank has labeled the BRICK nations. They are Brazil, Russia, India, China, and Korea. Notice that four of the five are from the Pacific Rim. These coming economic powers have three billion people, making America, but 10% of their power base from a human resource perspective.

Get inside the #'s to Manage Your Business

It is imperative that any business owner or top gun knows what the #'s mean in the firm's success or failure. What happens in an up market and in a down market? Few know! A CEO tends to rely on the CFO, but that is often the consummate C.Y.A. place where games are played more than most realize. If the top gun or an entrepreneur is not steeped in the Price Elasticity of their products and services, and the Break-Even in units and dollars, they are not savvy enough to manage a company when things turn volatile. Delegating such things to a Hired-Hand can prove costly or dangerous.

In the Buck Game the same rules do not apply as decades ago. We are immersed in an Internet Age. In this game, money is only how we keep score. It should not be the end all and be all as that is a short-term strategy sure to lose. Chase dreams and execute effectively, and the money will be delivered in trucks. That simple axiom is lost on most people. So many have been reared to worship at the altar of money it has warped their thinking. Gary Erickson of Cliff Bar fame did not follow tradition in this regard. That day in 2001 when he turned down $120 million for his company, most people - including he partner - thought he had lost his mind. Gary later told the media, "My investment bankers said the company would go under within 6 months. My partner thought Cliff Bar couldn't compete against the big companies and demanded I buy her out. I listened to my gut and said no to the offer." That is playing the Bucks Game with verve and panache. It is the ability to chase dreams even when family, friends, mates, or business partners tell you "no." This was never said better than Dr. Edward Deming who offered sage advice on this bucks game, "Managing by results, assigning reason to every result is fatal. This means the abolishment of the annual or merit rating or management by objective systems in order to become transformed." These simple words are absolutely lost on the majority of Western leaders. It is now time to look at the Brain Game. In that chapter you will learn how to manipulate your mind to think in a more progressive manner, or not permit it to dissuade you from your goals.

Chapter 4

The BRAIN Game – Mind Myopia
& Tunnel Vision

We become what we think and what we believe!

"Contrary to centuries of thinking the brain is not hard-wired. It is highly malleable like a muscle." – *PBS* Special (2008)

"Your behavior and environment can cause substantial rewiring of your brain or a reorganization of its functions."
Scientific American Mind (March 2009)

Mental masturbation is alive and well in America. Most leaders would deny that they are playing with their heads in their strategic decision-making, but they are. One such organization is the United States government. For many years it has cost 1.5 cents to make an American penny. The same irony exists with the nickel, which costs 9 cents to mint. With every one minted America increases her national debt by more than what the coin is worth. Why would rational people do this? They wouldn't, but card-carrying CYA governments would and does. Despite the depressed value of a penny, a Gallop Poll study found that 76% of people still bend down to pick one up. Edmund Moy, the Director of the Mint says, "We could save $100 million annually by changing the metal from copper and nickel to something like steel but congress won't approve it."

This is much like the CEO's being unable to see the forest for the trees or pilots crashing planes because of their inability to say, "I need help."

In spring 2009 *The Wall Street Journal* published an editorial titled "Is This the End of Capitalism?" It said, "Today's banking debacle had less to do with capitalism than with psychosis. Capitalism didn't tank the U.S. economy; overbuilt housing did the job in America, the UK, Ireland and Spain." It may not have been psychosis of the wannabes at the bottom, but it was certainly a mental malady of self-serving at the top. It is the Hired-Hand Syndrome at work again. The mind can be a friend or the enemy. It separates winners from losers, innovative leaders from the "Give it to me now" crowd.

In *iBrain* Gary Small wrote, "Hyperactivity, innovation and multi-task-ing, mania are just a few of the behavioral consequences of the new tech-no-brain." He was decrying the fact that Millennials are becoming repro-grammed due to their web surfing addiction. Altering brains is occurring at warp speed. "We see with our brains, not with our eyes" Norman Doidge told us in *The Brain that Changes Itself* (2007). This makes the mind the master of our fates and causes us to be C.Y.A. types or visionary types. Professor of psychology Peter Ubel wrote in *Free Market Madness (2009)*, "Conventional economics assumes humans are rational agents acting in their own self interest. That is deeply naïve and scientifically unrealistic." Ubel writes that such irrationality is responsible for the eco-nomic downturn that occurred in 2009. "The economic mess," he told the media, "is about fiscal foolishness. It's irrationality plus greed and a substantial dose of ignorance." That is so right on. The political pundits saying bring our jobs back should look within to find the problem.

Do You Have a Satori Mindset?

The Japanese have a word for personal motivation that is called *Satori*, meaning to have a "No Thought" concept of awareness. It is the ability to separate the mind from what is transpiring. A *Satori* State is when you are removed from the action in a kind of ethereal state of consciousness. It is a sort of an epiphany of the mind. In China they refer to such a state as "Chi." In America, especially in athletics, it is known as getting "In the Zone." When you enter such a euphoric wonderland, you tend to be special. Most people have had such an experience. It is when every single word you speak is right on the money, when each action you take is correct, when each Bridge bid is correct, and each backhand in tennis is a winner. *Satori* is when you are *Solution Focused,* not *Problem Focused.* Remember, a crocodile crawling in front of you will always distract you from watching the glorious sunset, but not if you are in *Satori.* When in a *Satori* State, you are able to encounter a sudden flash of consciousness that is a revelation. It can be a sort of mental catastrophe taking place all at once, after a lot of intellectual rubbish and then a sudden unveiling of truth. It is the integration of mind, body, and spirit into one flowing system of power from within.

Satori can be a powerful force from within. It can help remove the ego from an engagement and provide us an uninterrupted journey to enlightenment. There are times when events appear almost surreal. One of those was that morning on 9/11 when that plane crashed into the World Trade Towers. Watching the buildings burning and people jumping to their deaths are permanently etched into the minds and hearts of most Americans. Now think back about that time when you were the happiest in your life. You weren't trying to be happy. It is often a time when you were in a loving place with someone you love and doing what you love. Ironically, when you try too hard to get there, you don't. The mind keeps you from entering it; but by having Satori, you can find a "can-do" of omnipotence. It is a state of relaxed-concentration, a kind of transcendent reverie. As Mike Murphy wrote in *The Zone,* "Out-of-this-world experiences are really out-of-mind experiences." Chicago Bulls NBA coach Phil Jackson was a Zen-master who likened Michael Jordan's life force when he was unstoppable saying, "Michael is like a Zen student. He is relaxed and intensely focused in the midst of chaos."

Superstars Flip-Flop between Brain Hemispheres

Flip-flopping between brain hemispheres is a special talent not seen in the general population. Those with this ability are able to see the big picture and deal with what they envision in a quantitative way. It empowers them beyond the norm. Think about a golfer like Phil Mickelson who hits the golf ball with his left hand despite doing everything else right-handed. It gives him an edge, as it does Rafael Nadal who is a righty playing tennis left-handed. Russian tennis queen Maria Sharipova can be seen stretching to get a ball to her backhand and striking the ball very fluidly with her left hand. Why? She is a lefty playing tennis right-handed. This ability to cerebrally center makes them special. They have a prescient ability to flip-flop between hands and thinking without a lot of effort.

- ✓ *Leonardo da Vinci and Michelangelo* were both equally adept at painting with either hand and switched hands while sculpting or painting with ease.

- ✓ Mathematician *Henri Poincare* could write equally well with either hand. Harry Truman could do the same as well as former tennis great Martina Navratilova.

- ✓ *Babe Ruth* – Beat Yankee teammates bowling or playing other games like handball with either hand, and could do most things either way.

- ✓ *Maria Sharipova* plays tennis right-handed despite being left-handed in most other arenas.

- ✓ *Phil Michelson* & **Rafael** are right-handers playing golf and tennis left-handed.

Reprogram the Head – It's Plastic

In *The Brain That Changes Itself* Norman Doidge said, "We can change our brain anatomy simply by using our imagination." This has been validated many times. One study showed that if we think we are getting fit by cutting the grass we will and if we don't, we won't. When we are happy, we actually become healthier. If we believe we are using our muscles, our muscles become more toned and stronger. Sounds a bit mystical, but it is unequivocally true. Our minds are the masters of our destiny. Our health and happiness, and even more importantly, our ability to function at peak and more effectively lies in our heads. This is especially true when facing dire circumstances such as occurred in 2008 and 2009 when the world was recession bound. Why then? Fear becomes a catalyst for excess and self-destruction when things turn sour. There is a dramatic difference in the way the West typically deals with disaster and how the East deals with it. "Easterners perceive things holistically," writes Doidge. "They view objects in a context, whereas Westerners perceive them in isolation." Asia's ability to tackle the whole of a problem lets them see things from a much larger perspective and they're less likely to get caught up in the disaster of the moment. Those that get caught up in the moment are at greater risk of all kinds of things including suicide. Mark Twain wrote, "I kept crossing those bridges that weren't there when I arrived." Asians are not quite as inclined to let their minds mess with living. American politicians pontificate endlessly on such things as dumping and working conditions. That is seldom found in Asia. They see such things as part of everyday life and trivial compared to a larger context. Many politicians in the West see what the East sees as trivial as platforms from which to preach. In India the people are reared to use meditation and strong introspection as a means of controlling the mind. They know the mind is able to influence the body, pain, suffering, or one's station in life. The caste system is there to keep them in line, and so they stay where they feel fit. Americans are not so steeped in mind control as those in the East.

Brain Fitness

People are unaware that for every move or idea they are imprinting the mind in some way. Voracious readers have a facility with words, not because of some special acuity, but because they read. Reading and study is akin to a magical knowledge machine. A fit brain enhances the body and spirit. When it is not fit, it contributes to problems in work and play. Most people do not care to believe that they are the problem. That is another part of mental delusion. We are often the problem. We often cause ourselves to be sick. Studies have found that the same intelligence that we have for planning, hoping, imagining, and doing well in life are also the same ones that allow us to worry, fret, and become pessimists. Norman Doidge wrote, "Brain plasticity affects everyone without them knowing it. When we stop exercising mental skills, we don't just forget them. The brain map space for those skills is turned on to the skills we practice. Too many bad habits prevent the use of that brain space for good habits."

Research shows that those brains that fire together wire together, meaning that mental workouts lead to burning new brain neurons and growth. The bottom line is that the brain is susceptible to great change. It can be positive and it can be negative. For the brain to grow into a positive force within our heads, it is imperative that we begin thinking better. It is proven that it will lead to more viable thoughts and images. It is all a habitual exercise, mentally rather than physically. Positive stimulation has proven to develop more neurotransmitters in our bodies and a better blood supply than less stimulating environments. This could very well be why men like Irving Berlin and Bob Hope lived so long. They never retired, never slowed down until their late 90s and didn't get as sick as often or as seriously as those not so stimulated by their career paths. In the Brain Fitness world, they have a number of conditions to be followed to help us all change our brains. These are listed below:

<u>Brain Plasticity in Remolding Behaviors – + Attitudes</u>

↗ One must be in the **_Mood_** for Brain Plasticity to work; the neurotransmitters must be conditioned to fire for them to fire effectively.

↗ High **_Focus_** is essential for brain change to take place; believe in it for it to work.

↗ Brain Neurons that **_fire together will wire together_**—stability is the key for change to take place.

↗ The change must be **_Reinforced_** for an integrated change—keep on trekking to make it happen.

↗ Brains are malleable—**_Habitual Behaviors_** must be separated relative to the Good & Bad, Positive & Negative in order to change for the good.

↗ **_Memory Retention_** (Mirror-Neurons) must take place thus Success or Failure Patters in the head are a direct function of the experiential activities.

↗ **_Personal Motivation_** is the key for Brain Molding to work—get excited about change to make the change effective, as those not so inclined will resist the rigor necessary to change.

Manage Your MIND or It Manages YOU!

C. Northcott Parkinson told us, "It is the busiest man who has time to spare." The reason is such individuals are prone to manage their lives rather than reacting to what happens. Anxiety states are often the result of a kind of mental mysticism or sometimes exaggerated thinking. Walk a backyard balance beam with a $100 bill at the end of the beam as your prize for having balanced on the beam. Typically, it would pose few problems unless you had just finished off a six pack of beer or had chugged a couple of glasses of wine. Why? The mind is intently focused on the task at hand, balancing on the board and completing the task to get the $100 bill. Now raise the 2" x 6" board to ten feet in the air. Try the walk again at the new height. What happens? The mind is no longer focused on the beam or the bucks. It is focused on not falling–a fear thing. The solution? Blindfold your brain so you don't think about anything but the goal. The brain will sabotage your actions. Don't let it. The moral of this metaphor is that the brain must remain positive or the negative becomes the enemy from within.

Fishing in the stream of consciousness, researchers have learned that intentions are predictable. Our choices are self-evident, even prior to the time when we are aware of them. The brain makes up its mind 10 seconds before we become conscious of making a conscious decision--an eternity at the speed of thought. "We think our decisions are conscious," said neuroscientist John-Dylan Haynes at the Bernstein Center for Computational Neuroscience in Berlin, he is pioneering this research. "But these data show that consciousness is just the tip of the iceberg. This doesn't rule out free will, but it does make it implausible." Michael Merzenich found, "Contrary to centuries of thinking the brain is not hard-wired. It is highly malleable like a muscle. The brain can change in response to experience."

The Nocebo Effect is the inverse of the Placebo Effect. It is what can make you sick even when you aren't sick. The Placebo makes you think the pills you are popping will help you, and they do since the brain is wired for a positive result. A Nocebo Effect does the opposite. It makes you sick because you are thinking sick. In one experiment, asthmatic patients were asked to breath in a vapor that researchers told them was a chemical irritant or allergen. About half the patients experienced breathing problems. A dozen developed full-blown attacks. They were "treated" with a substance they believed to be a bronchodilating medicine, and they recovered immediately. In actuality, both the "irritant" and the "medicine" were a nebulized saltwater solution. It's all in the head, health and hurting.

Fishing in the stream of consciousness is where we come up with new ideas and fresh approaches to old problems. Researchers have discovered how to detect our inner most intentions and predict our choices before we are aware of them ourselves. At the University of California in San Francisco, researchers found out that the brain initiates free choices about a third of a second before we are aware of them. We know before we know.

Brain Wiring – Crucial to Altering Paradigms

I've often said, "It's okay to not know something; it's also okay to not know and know it; it's not okay to not know and not admit it; and *god forbid* if you don't know, don't know you don't, and don't care." The way we think is a function of how our brains are wired. Some are wired for adventure; others are wired for solitude; and others for overachieving. I'll never forget sitting in Hong Kong many years ago and espousing the rule of thumb multiples like ROI's and percentage margin differentials for break-even points. The owner of a Chinese manufacturing plant looked at me in awe. I was trying to motivate him to give me a good price. The strategy was a function of my American numbers-crunching background that was my mental wiring. Looking a bit exasperated the Chinese manufacturer said, "You Americans. I don't need all of this ROI stuff or percentages or nothing. I just need to make $1 on each of the million units a month you are buying. If I make that, I can run this plant profitably." I walked away thinking. Wow! All of this MBA stuff I have in my head may not be all that pertinent after all. The man's logic was 20/20. Make one buck a unit and he would have $1 million each month to cover his costs and make a profit. It was my educational indoctrination into the numbers game.

A *USA Today* (6-13-07) editorial offered prescient insight into such mind games. They were quoting an American politician from Michigan attempting to make a point and get votes. Democratic congressman Sander Levin said, "We're competing with a country with low wages, but with very high and heavy subsidies and a rigging of their currency." Even if that were the case so what? Is it any of our business? What does it have to do with the problems in Detroit? The root of the problem is that Fiat, Porsche, Volkswagen, Mercedes, or Hyundai were not uptight about what was transpiring in China. American politicians know little about the subtleties of world economics but love to become mired in a political pontificating so they appear that they care. The article spoke about the political pressure to impose duties on Chinese imports. What would it do? Dramatically raise the prices on all consumer products coming from offshore—clothing, tennis shoes, furniture, computers, and appliances. Cal Cohen, President of Emergency Committee for American Trade retaliated saying, "Our companies do not want to see a trade war with the Chinese. Our companies want to expand trade relations. It's a very, very good market for the U.S."

Market Myopia Reigns Supreme in Most Minds

When we are myopic we are unable to see what is transpiring right before us. This can be likened to a rat running a maze. After 100 times thorough the maze they gain a tremendous amount of expertise. The same is true of man doing the same thing, but like a rat, after 200 times they become hard-wired in certain arenas. It is the cause of those that we find who are rigid, inflexible and refuse to accept new ways. We think we are in control. Well we have run that maze in our life so many times we become rigid and inflexible to the point of becoming our own enemy.

This arms the brain with power, to create or to debilitate. It is true of leaders in any discipline. Most people have no idea what business they are really in. Such ignorance becomes their Achilles Heal. It interferes with their ability to implement the right strategies or the right marketing plans. Ray Kroc knew what business he was in from the start, and it wasn't burgers. It was real estate. But the Wall Street dudes kept insisting that food was his thing. Today they do the same with Starbucks and that is what causes the *hired-hands* to make bad decisions. Thinking that the sharp and well-educated Wall Streeter analysts know the truth is very misleading. They know the #'s, but the numbers are only part of the story. Businesses often listen to them so they can ensure the stock stays vibrant, but when the rubber hits the road relative to the true cause of problems it is often too late to turn the ship. Coffee is not the key to Starbucks' success. They are in the stimulating meet and greet business where a worker bee can feel special with a latte for $4. If they can't afford an expensive sports car or villa they can afford a special coffee that wires them for the day. Is coffee important? Of course it is, but it is but a vehicle to what will make or break them. In a similar way, Detroit has never been in the car business. They are in the transportation business. And the minute their cars aren't the best means of transportation they are gone. Gyms are not in the exercise business. They are in the self-esteem and feel good business where commiserating needs company since people could buy the equipment for use at home for far less money.

Many firms define themselves through the products or services they sell. At first look this seems plausible. It is not. Taking a product-based approach narrows your focus and limits your organization's ability to compete effectively. Harvard's Theodore Levitt wrote that companies that took a product approach suffered from marketing myopia. Although his classic article titled Marketing Myopia, was written in 1960, it is still relevant today. An excerpt from Marketing Myopia by Levitt from the *Harvard Business Review* offered insight into this:

> **"Let us start at the beginning: the customer. It can be shown that motorists strongly dislike the bother, delay, and experience of buying gasoline. People actually do not buy gasoline. They cannot see it, taste it, feel it, appreciate it, or really test it. What they buy is the right to continue driving their cars. The gas station is like a tax collector to whom people are compelled to pay a periodic toll as the price of using their cars. This makes the gas station a basically unpopular institution. It can never be made popular or pleasant, only less unpopular, less unpleasant."**
> *Harvard Business Review* **(July/August 1960)**

Market Myopia is a form of Tunnel Vision. This esoteric concept is really wrapped neatly into the more meaningful question, w*hat business am I really in?* What is the reason a customer buys what I sell? What services are the real benefits that I bring to the party? I am not in the exercise business; I am in the "Having a sexy body" business. Product focused firms become too wrapped up in the features and benefits of the hardware to truly understand the mind-ware. You don't sell "organic food." You are selling a long, healthy life. People get caught up in the old adage that if you provide the best product or service, people will beat a path to your door. But that is not necessarily true. Many ventures have made the best product and never survived. Look at the mainframe computer industry for dozens of examples. IBM never had the best product but for decades owned a 65% market share.

It is incumbent on leaders to analyze the customers' needs and wants. That will make them more aware of what game they are really playing. Levitt criticized the railway industry as being myopic. They erroneously believed they were in the railroad business. They were not, and consequently many filed bankruptcy. Railroads offered a very poor option for travel and were limited by their tracks in the shipment of products. They defined themselves too narrowly and some titans like the Pennsylvania Railroad bit the dust and went bankrupt despite having billions in assets. They made a very bad assumption, and as a result, permitted the automotive, trucking, and airline companies to steal their business. The founder of Revlon understood his business well. As head of Revlon International Corp., Revlon reflected, "In the factory we make cosmetics. In the department stores we sell hope."

America has suffered from tunnel vision in the mass consumer markets for a very long time. It would be nice to still be manufacturing labor-intensive products like tennis shoes and dress shoes, but that time has long since passed. America led those industries in the late 19th century, but since the advent of overnight deliveries, instant communications, Internet ordering and selling, and with a shrinking world economy, that is no longer possible. Politicians are constantly pontificating about bringing back manufacturing to America. It flies in the Rust Belt and a few union dominant markets. It should stop and get on to creating new jobs in new market arenas. Firms that were once best suited to make and sell Christmas tree ornaments and cheap shirts are no longer viable, so stop trying to chase what is past history. India, Taiwan, and China are better at building cheap widgets or cables than America. Leave them to those jobs and find ones that better fit you and your cultural background. America has a propensity for innovative services and creative ventures just as Mexico is more attuned to growing and picking oranges or other labor-intensive products. It is a mystery why so many people fight change and refuse to move on when their skill sets become obsolete. Those resisting reality are destined to be destroyed by their mindset more than anything else. Those caught up in a skill-based crossfire should find a new expertise in which to sell their time and talent. When your software job ends up in India, it is the perfect opportunity to open an ethnic restaurant. Start a Web business. Launch a 24/7 computer service firm, or better yet open a Brain Gym. The latest rage is clubs for aging Boomers like Vibrant Brains, Nifty after Fifty, and Vibrant Brains in California. Many use Brain Age games by Nintendo along with nutrition and mental or artistic regimens to maintain mental health. Within a few years you will be making more than you made as a software engineer.

Transactional vs. Transformational Leadership

There is a long history of traditionalism fighting innovation. Visionaries tend to lead when change is important. They tend to be armed with strong *Transformational* platforms. Traditionalists lead in static and *Transactional* venues. The reason one is innovative and the other is static is pretty basic. Transformational types have their feet permanently planted in outer space. They see the bigger picture and want to lead to what they envision. Traditionalists have their feet firmly mired in the safe present or past. The mind and the behavior that underlies all this is a function of past training and brain wiring. This wiring is crucial in a Web World where you change or find yourself mired in the good ol' days that are never going to return. This can be seen in the past when things were bad. In Depression-afflicted times, the party in power often remained in power. Why? The voters fear making a change during conflict or when at war. Some savvy politicos get that and figure if they can create conflict--god forbid that was George Bush's underlying motivation for invading Iraq--will often start a conflict to remain in office. Don't think Mr. Bush was that bright. A good example of this phenomenon at play is the housing debacle of 2008 and 2009. It led to a major recession with many predicting a Depression. This helped the Democrats to win easily in the 2008 election campaign. In the United Kingdom, the bubble bursting of housing and a growing recession crippled the incumbent Labor Party and put the Tories in power. When Fidel Castro led the revolution in Cuba, he remained in power for many decades. Fear keeps people voting for the incumbents for fear of change that could endanger them even more. That is about to change.

Sounds a bit trite, but it comes down to a head and heart thing. Are you a Qualitative or Quantitative thinker? Most traditionalists plan flippantly and operate rigidly. Not true of the visionaries. They do the reverse, planning rigidly and operate loosely. There is no right or wrong way, only what is best for any given situation. There are times when it is best to make gut decisions and there are times when it is prudent to be make more rational ones. Those saying "It's not in the budget, so you can't or playing the quantitative game. When you hear, "It's okay to try something new. Let's see where it takes us," are in a very qualitative decision making process. Each can elicit a far different response depending on the mindset of the organization. Each might be right in one situation and wrong in another. What is pertinent here is that understanding behavior is crucial to the way one leads and the leader cannot possible understand others until he or she understands what makes them tick. Carl Jung said the best in *Collected Works*, "Even when I am dealing with empirical data, I am necessarily speaking about myself." This preeminent therapist understood himself quite well and was telling us to make sure we understand others as well. When planning it is the common filter that everyone in that culture abides by that is crucial for producing an optimal plan. Do you have a *Transactional* filter? Or do you have a *Transformational* filter? I was told in grad school to "just run a business by the numbers, Gene," I then landed in Silicon Valley, and saw the movers and shakers disdain such a strategy. And most of them were physicists, engineers, and scientists. It proved a costly lesson, but I saw the light.

Traditionalists and MBA's tend to plan *Qualitatively* – big picture oriented and operate *Quantitatively* - by the numbers. In contrast, the visionary leader plans *Quantitatively* and operates *Qualitatively*. That leads to a clash when the two attempt to make deals or through a merger find themselves in the same firm. One type is highly grounded in a numbers and budgets game. The other is loose as a goose and functions in an autonomous "just go get em" fashion. When they hear, "You can't do that. It's not in the budget," they become riled. This occurred when traditional Sears acquired Lands' End, a yuppie group of techies that did not fit in the Sears Tower world. The quandary here is that traditionalists are prone to plan with a castle-in-the-sky mode, but operate very rationally while the visionaries tend to plan very rationally and operate very fluidly. For both, numbers are important. For one, it is in the planning stage and the other in the operating stage. Why has this been covered in such detail? Because it is not only a diametric difference between the visionary and the traditionalist, it is also a huge difference between how the East and the West operate. The West tends to elevate numbers to a godly state. Why? Quarterly bonuses and results are seen as success, not long-term viability. Not so in the East, where long-term success is far more appealing. There are some exceptions to each of these dictums. I'll never forget when Nolan Bushnell--the father of the video game industry and an electrical engineer by training--looked at me and said, "Gene, will you stop permitting the truth to interfere with where we are going?" Wow! What was he saying? It wasn't to lie. It was to stop being too grounded in logic or the numbers to the detriment of the possibilities.

Mind-Games & Labels

America became an enormous economic hyper-power. With that power, came the need to protect what they had garnered. That leads to elevating numbers-crunching and legal departments that will protect the asset base. Then came the military. It was created for protectionism during European and Asian conflicts, but with power comes the ideology of spreading your new-found fame and ideas to others in need of what you have found. Wrong! Due to their trying to curb Communism and promoting Capitalism, America has come to be seen as an imperialist nation. She earned it with billions of dollars and thousands of troops deployed in places like Korea, Viet nam, Iraq, Afghanistan, and many African nations. Consequently, many European nations that were once allies are now looking at America as a nation lost in their own reverie. They look at America's need to spread her influence as more of a threat than a value; more war-monger than peace keeper. Playing this game has cost American taxpayers billions each year. America is being portrayed as trying to sell her ideas, rather than as a peace arbiter. Any nation that becomes lost in their own need to sell their ideas and way of life to those that don't want it is setting themselves up for a fall. This is not about what is right or what is wrong; it is about any nation having the right to tell others how they should live. Every nation does not operate with the same mental filter, thus attempting to force one's standards on another is seen as arrogant.

Many former allies have declined to play in the American sandbox. Many politicians fear that any conflict has the propensity to explode into a nuclear war. There is no question that paranoia reigns supreme in a world where terrorism exists. For many years America was seen as the World's greatest military arsenal. Responsibility comes with such power. From travelling in Europe, it is more and more apparent that what was once an American privilege is no longer welcomed. The loathing rampant in most nations over the Iraq invasion is still alive in the minds of other nations. Some have labeled the Bush years as a sociopathic adventure. The inability to negotiate with others in that international sand box is a sign of inherent weakness. Why is this all little more than a brain thing? Because what we learn is how we function. Norman Doidge told us, "Unlearning is harder than learning."

IQ & Differing MindSets

Twilight states are what we experience just prior to going to sleep or waking up. It has been found to be the place where super-learning occurs. Thomas Budzynski wrote some years ago "It is in the theta state that the brain can learn enormous amounts very quickly, it is the state where super-learning takes place." It should not be a surprise that children are in this state much of the time. It is why they learn languages so readily. It has been found that old adage, "use it or lose it" is true, not only for the muscles, but also for the mind. Those individuals that spend their older years doing crossword puzzles, reading voraciously, and or playing chess are far less inclined to end up with Alzheimer's.

Many college-trained people still use interchangeably the words, intelligence, creativity, and genius. The words are in no way correlated. Paul Torrance--the preeminent psychologist on children--told us, "Above 115 or 120, IQ scores have little or no bearing on creativity. Creative giftedness may be found anywhere along the scale, except possibly at the bottom" (March 1987 *Redbook*). I have continually defined genius, not as some arbitrary number, but the ability to create something from nothing that others have not been able to do. Walt Disney is a prime example. Walt had an IQ of about 110 or at best 115. To be accepted in a Mensa organization, one must sport an IQ of 140. In American schools, to qualify as gifted, it is 130. Ted Turner created CNN with an

IQ of 118 about the same as President John F. Kennedy. IQ is merely a measure of academic capacity for logically comprehending symbols and words and not genius or creativity. When Henri Poincare--considered by Einstein to be the world's preeminent mathematician--took the Stanford-Binet IQ test, he scored at the imbecile level, not once, but twice. Psychologist Frank Barron said, "For certain intrinsically creative activities a specific minimum IQ is necessary to engage in the activity at all, but beyond that minimum, which is surprisingly low, creativity has little correlation with scores on IQ tests." Robert Toth, an eminent North Carolina sculpture wrote of the child-like characteristics in innovators in *The Flowering of Genius*, saying, "I'm ADD, as an artist I have always been drawn to things that are larger than life, themes that take on a meaning beyond themselves and fill us with memory and emotion." Toth confided in me, "I love your work. In reading it, I wasn't reading about the subjects. I was feeling me in your words." Being told being different was bad didn't deter Toth from chasing his passions. Never forget that normal is a synonym for mediocrity, making renegades the benefactors of creativity.

What is this Brain Game about? Change! If we are happy with our lives, we don't need to change how we think and how our brains are wired. If we are not, then we should take a close look at how to change. We all become what we *Think* and what we *Fear.* Polls continually show that a fear of making a speech ranks well ahead of a fear of death. Why? Humiliation is held higher than even dying. It is why soldiers in battle tend to fight when every nerve in their body says, "Run!" Safe dominates today's organizations in the West. Those in charge are to blame since their thinking is far too self-serving, risk-averse and short-term driven to overcome the inner need to feel secure. That is why America has a hard time competing with those that are not so inclined. Operate on the very *edge* with an *ethereal* mindset or wake up to find yourself as obsolete as a typewriter. Most leaders are not so programmed. In the mid-1970s, most middle schools and high schools in America along with many renowned universities actually banned the use of hand-held calculators with transcendental functions in their classrooms. Why? Fear! Not fear for the students, but fear for losing their jobs or demand in education. Would technology obsolete them? It was ignorance running rampant in our most cherished educational institutions. The irony is that today you cannot enroll in the same classes without buying the very same calculator that had been banned. Individuals must come to grips with those brain viruses that cause such poor or erroneous decisions. Dr. Gene says to look deep within and never forget that:

FEAR IS ANTITHETIC TO PROGRESS
FEAR DESTROYS FROM WITHIN
FEAR INHIBITS CREATIVITY
FEAR WARPS THINKING
FEAR DIFUSES TALENT
FEAR SAPS ENERGY

Don't Confuse the Map with the Territory or Metaphor with the Message

People get lost in the trees to the detriment of seeing the forest. They have trouble differentiating between the whole and its parts - the message and the metaphor. An example of this principle at work comes from the mid-20th century party matron Elsa Maxwell. She personified this precept as the madam of posh. Maxwell was the matron of Grande parties for the carriage trade in Paris, Monaco, Washington, London, and Manhattan. She had the money to buy a villa, Rolls Royce, or whatever car or house she wanted. To the amazement of the media, she owned nothing. Every home or car was leased if she was not being escorted about town in a chauffeured limousine. A *New York Times* reporter cornered her one evening, and bewildered about her strange lifestyle, asked, "Why are you ensconced in the Ritz Carlton Hotel and carless when it appears you have the wherewithal to own your own elegant estate somewhere and a very elegant set of wheels?" Maxwell looked at the reporter and said, "You don't own them. They own you." Is that insightful or what? For these types, the metaphor is the message. Most movie-goers never understood the larger message in the famous movie *The Wizard of Oz*. It was not about brains, hearts, courage, or getting back home. The Wizard was doling out hope and the need to know oneself. Once that happened, all other things are trivial.

Atlas Shrugged was a metaphorical masterpiece that made Objectivism a new philosophical tenet. To many, the book was not about a failing railroad. It was also not about the intractable John Galt. It was not about either. It was about political systems trying to make people into pawns of the state – telling them where they could work, live, and study. Ayn Rand's protagonist in the book was John Galt, a recalcitrant who opted to go on strike rather than capitulate to such autocratic governmental rules. Rand had Galt pontificating on what she called "rational self-interest" as the end all and be all of living a productive and meaningful life with Galt screaming, "The man who produces an idea in any field of rational endeavor - the man who discovers new knowledge is the permanent benefactor of humanity. Who do men fear most?" She wrote, "The brilliant loner - the beginner, the young man of potential and eminently ruthless integrity, whose only weapons are talent and truth." (Atlas Shrugged 1957 p. 171) In his famous radio speech, Galt says:

> **"In proportion to the mental energy he spent, the man who creates a new invention receives but a small percentage of his value in terms of material payment, no matter what fortune he makes, no matter what millions he earns."**
> *Atlas Shrugged* pg. 988

Messages are often hidden within the metaphor. Since communication is over 80% nonverbal, the way we dress, look, and speak is key to our ability to be effective. Studies have shown that creative people share a facility for using metaphors to communicate. Carl Jung said this a bit differently, but oh so right, "It is not Goethe who creates *Faust*, but *Faust* who creates Goethe. *Faust* is but a symbol." No better example ever occurred than the tragic story of a San Francisco high school art teacher named Jancy Chang. She became afflicted with left-brain dementia in her early forties after having painted since childhood. The doctors charted her mental decline and her art for the next twelve years. As her dementia progressed, her paintings changed from practical to imaginative–from left-brain rationality to right-brain surrealism, leading to progressive creativity –Realism to Impressionism. Dr. Miller wrote, "The more she lost her social and language abilities, the wilder and freer her art became–it allowed her to break the shackles of her realism art training and become increasingly impressionistic and abstract. Her paintings were much more emotionally charged." (Kraft SAM May 2005)

It has been found that half of all the caloric energy burned in children comes from their brain. Only 20% of the caloric energy burned in adults is brain related. That is one of the reasons why children are more inquisitive and learn easier than adults. Adults are far more relaxed. The bottom line in all this is that we too often become transfixed with our viral infections of the mind to take advantage of opportunities. The mind is not hard-wired. It is malleable and can make us or break us and far too often the latter is the result of our cogitating relentlessly over minutia. If it is lost on some wayward road, we now can right it. You wouldn't see a steak on the menu and eat the menu, so don't let mental mysticism or mind viruses mess with your success. For personal transformation, play the brain game. If unemployed the real fact is it is probably the very first time in your professional life you are free to do what you want, go where you want and restart your engine. Always wanted to sell real estate, open a picture gallery specializing in weddings and special events? This if your chance! It's a matter of dousing the negative karma that is associated with not working.

Chapter 5

The *BALLS* Game – Greed vs. Fear Prevails in All Venues

Risk & Reward is a Zero-Sum Game – Bet it All to Get it All.

"Only those who will risk going too far can possibly find out how far they can go." - T. S. Eliot

"Most educational systems honor those who play it safe. They're the ones who get good grades. Economic success is about the willingness to take risks." Farson & Keys 2002 – *The Paradox of Innovation*

Risk-taking is the only path to greatness. For some reason that is lost on the masses who avoid risk as if it's a plague. Risk is the only way to be great in any endeavor. And the ability to bet what you have to get what you want is a mind game as discussed earlier. Most people have been so indoctrinated in playing safe games they are ill-prepared to live further on the edge where fame and fortune are born. Many think edgy behavior is genetically based. Wrong! It never ceases to amaze me how a well-read, so-called scientist can make inane statements about our decisions being due to our genetics. It is akin to the many Marketing Professors in high-profile universities saying the best sales people are extroverts. Such characterizations are more about covering your ideology than your assets. The truth is that such statements are self-serving nonsense. The need to play the CYA game and reduce life's risk underlies most inane ideas. It is the ability to live a bit more on the edge and go with what is working that is the fuel of superstars. Economist Robert Gordon in 2009 told the USA Today, "New rules – less risks - mean fewer crises and less innovation." Touché!

A spring 2009 *Parade* article said, "Your DNA may reveal how much financial risk you're willing to take." The Northwestern University study was based on saliva tests to reveal the amount of anxiety and risk-taking in the genes of the subjects. It has been known for many years that risk and anxiety are due to the way we think, not some genetic factor. And the way we think is a function of our experiential profiles, testosterone, and to a limited extent, our genes, but not much–about 25%. An over-protective mother sheltering her offspring from risk will reduce the risk-propensity of them as adults. And anxiety is learned, not inherited. Harvard tests on winning hockey and other sports events show that the winners have higher testosterone than the losers. That would indicate that winners either come armed with a Big T personality or become more wired due to winning. Data shows that it is a bit of both. One in three American adults is in prison; five times that of the rest of the world. Does that say it is in the American gene? Don't think so. It has far more to do a permissive society gone amuck. It has more to do with inner-city projects, drug-laden, and gangs that have no parental influences or run amuck on the streets to show they are worthy and big-time. That big-time mentality becomes deeply etched in their psyche in what I have long labeled "Failure Imprints" and "Success Imprints" –all a function of early conditioning. Other countries have parental control not found in America. When asked why he emerged out of a bad Queens's neighborhood and didn't take drugs or die as most of those in that same environment, Colin Powell told the press, "My parents would have killed me." The Jesuits were right when they said, "Give me a kid until seven, and I'll own him for life."

Risk-Taking & Fear Emanate from Within

Inhibition is the mortal enemy of creativity. Harvard discovered this by wiring the brains of creative and non-creative students. Those with the least inhibition were 7X more creative than the norm. We see this constantly in charting those that make innovative leaps and those that become mired in the status-quo. Leonardo, Picasso and John Nash had little inhibition. This is apparent in their lifestyles and work. They were comfortable with ambiguity. It led them astray, but it made their work original. Thus, it is fear, not venturesome moves that are the enemy. Wall Street has had the anthem of greed versus fear. Are you greedy enough to bet beyond your fear, or are you willing to bet what you have on what you want? Are you inhibitions keeping you from going to that place where success is based on the bucks? Personal success and ultimate transformation are inextricably tied to such temerity. It is amazing how many leaders are vanquished due to opting for the safe roads where they are prone to serve at the altar of their anxieties.

We all fear something. It may be looking bad, losing our money, or getting fired. But it is those intrepid warriors who refuse to permit such ideas to program their lives that are more resilient and more prone to find the gold. In the quote *The Paradox of Innovation*, "Economic success is about the willingness to take risks" is a profound message on reaching the top. Politicians are unable to go to such a place for fear of ruining their career. We see it in students as well. Students unwilling to face the displeasure of their peers or parents are the ones that must get an A. Those not so driven for perfect scores are there to learn something they can use on the street more than how they can look good. Good grades do not correlate with eminence. They correlate with doing well in school. What is not often acknowledged is that those students that change the world were not so inclined to chase A's, but to chase knowledge. Visionaries always chase knowledge, which leads to long-term results. This is why B and C students are the one's most likely to alter paradigms.

Entrepreneurial superstars are so inclined. The four leaders of the information age – Bill Gates, Larry Ellison, Steve Jobs, and Michael Dell don't have the equivalent of a Bachelor's Degree between them. And if they had it is very unlikely they would be worth so many billions. For them it was dreams, not grades that charged their souls. They were rule-breakers, and rule-breaking is imperative for making a difference. That is the Balls Game. If you don't have the guts to be different, it isn't likely you will be. It is about thumbing your nose at established dogmas. Such a mindset in Japan was rooted in the words *Tora Tora*. It was also latent in that juggernaut that landed in our living rooms in the form of electronic products. They had the Balls to go where others feared, and that included their infamous bombing of Pearl Harbor. Such a gutsy act caught Washington asleep. Their product innovations did the same economically. In each case, the Japanese didn't need for some intrinsic motivation, it was latent within. Their success was not some accident of fate, but deeply rooted in a ballsy attitude.

Tora Tora was a code word used by the Japanese in their Pearl Harbor attack in World War II. In Japanese, tora is written 虎 for "tiger" and "to" is the initial syllable of the Japanese word 突撃 totsugeki, meaning "charge" or "attack." To Ernest Hauser--a Western journalist--writing about the Japanese attack on the American stronghold is a dichotomy. The typical Japanese is a "nervous, emotionally high-pitched, sensitive person," Hauser writes. But it's this inscrutable personality type energized from within that Hauser would label a split-personality. Japan is one of the oldest totalitarian systems on earth. When working in such a culture it is imperative to understand that they are unique and that is okay. Americans find it strange that in Japan there are no street #'s and a taxi takes you about looking for landmarks instead of numbers. In Japan imagery is everything. This is apparent with their alphabet. It is far more symbolic than in the West that is far more rigorous and absolute.

Kaizen Underlies Japanese Motivation

The Japanese have another word for internal motivation. It is *kaizen*. *Kaizen* is about continuous improvement throughout all aspects of life--becoming aggressive to become powerful. It is a fundamental philosophy of life in that little island nation. From it, come such business innovations as the Quality Circle concept of finding faults and fixing them. It had its origins in Dr. Deming's early quality control systems. In Japan, the *kaizen* mentality can be found as a pervasive force in their quest to be the best they can be. In Japanese, the word is 改善: the 改 meaning to change, improve, to renew; the 善 meaning good. Together, these symbols are about improving for the better. The Japanese life is centered on a philosophy of never ending improvement.

The West has an equivalent concept known as "Six Sigma." It is a statistically-based concept, rather than an intrinsically based one. It is about making all products 99.999% right with very few anomalies or errors. To get a bit technical on this, kaizen practices are aimed at attacking fear where it begins. In the brain, that is called "amygdala." This area of the brain is man's traffic cop. It is where inhibition originates. And as discussed above, inhibition is the enemy of creativity. It keeps us emotionally out of harm's way, but that is contra to the creative process. Left to its own ends, the amygdale in the brain is what keeps man from excelling in anything where risk is necessary. The amygdale makes fear more powerful than reason. In kaizen, the fight or flight of Hans Selye is no longer a problem. Selye found that stress from today's fast-paced existence causes the mind to make a choice. He labeled it a 'fight or flight' syndrome. In today's web-world, we face this dilemma constantly. Many of us find ourselves faced with some dilemma and don't know whether to fight or flee. Many of us are in a permanent state of arousal that takes its toll on our bodies. Selye called it a *General Adaptation Syndrome*. We face this in the early stages of having a new creative idea. The biochemical changes in our brains make us aggressive, fighting the new idea, or make us timid, fleeing from it. The Japanese have kaizen to quell their anxiety. America needs an equivalent word. The kaizen meaning of "educated wisdom" emanates from *"Kai,"* meaning continuous learning, and "Zen" meaning wisdom. Get smart and then get wise.

In Japan, every employee practices *kaizen,* from upper management to the cleaning crew. Everyone is encouraged to come up with small improvements on a regular basis. This is not a once a month or once a year activity, it is daily. Japanese firms like Toyota and Canon, have a total of 60-70 suggestions per employee per year of contributing ideas. Suggestions are not limited to any specific department such as production, finance, or marketing. They are expected to come from anywhere, anytime, and hopefully all of the time. Western philosophy is often summarized as, "if it ain't broke, don't fix it." The *kaizen* philosophy is the opposite. Keep breaking it to make it better. Improve it even if it isn't broken. If we don't, we can't compete with those who do. We saw this in Sam Walton whose philosophy of business was, "Break the rules." Any Westerner that has spent time in an American factory and then walked through a Japanese factory comes away transfixed. They immediately know why the East dominates the West in this arena. I was personally shocked when I left a California factory and walked through a Hitachi factory. It was 1969. I was young, naïve, and oblivious of behavior and motivation, but it was a real eye-opener. Our Washington politicians pontificating on this subject should go and take a look at the competition. American factories find people chit-chatting, making jokes, and flirting. Not so in a Japanese plant. There is an eerie silence pervading all production facilities. It is akin to a controlled-aggression married with relaxed concentration--a mind--controlled experiment that worked. I came away transfixed, wondering just how they could maintain such intensive concentration for eight hours.

U.S. Trade Deficit

In 2008, America's trade deficit reached $277 trillion and climbing. In the mid 20th century, the trade deficit had been positive, not negative. At that time, the dollar was very strong. As the dollar began shrinking relative to other currencies, the balance of trade began heading in the opposite direction. It has continued down this perilous path for some decades. When the dollar is strong, it makes other nations' products far cheaper in America. When it is weak, it makes American products cheaper in those nations, and attracts foreign investment. It doesn't matter if our products become cheaper due to a cheaper dollar if we aren't making them.

America is known throughout the world as a "shopaholic nation." It has been one of the most acquisitive societies known to man. Americans love to buy the newest widgets and have a reputation for conspicuous consumption. It has made America a very lucrative target for many foreign nations trying to improve their relative stations in life. Beginning in the 1970s, America has gone from a trade surplus nation to one in a deficit position with most other nations. That is when Europe and Japan began competing with the U.S. in many different industries, most notably consumer electronics and automobiles, the resulting loss of jobs made for political bantering. America was still in a state of prodigious growth, so no one cared that many workers had to change careers. They found jobs in the new dynamic fields of computers, communications, and aerospace.

This has come to sudden halt with the loss of industries and the need for politicians to fund foreign hostilities. With the decline in growth experienced after the millennium, the loss of jobs has suddenly become a serious problem for America. The trade balance deterioration became fuel for the political pundits screaming about the loss of employment, especially in manufacturing and other industries producing traded goods. The trade surplus in the 1960s had suddenly become a huge and growing deficit. The deficit reached 2.9% of the GDP by 1998, and has continued unabated since that time. The trade deficit problem has led to the loss of millions of high-skilled manufacturing jobs in America. It has caused workers to find new careers, often at lower wages, since when we don't bring tons of job expertise to a position we must accept the wages of that role. This has led many to start their own businesses. Many have opened their own coffee shops or gone back to nursing school, since health care is a burgeoning industry with many openings. Others have opted for a web business. By 2009, the U.S. had lost nearly 500,000 manufacturing jobs since March of 1998. Most of those job losses were attributed to the increase in the trade deficit. America is a net importer of capital because Americans do not save enough to finance all the available investment opportunities. That has led to an influx of capital from abroad, allowing us to pay for imports over and above what we export.

International Trade Myths

Why does America lose jobs? Many in Washington continue to attribute it to the trade deficits, blaming China, Korea, and India. It is interesting that they don't mention Canada, as they are friendly neighbors to the North, yet they are the largest importer of goods to America. The following myths are a reminder of why we are where we are.

MYTH #1: The first myth is that the overall U.S. trade deficit leads to the loss of job security in the United States. There is no job security. The security is within a person who has not identified with his job to the point that he self-destructs when that job is no longer viable. This tome has numerous examples of those who lost their job and it made them rich and famous. It was true of such icons as Walt Disney and Buckminster Fuller. Had Walt not been fired as a cartoonist, he would never have launched Disney Studios where he would become the maven of animated films like *Snow White*. Had Bucky Fuller not been fired from his Chicago job, he would not have created the geodesic dome.

MYTH #2: There are unfair trade barriers abroad, and that has been the genesis of American problems. Foreign tariffs and other barriers are certainly a problem, just as American import tariffs are merely masking a larger problem. But trade restrictions are not what determines U.S. trade deficit, nor do they fully account for the differences in bilateral trade balances. An example is the large trade surplus with Brazil, a country with relatively high tariffs on many products. And of course our NAFTA partners, Mexico and Canada, are where the nation has huge deficits, with Canada being the largest single importer. Both nations are virtually open to U.S. exports and imports.

MYTH #3: The myth that trade deficits are caused by an inability for America to be competitive is sheer nonsense. America is one of the most competitive nations in the world, far more than many of the Pacific Rim nations. The myth has been refuted by the performance of the American economy that remains one of the world's greatest examples of how to rebound from adversity. Since 1992, the U.S. trade deficit has tripled, but its industrial production has grown by 24%, and its manufacturing output has improved by 27%.

MYTH #4: Another myth is that trade deficits destroy jobs. No matter how many products and services move offshore, the American employment remained vibrant until the 2009 recession. When an economy is expanding due to chasing new innovative products, they create new jobs, even if the obsolete ones are gone. Even the exporting of diagnostic services to places like India leads to interfacing jobs in America. The incredible American economic results in the recent past should lay that myth to rest. While the trade deficit has expanded, so have American payrolls during the same time period. But as we have noted, there is a strong correlation between rising trade deficits and falling rates of unemployment. The reason is simple: The same expanding economy that stimulates demand for labor also raises demand for imported goods and capital.

MYTH #5: This myth is the idea that trade deficits drag down the U.S. economy. Since 1980, the American economy has grown an average of 3.1% in those years in which the current account deficit has expanded from previous years. When the deficit shrunk, the average decline was just 2%. If trade deficits were bad for growth, then how could the economy grow more than 50% faster when the trade deficit expands? One example is the African aid from rich nations to help them grow. It did the reverse. Evidence shows that aid to Africa has made for slower growth and the poor are even poorer. *The Wall Street Journal* (March 21, 2009 p. W1) wrote:

> **"The insidious aid culture has left African countries more debt-laden, more inflation-prone, more vulnerable to the vagaries of the currency markets and more unattractive to higher-quality investments."**

What America needs is export-led growth, not import-driven consumption. America has had a long run of trade deficits due to a need to sate their huge appetite for new products. The nation suffers from trade deficits due to printing money to finance wars and to fund downturns such as took place in 2009. Large trade surpluses in Asia led to most of those nations over-saving; the exact opposite of what took place in America where the people and nation were caught up in a debt-oriented lifestyle. In China, consumer spending represents 35% of their GDP. That is half of America's debt to GDP ratio. The average person in China saves half of what they earn. That is a fraction of what an American earns, but the American has had a negative savings rate for some years.

Risk-Takers, Care-Takers & Under-Takers

There are but three types in the world. Those that risk are a very small percentage—between 2% and 10% of any given cohort. They are willing to bet what they have to get what they want, but most people are unwilling to play that game. The Care-Takers are those caring followers who are infected with the C.Y.A. disease. They represent about 75% of any cohort and are unwilling to risk losing their job for any rewards. The

Under-Takers represent about 15% of any organization. They are misfits at some level or devious to a fault and should be found and dismissed.

Those that change the world tend to fit the Risk-Takers category. Warren Buffet is normally not classified as a Risk-Taker, as is someone like Rupert Murdock, Ted Turner, or Amelia Earhart, but he fits the definition when he says things like, "A simple rule dictates my buying. Be fearful when others are greedy, and be greedy when others are fearful." That is similar to what billionaire, oilman J. Paul Getty once said, "I buy when everyone else is selling and sell when everyone else is buying." Age is usually a factor in risking, as most people bet less and drive slower as they age. But that doesn't hold for what I label "entrepreneurial spirit." The age factor is why they put 18-year-olds in foxholes. The young seem to accept the new long before older people do. Why? Age leads firms and people to protect what they have accumulated. With more assets, there is a tendency to take fewer risks and as maturity happens, there is far less speculation going on. As Burton Klein told us in *Dynamic Economics*, "Those who leap before they look are more successful than those who look before they leap." People who leave an imprint on the world tend to be on-the-edge types. This can be seen from both a positive and negative perspective. Mark Twain, Thomas Edison, and Frank Lloyd Wright were broke at sixty due to their on-the-edge behavior that led to betting on new venturesome ideas. But by the time they passed, they were rich and famous. They left a positive legacy due to their ability to risk, and when it failed they wrote it off as a loss and moved on to another opportunity. Such people are known as Big T—high testosterone risk-takers. The *San Francisco Chronicle* (Nov. 19, 2006) wrote:

"People with power are more oblivious to what others think, more likely to pursue the satisfaction of their own appetites, poorer judges of other people's reactions, more likely to hold stereotypes, are over optimistic and more likely to take risks."

Such rhetoric has had a long legacy. Catherine the Great arrived in Mother Russia as a teenager from Germany and wrestled power from her imbecile husband, Peter. "There is no woman bolder than I" she told a British envoy, "I have the most reckless audacity." This indomitable spirit wrote in her memoirs about taking the reigns from her dim-witted husband, Peter: "I was sustained by ambition alone. There was something within me which never allowed me to doubt for a single moment that I should one day succeed in becoming the Empress of Russia, in my own right." One of her biggest detractors and political adversaries was Professor Masson who wrote, "Catherine combined corpulence with elegance and an air of great nobility with a very gracious manner." When the spirited lady heard that Peter was on his way to arrest her, she donned a male Captain's uniform, replete with sword, and mounted her steed--full saddle, an unheard of thing in 17th century Europe. She told the imperial guard to follow her into battle. They did, and defeated Peter, and made sure he never returned to challenge her rule. It is unlikely the soldiers would have followed a woman donned in dress and bonnet seated side-saddle.

A very similar moxie mixed with a gambling spirit is always found in the minds and hearts of almost every single individual that has made a difference in the world. Why? The entrepreneur spirits view risk as part of the process. They often begin at the bottom and know that the only road to the top is paved with many barriers and problems. Asians know this and accept it. Strangely, many Westerners see risk as something to avoid, not as a weapon for winning. That is precisely what has led to their Mass Market Myopia. George Gilder said it quite eloquently on the subject of America's penchant for getting lost in cost as a means of pricing a product in mass consumer markets. The Asians seem to know that there are no fixed costs in the long run. That seems to be lost on Americans. What is fixed is always fixed to the traditionalist mindset. It is also a road to disaster in mass marketing. Traditionalists get so grounded in what they think is a truth they have difficulty with what is often counter-intuitive. George Gilder saw this in speaking of the *The Spirit of Enterprise*:

"Selling below cost is the crux of all enterprise. Today, the Japanese dominate market after market by obsessive use of the curve while many American companies and business experts believe that the strategy is somehow obsolete or reprehensible."
- George Gilder

Sounds pretty simplistic, but it is deeply imbedded in Western pricing strategy. In the early days of the Chuck E. Cheese start-up, I was told by a Harvard trained CEO that I could not afford to have a rat costume character that had cost me $5,000 to buy. This scenario happens daily and is what Gilder was talking about. The first of anything is always exorbitantly expensive. I told the expert, "I didn't buy that rat for one store. He is a test vehicle, and if he works, I will figure out how to buy him in volume at some lower cost. In economics, cost drops by 30% with each doubling of volume. In the case of the Chuck E. Cheese costume--after twenty stores were opened--he cost just $300 to buy. So many firms base their decisions on early data, and that leads them totally astray.

The Dumping Myth

For many decades, the word "dumping" had a very negative connotation in America. Laws were passed to make it illegal to sell any product below its cost. What is wrong with such a law and most have a similar genesis is that cost is very different in different organizations and radically different in different nations. In America there is a fringe benefit cost of approximately 40% - 45% on top of every hour of labor in that product. It is a fraction of that or sometimes non-existent in Asia. Thus when cheap Asian products started hitting our shores in the 1970's and 1980's politicians began screaming about "Dumping." since it was undermining American jobs. Who decides what something costs? Those in power! Thus it can be and often is a moving target. Too often the dude pontificating on dumping is some government official who has never built anything. Give me a break. In America, the fringe benefits are considered a joke in struggling nations like Mexico, China, Taiwan or India. An American worker earning $40,000 will cost the business almost $60,000. How do you ever equate that with the direct or indirect cost of products in other nations where there is no such overage added to labor? Politicians are on their soap-box telling Americans that it is un-American to buy something below cost. Yet they don't even understand the differing nuances of how cost is computed in other nations. They've never run a factory there. What gives them the right to act like they know? They need a platform from which to get blue-collar votes.

Just because a stereo system or TV sells below cost, should some politician have the right to outlaw the consumer from saving money to have it in their home? Besides, the basic rubric here is about the word "cost." One man's cost is another man's profit. In China, Taiwan, and Korea they laugh at this dumping argument as self-serving at the very highest level. Many pompous politicians--including former First Lady, Hillary Clinton--told China to stop abusing the Humanitarian Rights or pay the consequences. That is tantamount to a Chinese official telling America to make it safe to walk the streets of Detroit, New York, and Los Angeles at 2A.M. or they will stop shipping tennis shoes to America. Cultures are different. That is the nature of the world. Any nation with the unmitigated gall or arrogance to tell another nation how to live is why America is looked upon as imperialistic. No culture has the right to tell the other how to live. President John F. Kennedy saw this while in office and told the media, "The U.S. is only 6% of the world's population. We have no right to impose our views or even system of government on the other 94%." In today's diverse world, this is even more relevant. Today, there are 185 million Americans (61%) that are overweight with 80 million (27%) clinically obese. There are 30 million Americans taking tranquilizers for depression or other anxieties. These tragic numbers are not true in other societies. What if India said they will no longer do business with us if we don't get skinny or stop drugging ourselves? Politicians should take a gander in the mirror prior to pontificating on how others should mimic America.

China produces 75% of the world's toys, with 78% of them coming from Guangdong Province where 5,000 of China's total 8,000 toy factories produce export revenues of $15.2 billion annually. For the uninitiated, that is approximately 25% of the total American retail toy sales' revenues, or about $60-$70 billion. Their wages are a fraction of American wages. In 2006, they were paying $88 per month for a factory worker who works an 8-hour day and 21-day month. That is still far less than is desired in America. The United States has held the title of the most competitive nation in the world. Many times, Japan comes in as #2. But the U.S. places very low on People Skills, Education, and Training.

RISK & REWARD – A Zero-Sum Game

Risk and reward is a zero-sum game in that for every risk we attempt to remove from any decision or idea, the more reward we remove. That means that for every bit of risk the CFO or legal counsel encourages you not to take, the less chance you will have to make a big hit in the future. This simple axiom is often lost on many leaders and most politicians. I like to use a family metaphor to make the point. Lock your children in their room and never let them see the light of day, and all risk of getting beat up, breaking an arm, or suffering defeat from an adversary are eliminated. The price you will pay is your children will never amount to anything since we learn and grow through adversity on the streets of life. Conversely, the more risks you take the greater the potential rewards. Babe Ruth broke all of the homerun records. He also set all of the strikeout records in his era. Had he declined to risk striking out, there would have been no chance for him to set the homer records, but he would not have suffered the indignation of holding all of the strikeout records in major league baseball. The moral here is that risk should be elevated to the highest in everyone's life. Take the greatest risk you can tolerate and you will be able to achieve the highest rewards. We cannot grow without facing problems and getting a bloody nose. This is precisely why the children of eminent people seldom become great. Life is too easy. They are not faced with the huge obstacles and risks that other children face. They must learn to fight in order to learn how to win when things get tough.

The vast majority of people are programmed to play it safe. That program was written when they were growing up and told, "Be prudent honey" or "Riding your bike alone to school is dangerous." Those are well-meaning statements by a caring parent. But the program in the child's brain is "No," "Don't," "Fear," and so on. The child is being programmed for surety and mediocrity. Tennis amateurs validate this. Most try to keep the ball in play rather than trying to put it away. The latter is fraught with unforced errors and the former with not looking bad. Female players tend to be guiltier of this than men. The macho dudes don't care if they look bad if they can hit an uncontested winner. The lower testosterone females tend to want to not err and thus they don't nearly as often as men. The men's rallies are shorter and the women's rallies are longer. We do the same with our kids. We overprotect them so they won't get in trouble, kidnapped, or lost. By doing this, we do not groom them to compete on the streets. Why are some kids from the projects more fearless? It's not an accident or due to any ethnic system. They grew up on the streets and learned to be street-smart early in life. They missed out on many other things by being out there, but some kids that lived within the safe cocoon of the home and classroom did not learn how to compete on their own. The adage is true. If you haven't fallen off that bike enough, you will never learn to be really good at riding that bike. Alpine skiers know that when a family friend says, "I skied all weekend and didn't fall once," the fact is they never pushed themselves enough to fall, and thus didn't improve one iota that weekend.

In the Brain Game chapter we spoke *of thinking* being the mortal enemy of *eminence*. Using the Alpine skiing metaphor, you think and you are in trouble. Thinking interferes with the body's ability to function at peak. It tries to protect us from failing and falling. It leads to erroneous decisions. In contrast, the gut is without inhibition, and thus far more providential. Neophyte alpine skiers almost always lean backward toward the hill. Why? That seems safe to their mind's eye. It is not! You should lean forward, because leaning down the hill permits the skis to turn much easier and it makes the task safer than leaning backwards. Fear is the culprit and therefore the catalyst for most major injuries on ski slopes. It is also true for boardrooms. Biologists who have studied boldness in animals find that those acting bolder experience preferential treatment by the opposite sex. That is certainly the case of man with many examples like a bold Bill Lear inventing the "auto-pilot" just so he could have a mile-high liaison, or Bill Clinton daring to have a young intern spend time in his White House office while Hillary was in another wing. Frank Lloyd Wright was the poster boy for blatant sex acts. While designing for a wealthy Chicago businessman, he took up with his wife Mamah Chaney—a well-read woman with a Masters Degree in education. Just after the birth of Wright's sixth child, the two surreptitiously split for Europe in a scandalous act that even shocked the media of the time. An example of Wright's willingness to bet on his passions was the fact that he borrowed $10,000 from a friend to finance his wild affair. The two lived in Berlin and Florence with Wright's flourishing architectural business abandoned to sate his need for love and adventure.

You hear people speak of playing it safe. Why do they say that? Fear! Moderation is the ultimate path to mediocrity. Doesn't sound politically correct, but moderation is the enemy of excellence in any venue. It is true in sports, business, or romance. In *The Way of the Peaceful Warrior*, Dan Millman opted for a metaphorical protagonist that he named "Socrates." It permitted him to wax philosophical with ideas and morals for his young protégé. Socrates eulogizes to his young Berkeley protégé:

"Moderation! It's mediocrity, fear, and confusion in disguise. It's the devil's dilemma. It's neither doing nor not doing. It's the wobbling compromise that makes no one happy. Moderation is for the bland, the apologetic, for the fence-sitters of the world, afraid to make a stand."

People often speak of compromising, rather than risking. Well this author believes that a compromise is a no-guts emotion without merit. An example is when you're new fledgling business needs a pick-up truck and a car. Each has its own merits. With a truck, you can haul or deliver your wares. So you compromise and buy an SUV or a station wagon. What do you get? You have a half-assed car and a half-assed truck. The compromise is a no-risk decision that is almost always an error. It brings to mind Canadian researcher David Viscott's words: "The driver most likely to be killed at an intersection is the one who hesitates, loses his nerve, and can neither accelerate nor apply his brakes. He cannot follow through on a commitment to act." Even more profound was George Gilder's analysis of America versus Asia in the war of fear versus greed:

"The investor who never acts until statistics prove his choice, the athlete or politician who never fails to move until too late, the businessman who waits until the market is proven - are all doomed to mediocrity by their trust in a spurious rationality and their feelings of faith."
George Gilder, *Spirit of Enterprise* (1984)

Anxiety & Eminence

Inner anxiety plagues most people in every discipline and in every culture. Anxiety and stress eat away at our ability to function without remorse or apprehension. It is why many of us lead lives of quiet desperation. The cause of such thinking can be found in our minds. I call them "viral infections" (see *Paranoia & Power*). We all have security-viruses running around in our brains trying to keep us safe and secure. They were put there by caring parents, preachers, and teachers. But safe is never remotely related to happy or healthy. *Wanna become an Icon?* Identify the enemy within and destroy him before he ends up destroying you. The mind is a con-artist of incredible power. It tries to keep us safe, but it is often what makes us weak. In business, this fear-freak from within is what makes us hide behind policies, procedures, budgets, job descriptions, and organizational charts. Ever notice that such things are verboten in firms run by superstars? This was the case in the incredible climb to success of Gore-Tex. Bill Gore refused to operate like the typical corporation, and his guts to implement his ideas led to unprecedented growth and profits. Gore pioneered *no organization charts, no bosses, no titles, no budgets* By going where others refused, it would lead to 50 years of continual profits and one of the very top U.S. firms to work for. Gore-Tex has a fraction of normal turnover in their industry.

Surety Mantras

Think Edison or Einstein ever kowtowed to such things as budgets or job descriptions? No chance! Sam Walton was famous for refusing to follow rules or policies. When the board insisted that he have a policy manual for his billion-dollar firm, he gave in and hired a specialist. The consultant had just finished Sears's policy and procedures manual. It had taken him a couple of years to write and implement. Sam gave him a couple of months, and the man looked at him incredulously. This mental mindset is telling since Wal-Mart would pass Sears as if they were standing still. Within a few years, they would be the largest corporation in the world. A Hired-Hand would never have had the guts to do what Sam did. That is precisely why they will never have the bucks he had. Hired-hands hide behind policy manuals, budgets, and job descriptions. Not a Sam! They use policies to keep the herd in line, but that is never important for a Sam

Walton. Surety is nice, but it isn't correlated with eminence. No one ever said this better than William Arthur Ward who told us that risk must be taken because the greatest hazard in life is to risk nothing:

The person who risks nothing, does nothing, has nothing, is nothing.
He may avoid suffering and sorrow,
But he cannot learn, feel, change, grow or live.
Chained by his servitude he is a slave who has forfeited all freedom.
Only a person who risks is free.
The pessimist complains about the wind;
The optimist expects it to change;
And the realist adjusts the sails.

It's okay to err. It's not okay to beat yourself! Making fun of our ineptitudes is the panacea of success and happiness. The only people who don't fail are those who refuse to test the limits or attempt new innovative concepts. Failing is the pathway to succeeding, but most people view it as weakness. Wrong! Mistakes are part of living and growing. In fact, the definition of Innovation is Creative Destruction--the willingness to destroy what is to get what isn't. Behavioral psychologist Alfred Adler offered a psychological take on this saying, "Behind every neurosis is a weakling incapable of adapting." Admitting, "I goofed" permits you to walk away mentally, emotionally, and financially intact. Few people are ever fired for messing up. They are fired for trying to cover it up. Clinton would have saved everyone much strife by just saying, "Yeah! I did it and I'm sorry." What would have happened? Not much. What if you walked in and told your boss, "I am truly sorry, but I screwed up that last assignment, but I really learned a lot and you can bet the farm that I won't do it again."? What can a reasonable executive say but, "That's okay. I understand. Thanks for letting me know and try not to let it happen again."? Being forthright buys freedom. When you mess up, confess to it and move on. Bitching will not make it go away. It can only go away by taking ownership.

Production & Pricing – A Mental Dichotomy

Why did America lose the consumer electronics industry to a small is-land nation like Japan? It wasn't about the cheap labor, as disillusioned politicians say. It is far more related to guts and bucks. It is correlated to risk-adversity and short-term thinking than labor. How does the typical American manager or executive price their products? As dis-cussed in the bucks section, they take little risk and thus look at the best cost they can eke out in their existing manufacturing plant. That is the traditional and conservative path to take to estimate manufac-turing costs. It is wrong. Why? Because in the beginning of any new venture, the first costs are high, too high to build a strong market share to compete. It is like my Chuck E. Cheese costume example. In the beginning, all things cost more. The stage show in the very beginning cost about $750,000. After twenty stores it cost about $50,000. That is what happens in volume operations. Thus, initial costs should never be the determining variable for moving ahead.

An important factor in pricing is the nature of long and short-term thinking. Americans are almost always guilty of short-term rather than long-term thinking. The Japanese are just the opposite. They look at a new product opportunity and the very first act is to see how they might be able to dominate the market in five years. That is never the first act in America. That thinking leads inextricably to the pricing question that will ensure market dominance. What price will it take to achieve that objective? Once the price question is solved, the size of factory to build them is next. What size factory will be required to build the volume at the cost necessary to sell at that price?

Let's look at an example of such a holistic pricing strategy. The as-sumption is that dominating the market demands a selling price of

$100. That leads to the demand of an ex-factory cost of $25 each. Notice that the plant is not the given, but the by-product of pricing and cost, the diametric opposite of how such decisions are formulated in America. American executives, with a short-term vision, look at the existing plant and figure out the cost they can build it at and the price is a by-product of the existing plant. The Japanese know this, so they do the opposite. Their strategy is, "What size plant do I have to build to get the lowest possible price? And then I will own the market." They have done this very, very well for many decades. They tell top management, "We need a 200,000 square foot, new factory working three shifts to produce one million widgets a month at a cost of $25 each." Their backward strategizing has led to them dominating market after market. The East is future-oriented; the West is now-oriented. Thus, they have owned the future, and we have lost out to their strategizing. The lifetime employment in Japan is a contributing factor since they make long-term decisions, while the hired-hand in America is prone to short-term ones. This simple difference has permitted them to own the mass consumer products business in the world.

Global vs. Local Decision-Making – a Plague for the West

The 2009 financial debacle that hit the world and threatened the very core of America—-Detroit, Wall Street, and the banking industry--was fundamentally grounded in too many people wanting it now instead of a willingness to wait. When President Obama and congress printed money to fix those that caused the problem—-Banks and Detroit--it caused many astute individuals to begin to worry if the inmates had taken over the institution. The U.S. government printed money to go into Iraq, a nation that was not a threat, but was operating beyond the ethical and moral codes of American politicians and a president that was not the brightest tack in the box. Spending billions a month on a war that could never be won for a people that did like the American way of life was ludicrous. If you are going to fight, then fight. If you are going to enter a place like Viet Nam or Iraq and settle into a guerilla conflict, you are going to pay very dearly, especially when it is grounded in ethnicity and religious dogmas or cultural nuances. Just look at the centuries of religious conflict in Ireland or African nations. Such a war has a deleterious effect of huge economic proportions. The price of printing money to pay for such a conflict could have been used to rebuild American bridges, schools, highways, or even for industries in plight. The savvy billionaire, Warren Buffet, put his finger on what had transpired saying, "When the tide goes out it reveals those swimming naked." A research project at Duke University found, "80% of managers would 'decrease discretionary spending on research, advertising and maintenance to meet short-term targets' to enhance stock price."

Why Are Top Dogs Sales Superstars?

As discussed in the Hired-Hand Syndrome, those working for others are not always aware of their actions. They are deeply ingrained with a need to stay employed at all cost. Thus, they are without the same kind of verve found in an owner or entrepreneur. That is why the top dude is always the best salesperson in any organization. They are not afraid to make a deal outside the bounds of the budget or policy. They are never guilty of telling a customer, "Let me check with legal or accounting." That makes the top dog powerful. They can make a deal on the spot, whereas the hired-hand cannot. They are more self-serving than is politically correct in most organizations. Psychological studies have repeatedly shown the hired-hand is prone to make 95% of their decisions, not on what is correct or right, but on how they think it will be best for them. Ugh! They creative approach is always outside the mediocrity box. Joseph Campbell in his The Power of Myth offered prescient insight into this when he told us, "You can't have creativity unless you leave behind the bounded, the fixed, all the rules."

Self-Serving agendas are contra to long-term viability and is endemic in all organizations. The sad commentary is that most people don't know or won't admit that they are so inclined. Sam Walton's incredible success at Wal-Mart was due to his refusal to think short-term. Why? Because he intuitively knew that by such thinking they would take a more personal interest in the store and when there was a serious problem on Sunday evening, they would not be sending some underling. Charles Tandy, the entrepreneurial founder of Radio Shack did the same thing. Tandy told the media, "I force my managers to be partners. To purchase 25% of the store cost for 25% of the monthly profits. Retail is a 7- day a week business demanding diligence and an owner's mentality." He went on to explain, "If a guy has his own money tied up in a store, he's going to work a lot of extra hours, not for you, not for the company, but for himself. Why? Because it is his own money at risk."

Visionaries v CYA Leaders

Visionary leaders from time immemorial have been willing to walk the talk and lead from the front. The reason the troops followed Napoleon is that he was right in the heat of battle with them. For him, what was safe was far removed from what was best. Hired-hands have a hard time with that simple axiom. Visionary entrepreneur, Bill Lear of Lear Jet fame, as well as the first auto-pilot, could always be found walking around the factory floor. To the chagrin of his supervisors, he would look at a procedure and change it right there without asking. The boss never has to ask permission. That tends to cause conflict in the ranks, but it is a fast way to make corrections in any organization. An example of this in retail can be seen in getting a better deal than your competitors. If a Sears executive cuts a sweetheart deal for a high volume product, their propensity is to keep the retail price intact and let the improved profits flow to the bottom line. Why? That will make the company look better in the short run and ensure his bonus. Guess what an entrepreneur like Sam Walton would do? He will cut the retail price, advertise it to the world, and dominate the market share. This is subtle, but a crucial difference in the way hired-hands and entrepreneurial executives operate. At Kodak, a firm that owned the film industry for 100 years saw the digital cameras on the horizon. Those in the executive suites voted not to jeopardize their current profits by delving into that new arena, an arena that would destroy them in a few years. The visionary would have not gone the CYA route and bet some of today's profits on tomorrow's opportunities.

MBA'S are the quintessential example of such a hired-hand philosophy. They are trained to be. They are groomed to raise short-term numbers and profits to a godly status. They do plan loosely, but operate tightly. They *plan* using the right brain and *operate* using the left via budgets and quantitative analysis. That is the exact opposite approach taken by visionaries like Steve Jobs, Bill Gates, and Michael Dell. This is still lost on many graduate school professors. One example is when Akio Morita of Sony retired and his role as new product maven was taken over by new MBA's. Sony had been renowned for its continual flow of new innovative products such as: transistor radio (1955), 12" TV (1959), Walkman (1979), and 3.5" disk drives (1981). Morita retired to politics in 1981, and during the next 19 years, the firm introduced no new breakthrough products. Research into this discovered that the reason was the new individuals responsible were bright young MBA's serving self-assured success by improving what they had, but never venturing outside that box of safety.

MBA's learn to chase numbers and treat them with reverence. They opt for what is safe, not what is innovative. Great entrepreneurs are of the exact opposite persuasion. They plan quantitatively, but operate qualitatively. They envision life's possibilities by planning by the numbers and operating in a free-form manner without budgets, rules, job descriptions, or other inane policies. Innovative wunderkinds are different, but the traditionalists don't get it and don't get them, and that is why such people never last long in bureaucratic environs. When Bill Gates was being prosecuted for a monopolistic operation in 2001, the traditionalist judge, Thomas Penfield, told the *New Yorker*, "Bill Gates has a Napoleonic Complex, an arrogance that derives from power and unalloyed success. Microsoft employees don't act like grown ups." Such a statement would have made Freud stand up and cheer and Einstein to smile. *Business 2.0* once wrote a profound editorial on this:

"The management philosophy of corporations is based on the assumption of continuity, with a focus on operations. Capital markets are built on the assumption of discontinuity. They focus not on operations but on creation and destruction. Most, 80%, only allow change that is incremental, not substantial or transformational. They die by their passionless "rational analysis." They dead end in a *cul-de-sac* of mediocrity."

Such traits are ubiquitous in Silicon Valley. The people there are different. They have learned almost by osmosis that it is alright to show up without a white shirt and tie. It is okay to be different. They have seen this for many decades at Apple, Google, Netscape, and Costco. In those institutions, the personnel are encouraged to take new paths, to dare what others fear. This makes Silicon Valley an anomaly. It also made them the home of the first of many innovations such as: the first stereo, IC chips, microprocessor, programmable computer, home-games, and internet browsers. How could all those things come from one small geographic area? It wasn't the water. It was a mental game of permission to be different and to take risks. Berkeley psychologist, Cameron Anderson, noticed this and wrote, "The powerful take risks more than others, are more likely to minimize their chances of being affected by an accident, more likely to gamble on a lower blackjack hand, reveal vulnerable information in a job interview and engage in sex without a condom than are people with less power." What is different about Silicon Valley innovative leaders from the ordinary?

Silicon Valley Visionaries Are Different, but in Very Similar Ways!

↗ The *Vision* of a mystic

↗ An *Ego* bigger than God

↗ *Attention-span* of a hungry fly

↗ The *Charisma* of a wired evangelist

↗ The *Passion* of a 16-year-old on Viagra

↗ The *risk-taking propensity* of Evel Knievel

Innovative Wunderkinds

Nietzsche offered lucid insight into the nature of those that alter paradigms and change the world when he wrote of the inner will-to-power. In *Zarathustra*, Nietzsche offered prescient advice to those afraid to be different saying, "If one is not half mad how can one give birth to a dancing star?" They can't! That is the message. No one said it better than Jacques Barzun in, *The Paradoxes of Creativity* (1990), "Mad passion or passionate madness is the reason why psychopathic personalities are often creators and why their productions are perfectly sane." The University of California in *The Art of Disease* said, "Artists able to lose their inhibition become wilder and freer and more original. The ability to transcend ordinary social, physical and cognitive constraints is a feature of great artists."

Live on the edge or you will never have an edge. Those unwilling to bet it all can never have it all. It's easy to talk about being a risk taker, but ask the dude to write a check to bet on a new idea and you suddenly separate the talkers from the doers. Risk is one of those words that vary dramatically by individual. What one person sees as risky another sees as a walk in the park. Many business people think they are risk-takers, but when the chips are down they are care-takers. Why? Risk-takers keep on pushing the window of opportunity even when they are older. Mark Twain, Frank Lloyd Wright and Thomas Edison were so inclined. All were insolvent in the 50's but made it all back before the end. Their work shows that age doesn't have to stifle risk-taking although it is prudent to take manageable risks when your hair has turned grey. The innovators tend to fit my label of a Big T personality. The general population does not fit the profile and thus tend to drive slower as they age, protect what they have amassed and would never bet their savings on a dream. I have labeled these types Little t's. They demand surety at all cost. *The Story of Psychology* wrote on the potential for behavior relative to risk-taking and said, "Psychological studies have discovered that most people would rather bet on a sure thing when the most prudent decision is to go with the odds. In most cases fear interferes with their logic." Even Angel investors, those that look at putting seed money into new start-ups, think they are risk-takers but they seldom are as they insist on exit strategies and guarantees. They like to play the role of gambling on the new but keep insisting on things like 'barriers to entry' a term that keeps them warm and fuzzy like patents. Data shows that the need to be positively certain and have a barrier to entry or an exit strategy is important. They are wrong. Had this been crucial Xerox would never have been born or IBM or Microsoft.

Chapter 6

The *PASSION* Game – Get Excited or Change Venues

Pass Dr. Gene's Tumescence Test or Live a Mediocre Life.

"Personal magnetism is nothing more nor less than sex energy."
Napoleon Hill, *Think & Grow Rich* (1960)

"Men who are high in stimulation-seeking also have rather high testosterone levels. The Big T person will become either a creator or a destroyer, they are often unhappy and tend to very strong sex drives."
Frank Farley, psychologist who labeled risk as Big T

Passion makes the world go around. If those key to your success are not wired with incarnate energy look out. A person must be excited to do well no matter the endeavor. Honore Balzac is recognized as the father of the modern novel. When Balzac entered a room it virtually shook by his passion. Others are not quite so vivacious. Gandhi and Mother Theresa were driven but their drive attracted disciples to follow them towards a dream. U.S. President John F. Kennedy was so magnetic he was irresistible to both voters and ladies. Bucky Fuller was so incredibly jacked he could be asked to say a few words and not sit down for hours. Such individuals are driven by a seething psyche that makes them special and wires those in their presence. Dopamine flows through them at warp speed. Much data shows that passion is highly related to libidinal drive. This was never more apparent than in past White House dalliances by American presidents. What most don't want to hear is that what got them elected, made them into lotharios while there. Franklin Delano Roosevelt came to power in a wheelchair, a man who few would ever have suspected as the man about town. This caring, married man carried on like some college fraternity dude. One of his affairs was with Lucy Mercer, his wife Eleanor's social secretary. Five years later, a befuddled Eleanor discovered a bundle of love letters from Lucy to her husband. It led Eleanor to say, "The bottom dropped out of my particular world." Records show that Lucy visited FDR 40 to 50 times in the White House, usually under a pseudonym "Mrs. Paul Johnson." Strangely, it was not Eleanor that was present when the President died in office in 1944, but his faithful courtesan, Lucy. Such White House liaisons have been left out of the mass media, even those of John F. Kennedy. This all changed with President Bill Clinton's Lewinsky affair.

Why are White House sexual encounters of importance in this work? Libidinal drive underlies the passion that leads to the pinnacle of power. What gets them to the top is passion beyond the pale of the ordinary. That was certainly found in the lives and loves of John. F. Kennedy and Bill Clinton. You hear some voters say, "Yeah, they had raging libidos, but why in the White House?" Well, needs to sate passions have far less to do with the color or majesty of the house than with their passions. Such passion is what got them voted into office. It wasn't about to change once there. Conservatives would like to believe that once you get to a position, you can and should change from what you were. Good luck! We dance with the inner damsel that brought us to the dance. The leopard does not change his spots when he ages or alters his environment. It is a fact that male CEO's and presidents use power to get sex just as they do to get votes, and many women use their sex to gain some inner sense of power.

Superstars that leave a legacy of power are uniquely different. They don't need as much sleep as the norm and are still vibrant workers. The fuel driving this train is an inner psychic energy fueling their drives far beyond the ordinary. Many tend to be ADD. Most don't get ill as much as the masses. Examples of this can be seen in studying the lives of Leonardo, Edison, Ford, Irving Berlin, or today's Martha Stewart. Passionate people are truly different than the so-called normal person. They have a kind of rushing sickness and must work even on Easter Sunday or Christmas Day. On vacation, they can be found phoning or texting. Despite such a frenetic lifestyle, they achieve far more in less time. Their vitality releases neurotransmitters from an over-charged libido, and that seems to imbue in them a kind of energy incarnate. It implies that you should light that inner energy pit and it will light up you.

Passion, Power, & Zeal

History shows that powerful people are armed with passion to burn. Strong sensual energy is pervasive in both powerful women and men. The Russian Empress, Catherine the Great, was such a person as was Napoleon and artisans like Isadora Duncan and Picasso. In 1990 dollars, Catherine the Great spent $150 million on various paramours to sate her raging urges. This German-born lady used passionate power to control Mother Russia. Napoleon met and fell madly in love with the Creole beauty, Josephine, and wrote this impassioned letter, "I have awakened full of you. The memory of last night has given my senses no rest... what an effect you have on my heart. I send you thousands of kisses, but don't kiss me. Your kisses sear my blood." Golda Meir, the first female Prime Minister of Israel had the nickname 'the mattress" in Tel Aviv for her many assignations. As Freud pointed out, "Unsatisfied libido is responsible for producing all art and literature." And this was found true in such people as Lord Byron and the American fantasy of romance, Danielle Steel.

Passionate people vitalize those in their sphere of influence. If their energy is low, the same thing happens in reverse. Margaret Meade was passion incarnate. She became the world's first female PhD in anthropology, was bisexual, and she dominated many Alpha Males such as Gregory Bateson. At 72, Meade spoke to a large group. In the audience that day was a young fan of her work. He was 30-years her junior, but was mesmerized by her words and passion. When Meade left the stage, the young protégé told the press, "The sex appeal of that mind of hers was absolutely captivating. If she had pointed to me and said, 'You! You're the one I choose! Come off with me!' I would have gone with her, anywhere." Napoleon Hill validated such words in his classic *Think & Grow Rich*:

> **"Personal magnetism is nothing more, nor less, than sex energy. Sex energy is the creative energy of all geniuses. People who lack sex energy will never become enthusiastic nor inspire others and enthusiasm is one of the most important requisites in salesmanship – no matter what one is selling."**
> (Think & Grow Rich p. 187)

A seething psyche is magnetic and a driving force that befuddles those who have it. Existentialist Albert Camus wrote, "The whole question is can one live with one's passions. For a 10-minute love affair I would have renounced my parents." This kind of ardor is found in many who make it to the very top. Picasso had such passion, as did Carl Jung and Bertrand Russell. It appears that what turns you on is what turns others on —so get excited or don't bother playing the game.

The World is on the Fast Track – 24/7 is In

Looking at the behavior of the superstars it is evident they are wired to work. Danielle Steel told biographers about waking up as the sun was rising with the typewriter keys imbedded on her forehead since she typed until she dropped. For such types sleep is a waste. That was the thinking of Bucky Fuller who trained himself in his Dymaxion Sleep system where he could work six hours and take a 30-minute catnap and they reawaken to keep on working. Edison was infamous for sleeping on his lab counter. Bill Gates had been programming non-stop for seven consecutive years when he quit Harvard and launched Microsoft at age 19. At Microsoft for ordered dinner at midnight while still in the office. The Internet maven Bill Joy told reporters, "I programmed eight or ten hours a day. By the time I got to Berkley I was doing it day and night – sometimes I'd fall asleep at the keyboard." What causes such passion? An inner need that becomes an inner driving force – what I have labeled a tumescence test – and fuels their engine more than so-called normal people. Obsession reigns supreme.

Psychiatrist David Hawkins wrote, "One characteristic of genius is the capacity for great intensity. To remain in power high energy is key." This high energy is then translated into outputs. It also appears to be increasing with the Internet Age. Validation of this comes from TV sound bites. Between 1965 and 1995, TV news sound-bites dropped from 42 seconds to 8 seconds—an 81% drop in just thirty years. Jobs and communications are now on the same fast track—24/7 is in and it is altering the way we live and the way we work. Those unable to keep up with find themselves in the back of the pack. Charles Darwin saw this coming saying, "It is not the strongest of the species that survive, nor the most intelligent, but the one most responsive to change." Business guru, Tom Peters, spoke of this saying, "The world is going through more fundamental changes than it has in hundreds, perhaps thousands of years. You must put yourself in harms way a dozen times a year or go hopelessly stale" Change and passion are cousins. The passionate have been found to thrive on change. The dispassionate fight it to the bitter end. Studies show that ADD types lead the way in change. In *The Age of Spiritual Machines* (1998), futurist Ray Kurzweil told us,

"Sexuality and spirituality are two ways that we transcend our everyday physiological reality." He went on to say:

"When a rat presses a button and directly stimulates a pleasure center in the limbic system of their brains, the rats press the button endlessly, as often as 5000 times an hour, to the exclusion of everything else including eating."

Studies show that moving mice from a sterile, uninteresting cage to a stimulating one doubles the number of dividing cells in the hippocampus. Rats that solve a puzzle 100 times will gain tremendous expertise and doubling that permanently wires the behavior and have altered their brains with a habit that becomes rigid and inflexible. That can be seen as a pervasive trait in Detroit. In contrast, those intrepid warriors who keep learning new things are programming their brains to accept change. The mind becomes reprogrammed and conditioned to accept change, and at some point, to become infatuated with it. In such people, the brain is not prone to atrophy, since both muscles and the mind atrophy without continuous stimulation. Staying active and learning adapts us to a viable lifestyle.

Speed is a Web World phenomenon. When time is of the essence, we adopt slogans and one-liners to describe our lives. Cyber-talk on e-mail is an example as people speak in phrases or acronyms. Text messaging has become a system of abbreviated aphorisms that only the in-group understands. The sagacious Greek Heraclitus said, "You can never step into the same river twice." That sage advice is truer in the Internet age than ever before. Kurzweil wrote, "The Singularity is technological progress so rapid and so profound that it represents a rupture in the fabric of human history. The price-performance of computation and communication is doubling every year." When your job is taken by an Indian or Chinese worker willing to work for $10 a day rather than

$10 an hour, or in lawyer terms, $300 an hour, then you should find another job that is far more needed in the new Web World of today. The buggy whip manufacturers were wiped out by the automobile industry and those individuals that were willing to change went to work in an auto plant. When the individual trained to sell stereo systems faced the world of iPods and iPhones, they went to work selling that which had displaced them. In the modern world, one must change or pay a horrid price for refusing to change.

The Inscrutable Japanese – Non-Verbal Messages

Westerners have a propensity to show emotion, get excited, get mad, and get happy and to show this when in a social setting. Not the Japanese. They find such emotions as a sign of weakness. They hold emotions in and is one reason many firms in Tokyo have punching bags in the basement. It is a way for their executives to release their inner tensions, since it is verboten to do so in front of their fellow workers. When they negotiate, they come off as inscrutable, since no one ever knows if they like or dislike what they are saying. That is known in Vegas as a poker face. To be so inclined is said to be difficult to fathom or understand; impenetrable or mysterious. There is a vast divide in the East and West in this area. In Japan, it is considered rude to disagree. You speak about your point of view. They speak of theirs, and then each group will caucus. But it is not polite to tell someone they are wrong. Japanese people tend to avoid any form of confrontation. In their culture, negotiations and quarrels are all "disputes," and bad for society, so they refrain from such emotional things.

The Tokyo public transportation system is so crowded everyone is bumping into others, and it is so prevalent they have learned to accept it and say nothing. Americans are trained to say, "Excuse me." If you did that in Japan, it would be a constant refrain, so no one says anything. Such behavior is a way of life. For the Japanese, it is the price paid for urban living. Due to living in a frenetic and crowded environment, total strangers sit at your table, something that is never done in America. Direct eye contact in Japan is only done in aggressive action. A Japanese teenager looking at his father in the eye will be punished much more severely for daring to be aggressive. That is why a Japanese businessman will look away, leaving the American negotiator to feel as if they don't care. They feel a smile is not to use to display joy or agreement, but to use to mask embarrassment. That irks the American tourists in the Ginza district shopping as the sales clerk makes a mistake and smiles while apologizing to the customer. The dress in Tokyo is so formal as to have Americans writing home about the penguin look as virtually every one they see on the street has dark suit, white shirt and dark tie with black shoes.

Years ago I spent weeks negotiating multi-million dollar contracts in Tokyo. The Japanese business men were very polite and cordial. When I spoke, they were attentive and nodded their heads up and down as if in total agreement, and said, "Hai!" Being a young optimist, I thought they were agreeing with me. Wrong! It only meant they understood what I was saying. It took a while to figure out that very important point. The Japanese operate in a Ringi style management system that is bottom up in contrast to the American style. The lowest in the management tree speak first, then the next level up the hierarchy, and finally the top dogs speak. This can prove to be a very long and arduous ordeal for Western executives. An American wants to say, "Let's get this train moving." But they are very in to perfectionism so no one ever loses face. What I didn't realize at the time was that this bottom-up approach ensured that everyone in the room would finally agree before that older gentleman at the end of the table would nod his head and then and only then was the deal done. In management jargon, this process is known as "Theory Z."

The Japanese often smile when they are really upset. A Japanese executive may smash his Lexus and laugh it off. Not so in the West, as such an act elicits anger or tears. That can be very confusing to the more effusive American who will show emotions to communicate agreement or disagreement. A Japanese student shows respect to the professor by never looking directly at them, disagreeing, or even asking questions. Not so for the more direct American student. Humility and bowing is a sign of humility in the East and is programmed in at a very early age. This tends to communicate a sign of weakness or lack of confidence to an American. It is merely a cultural nuance and not what it seems. So be very careful when in a foreign culture like Japan, as what you see and hear is not necessarily what you think it means or is being communicated.

Chasing Dreams with Passion

A strong libidinal drive is what Freud described as psychosexual energy. Others call it ardor. Those with it are zealots on a mission to achieve an impossible dream. It is a fact that these types are often on a maniacal mission and willing to go where the meek fear. They often get in trouble in the process. Those armed with such fervor tend to be obsessive and reek of enthusiasm. It is what underlies comments like Thomas Edison's tormented yell, "It will be factories or death," when J. P. Morgan refused to finance his General Electric light bulbs. Edison was so perturbed he took the money out of his pocket to finance the factory for those first light bulbs. Such passion comes from those with a very strong sex drive. It is what Napoleon Hill found in America's most eminent industrialists. This kind of passion was latent in Leonardo and Michelangelo, despite both being gay. It was the underlying element in an aging Michelangelo to lie on his back for years to paint the Sistine Chapel.

Passion is an inner fuel that fuels workaholics. Writers often define it as being empowered. If you are not empowered then you are not pursuing something that lights that inner fire. If you don't love your job enough to work some weekends, quit immediately. If you are not sufficiently energized by what you do for a hobby, take up one that will light that fire. If you are unwilling to give up food, sleep, or sex for a new quest, find something else to pursue. Life's way too short to be spending time in a place that doesn't turn you on. Passionate failure is preferable to indifferent success. Balzac was asked about not being married, and he told the media, "My orgies take the form of books." They did! But he paid dearly for the chase as he burned himself out on 100 novels in twenty years and died at age 50. Carl Jung, the Swiss psychotherapist wrote "Sexuality is the *sine quo non* of spirituality." Jung created what he labeled a Shadow to explain the ability to deal with inner fears that plagued so many of his patients. He described this inner foe as "the beast within." Confrontation with this inner Shadow is essential for self awareness. We cannot learn about us until we learn about our Shadow or about others, as we are deluded by our own self-deception. Jung's insightful words on this inner fiend:

> **"It is a frightening thought that man also has a shadow side to him, consisting not just of little weaknesses- and foibles, but of a positively demonic dynamism. The individual seldom knows anything of this; to him, as an individual, it is incredible that he should ever in any circumstances go beyond himself."**
> *On the Psychology of the Unconscious* (1912) pg. 35

Ever notice that passionate people don't sleep as much as the normal population? Martha Stewart is much like Margaret Thatcher in that neither woman slept more than four hours each night, despite a rigorous agenda. Such zeal is found in all disciplines. They see sleep as a waste of time. One such individual was Arthur Jones--the founder of the Nautilus Empire. Jones's motto tells it all, "Younger women, faster planes and larger crocodiles" from a man who married five teenagers, flew his own 707 jet airliner, and wrestled crocodiles by hand. This maniac on a mission told the media, "I've killed seventy-three men and 600 elephants and I felt worse about the elephants."

Life Energy: The Power Within

The principle of energy has been likened to flowing into the moment. In Japan it is called *ki;* China calls it *chi* or *qi.* In India it is labeled *prank.* Bergson labeled it *élan vital* or vital force. Often it is called Flow or Getting into that Zone place. Superstars are energized from such a state. "Divine self-visualization empowers us," says Lama Yeshe, "to take control of our life and create for ourselves a pure environment in which our deepest nature can be expressed." Ancient healing practices, shamanism, miracles, and spirituality are all impossible without an inner ethereal energy. William Reich defined this power as *Orgone Energy,* "Man's 'upward strivings' are nothing but the biologic development of vital powers." Energy embodies all that we do and what we become. Validation comes from Michael Merzenich, who told the media, "We choose and sculpt how our ever-changing minds will work. We choose who we will be the next moment in a very real sense the leave an imprint on our physical form." A Cookie Crumble experiment at Stanford confirms this. They found that powerful students eat more cookies. Stanford professor of Organizational Behavior, Roderick Kramer says, "The lowering of inhibition frees the powerful to shake up organizations, fearlessly challenge the status-quo, do the right thing regardless of unpopularity and follow a more daring vision."

Psychiatrist John Diamond studied life energy extensively and wrote in *Life Energy,* "Life Energy is high when both hemispheres are active and symmetrical – cerebral balance." Cerebral imbalance is crucial in tennis. Racquet sports players--like tennis-- have more difficulty hitting backhands than forehands. Why? The right-handed player hits a forehand by stepping forward with left leg and hitting the ball with the right arm. Think about this. The left leg is moving forward as the right arm moves forward. It is cerebral balance and the body is in synch. Not so when hitting a backhand. The backhand has the right arm moving forward to strike the ball while the right leg is moving forward. This is asynchronous as the player is out of balance. To be in balance mentally and neurologically, it is important to have a mental balance, or what Diamond called "cerebral centering." Diamond wrote, "Centering can be achieved by using the left-hand between games or hitting the ball a few times with the offhand." (Diamond 1979 p. 80) This lets the brain become more centered.

Sybaritic Sex & Success

In *Sybaritic Genius – Sex Drive & Success* (2001), this author used a word not too familiar to most people. Why sybaritic? It has a romantic history coming from an Italian tribe in the dark ages. The Sybaritic tribe was Italy's most hedonistic society. History tells us that they were so passionate they even taught their horses to dance to music. Love, fun, romance, and pleasure were the fuel that charged their lives. Passion was their god, and it would prove to be the agent of their demise. Why? Their adversaries were the highly intellectual Pythagoreans. During an important battle, the cunning Pythagoreans played a happy melody causing the Sybarite's horses to dance. That left the Sybarites without a cavalry defense, and they would go down to defeat by the very thing that had fueled their climb to the top. As we spoke of in Chapter 1, be very careful what makes you as it could be the agent that breaks you. The Sybarites had elevated passion above their wellbeing. This can be seen from those emotional individuals who see life as a tragedy while their more rational counterparts see it more of a comedy. Addictive personalities tend to overindulge in booze, food, or drugs and they are more likely to be highly emotional or what Carl Jung labeled as "Feelers." Not so for the more rational types.

Studies show that powerful people come armed with high psycho-sexual energy. They are passionate and seldom tire as so-called normal people. They do not get ill as much as the norm, and consequently achieve far more in less time. Bucky Fuller was a man armed with a kind of rushing sickness. It led him to coin the term, "Ephemeralization," meaning to achieve more and more in less and less time. Bucky was imbued with insatiable libidinal energy, admitting in his memoirs to having had sex with 1,000 prostitutes prior to his 30th birthday. Research shows that the libidinal energy emanates from the brain, where neurotransmitters imbue such people with an abnormal amount of sex drive. John F. Kennedy and Bill Clinton were examples. These two U.S. Presidents pushed the very limits of decorum due to an unquenchable sex drive. Both engaged in numerous White House trysts with their wives in the building. Why would they do such a thing with a chance of getting caught with their proverbial pants down? It was more about ego than sex. They could have had sex anywhere. It is what I have labeled "the invisible syndrome." It had nothing to do with the sexual act and everything to do with proving they were special and above the rules of ordinary men.

In *The Female Brain (2006),* Louann Brizendine wrote about such drives in men saying, "Men fall in love at first site more easily than women. They have 2 1/2 times the brain space devoted to sex drive as a woman has. Sex thoughts enter a women's brain every couple days, for men thoughts about sex occur every minute." Brizendine also found that "Men utter an average of 7,000 words a day, women a whopping 20,000 or almost three times as many words as a man." It turns out that men take seven times as long as women to process emotions. So if men are more prone to the sexual game, women get even. The female is far more adept at audio sounds, taste, touch and smell and verbalizing their feelings. A primal example of gender differences took place in the banking debacle of 2009 when every single bank tanked in Iceland. The only surviving bank was the one run by two females.

It's Okay to be Different!
Different cultures view passion in different ways. America has long led other nations in risk-taking but the ranking is probably based on variables that are not always self-evident. Social risks and physical harm risks are not the same. Using drugs and binge drinking or eating toxic foods is risky, but not necessarily the areas looked at in such tests.

Americans take business risks, but their personal risks are much greater than found in the East. Their risky personal behavior has led to much obesity, stress, anxiety attacks, and a higher death rate from heart disease and diabetes. Many Americans are steeped in a strong Christian ethic that demands that others live and operate as they do. It is a constant theme in newspaper editorials in America to see, "Do you realize how many products have been manufactured in Communist China where workers are denied free speech or the right to withdraw their labor? A place where they tolerate human rights abuses, religious persecution, forced abortions, selling of body organs, and assaults on Tibet." This article appeared in the spring 2009 when the nation was in turmoil. It was written by a Middle-American who had never been to China, India, or Japan. Such people get lost in their personal dogmas as to what is right and what is wrong. China is becoming more capitalistic than many European nations and South American nations such as Venezuela. Americans, without thinking, often speak emotionally about Asian and Middle Eastern parents telling their offspring who they can marry. Arranged marriages in Asia are a way of life. It is deeply mired in those cultures and closely tied to economics and family heritages. Well, to be the devil's advocate, the parents just might have a better feel for what is right or wrong for their offspring than the raging hormones that tend to lead many teenagers astray.

There is a vast divide between how the way the East and West deal with parental care. Assisted Living facilities are a big thing in America. They are non-existent in other nations where they are verboten. For them, the parents reared you and it is your responsibility to care for them as they age. Assisted living homes are considered an outrage in the Middle East, Asia, and South America. In those nations, the parents are the babysitters when they go to work. Why? They want them to have the same chance to succeed as they did when they were young. Child-care centers are non-existent in those cultures. The grandparents expect to be a built-in baby sitter. This is not out of desperation, but out of a cultural need. Such are the cultural differences of societies that many Americans don't understand or find offensive. I am not arguing one way or the other, merely making a point that cultures are different and deserve that right to be different. No one culture has the right to dictate their standards on another, but many American politicians feel it is their right to tell other cultures how to live. You tell someone they must buy into what you think is right, and they may just come back and say you must believe in a Hindu Shiva God, or make Buddha or Mohammed your savior. What if your system is mystical or black magic, as exists in Haiti? Stop preaching and start being was the subtitle of *The Innovative Mind* (2008). A psychology professor at the University of Michigan, Richard Nisbett writes:

> *"Asian cultures differ from ours. Family honor is so important to the Chinese that students work hard not only for themselves but for the glory of their families. In the West, where achievement is a more individual accomplishment, students who struggle don't have the same incentive to persevere."*

Fear & Passion

Fear can make us stop pursuing things and it can be the fuel that lights our fires. Those with bravado look at problems and attack them head on with bravado. Will Smith, the Hollywood actor, was such a man. Will told the media in 2008, "My fear fuels me. I keep going because I doubt myself. It drives me to be better. My self-confidence is actually my reaction to fear." That is the fuel that has no limits. Others in Hollywood were also so inclined. Frank Sinatra, Sammy Davis, Judy Garland, and Irving Berlin were driven by inner fears—not one of them could read a note of music; insecurity drove them to do what was otherwise impossible. This same seething inner power was seen in others like the mother of modern dance, Isadora Duncan. In her memoirs, Isadora wrote:

"I feel the presence of a mighty power within me which listens to the music and reaches out through all my body, trying to find an outlet, this power grows furious, sometimes it raged and shook me until my heart nearly burst from passion."
(Landrum 1999 p. 224)

The Love Generation – Boomers Have Come of Age

Most of the world leaders at the millennium were Baby Boomers. These boomers were born between 1946 and 1964, and number 76 million strong. They are fast approaching retirement age, but many are still *individualists.* Many of these iconoclasts grew up on *hoola hoops* and *granola,* and trusted no one over age thirty. The leading edge of the cohort came of age during the turbulent 1960s. They worshipped at the altar of sex, drugs, and rock and roll. Their statement was shown in tie-dye and hip-huggers, where getting stoned was preferable to getting an education or taking responsibility. Hippie vans were more of a defiant statement than transportation. VW buses screamed out defiant words like "**TUNE IN, TURN ON, AND DROP OUT,** and **MAKE LOVE NOT WAR!**"

The boomer cohort immortalized the spirit of freedom and the search for a way to deal with a Cold War and daily threats of annihilation. Walking on the moon didn't deter them from the horror of a world that dared eliminate President John F. Kennedy, Martin Luther King, and Bobby Kennedy. Many dropped out, escaped into the fantasy of Ian Fleming's 007, or tripped out on marijuana and Cold Duck. Flower Children adorned the streets of San Francisco's Height Ashbury district. At Esalen, they attended sessions, including the Gestalt Prayer of Fritz Perls, listening to him preach why everyone has the unimpeachable right for, "You do your thing, and I'll do mine." Head shops and nude beaches were favorite haunts of those burning their draft cards, bras, and textbooks in a ritualistic tribute to freedom. It was a symbol of defiance for a world gone amuck. Hedonism and Narcissism flourished back then. These free spirits worshipped rock & roll Woodstock, but would grow up to become part of that world they denigrated. Many became lawyers, doctors, CPA's, teachers, and business types when they had to cope with paying mortgages and rearing a family with some values. They are now reaching retirement age and hand the gauntlet to another generation not so steeped in love and defiance. Their children are about to take over, and passion is somehow deeply ingrained in their psyches.

Extremely gifted children often do not fit in with the mainstream. They don't abide by the societal rules, don't fit well in school, and are labeled misfits by most teachers and friends. In his student days at Harvard, Bill Gates played poker all night instead of studying. Walt Disney and Dr. Seuss didn't make it in art class. Einstein was sent home repeatedly with the headmaster telling his parents that he was a loser. These type individuals were labeled *The Indigo Children: The New Kids Have Arrived (1998)* written by the husband-and-wife team of Lee Carroll and Jan Tober. Such people supposedly have an indigo-colored aura surrounding them. Many of the individuals this author has studied fit the profile of having psychic-like powers with high creativity and polyphasia – multi-tasking ability. Psychiatrist Gary Small in *iBrain* (2008) listed their qualities as:

- ✪ **Exceptional Creativity, IQ, Intuition, Abstract Learning**
- ✪ **Lack of interest in traditional schooling**
- ✪ **Bored with assigned tasks, homework, rituals, or policies**
- ✪ **Elevated Self-Esteem**
- ✪ **Difficulty with authority – mavericks**
- ✪ **Anti-Social behavior**
- ✪ **Difficult adapting in school**
- ✪ **Introspective and Intrinsic thinking styles**

The message in this chapter is 'get excited or pay the consequences.' If you don't have something to make you get up early and excited each morning you need to find something that lights your fire. Individuals with such fire are energized to leap the obstacles. Little of note happens until someone gets excited and then they are driven to push the limits. Such people sleep less, live longer, and achieve at a much higher level than those not so driven. Passion is a panacea for all productivity. It is the fuel for transformation. The caveat, however, is that we all pay for our excesses in one way or another. Excess has a latency that can come back to haunt us. Indulging in too much food, alcohol, romance or even golf takes its toll. As I preach, if you are really good, you can be bad, but too much of either leaves an indelible mark on your body, mind, or spirit. Don't forget that psychic energy is the underlying element in the success of superstars, no matter the discipline.

Chapter 7
The STREET SMARTS Game:
It's Bred Not Born

Superstars that Alter the World Walk the Talk.

"75% of development occurs after birth in contrast to a baboon that is only 30%." Homer-Dixon, *The Ingenuity Gap*

"20% of the variation in risk-taking is genetically determined; the rest comes from our upbringing, experience, education and training." *Wall Street Journal* (April 4, 2009)

Being street-smart is much more an art than a science. Psychologists preach that eminence is talent plus preparation. But as we learn more about the role of experience – street-smarts if you will - the more we find that preparation is the most important factor. Once you eliminate other variables those that have an inner need to win tend to be winners. They work harder than their peers. In Outliers, Malcolm Gladwell spoke of it as "The 10,000 hour rule." Neurologist Daniel Levitin wrote, "In study after study of composers, basketball players, fiction writers, ice skaters, concert pianists chess players and master criminals, 10,000 hours of practice is required" (Gladwell p. 40). Even prodigies like Mozart fit this model as he didn't compose his greatest works until he had been hard at work for more than twenty years. Put in your 10,000 hours and you will be on your way.

As the above graphic illustrates, you are the driver of the bus, so take the wheel and guide the bus to where you want to go. If in charge, take charge. Peter Senge in *The Fifth Discipline* told us, "Rigid authoritarian hierarchies thwart learning." He was dead right as was the *Wall Street Journal* when they said that success is but 20% genetically determined. This makes experiential savvy the driving force for eminence. No better example can be found than the success of Tiger Woods. Does he have innate talent? Sure! But it pales compared to his dedicated training regimen. Tiger begins his daily workout at 7A.M. After an hour, he stops for breakfast and an hour later heads for the driving range. After intense practice he plays 9 holes of golf. After lunch, he goes back out to the putting green for an hour. That is followed by another 9 holes of golf. That should placate his need for training, but it does not. He then goes back to the driving range to fix what was amiss on the course. This is the work ethic of a man who had earned in excess of $100 million for the past few years. In addition he is already ranked #1 in golf. It is testimony that Tiger knows that the street is where he hangs his hat. What does this mean for business? Carl Schramm, of the Kaufmann Foundation told *The Wall Street Journal* in 2009, "In the last seven re-cessions it's been entrepreneurs who essentially restarted the economy." These are the Hands-On not Hired-Hands.

In any discipline, those with street smarts have an edge. Any road warrior who had launched a new venture knows this without being told. They are far better equipped to tell someone how to do it than some professor that has only studied the process. Having run a factory in Hong Kong, or Europe, is far more instructive than studying how to run one. They will have forgotten more about how to run a plant and the nuances of importing and exporting than any political pundit pontificating on the subject. It's akin to taking a golf lesson. Would you take a lesson on blasting out of a sand trap from someone who had never done it? Don't think so! Politicians rant about leveling the playing field. Guess what? Trying to make everyone equal is antithetic to life. Everyone is different. That demands that we treat everyone different, not the same. Treating everyone the same is like saying the sky is blue. Yeah, sometimes it is blue, sometimes teal, and other times it's black or grey.

There was a time when Affirmative Action made sense. That time has long since passed. Trying to fit all people and all systems into one neat package is a form of mental masturbation. When that happens, we are playing with our heads. Those that say it is bad to discriminate have never run a business. In every business, there are the super people who make it hum and there are those that should not be there since they are druggies or worse. It is incumbent on the leader to discriminate against those individuals that are intent on destroying the place. They must be found and sent on there merry way. Treating a druggie the same as a conscientious worker is not the way to run the airline. It isn't right morally or ethically to discriminate based on how someone dresses, or their race, ethnicity, or creed. Affirmative Action Laws were created to stop bad discrimination, but they expanded into an arena where they tell communities to hire in the same identical relationship as the ethnicity of the geographic area. That is rank stupidity. What if those ethnic types are not qualified or refuse to work in that given arena? What if we said the NBA must match the ethnicity of the city in which they play their games?

Life is Unfair. We're not All Equal

Abraham Lincoln offered cogent advice on governments attempting to level playing fields when he said, "You can't strengthen the weak, by weakening the strong." Leveling the field of play is tantamount to placing weights on Michael Jordan or LeBron James so they can't jump as high as the other players, or forcing Tiger Woods to carry fewer clubs in his bag so he won't dominant golf tourneys. It would work, but only for a short time. Once the weak have been given an edge over their adversaries they actually become weaker. When that edge is removed they can never again compete favorably. This is seen in the welfare world. Give the disenfranchised food stamps so they don't have starve and after a while they learn to live on the doll and will never work or look for a job. When handicaps are removed, the game is over before it begins. The children of many wealthy people seldom do as well as those needing to work to earn their keep.

Treat everyone equally, but not the same, since they are not the same. Let's look at a teaching metaphor. We decide it is not good to give students really bad grades or really good grades so we'll grade everyone the same so no one will be offended, no one will fail, and no one will receive an A—the ultimate level playing field. After the first test, the grades are averaged, and everyone gets a B. The students who studied hard will be upset. The slackers will be very happy. On the second test we find that the diligent students that study hard didn't study nearly as much and the slackers didn't bother opening their books. The message here is that leveling the playing field destroys both the diligent and the slackers. Are you listening Mr. and Ms. Government?

It is unfair that the stronger and swifter tiger eats the deer. The birds feast on the worms. This is unfair to the deer or worm, but it is the Darwinian survival of the fittest. This is seldom viewed from a philosophical perspective. An example of this is the word *discrimination.* It has recently become a lexicon associated with bad. It's not bad. It's a leader's responsibility to discriminate against those that would destroy the organization. They should not be unfair or be prejudiced against race, ethnicity or creed. But they are responsible for finding those individuals in a firm that would destroy it. Studies find that about 5% and 12% of any organization is dysfunctional. They need to be weeded out before they can destroy it. Small firms fit the 5% category. Bureaucracies fit the 12%. All organizations have their fare share of alcoholics, druggies, derelicts and misfits.

Some people are smarter, stronger, taller, faster, and quicker and others are more well-read or well-bred. That is the very nature of life. Others begin with few expectations other than from their hard work. That is life. Get used to it. I have heard bar talk where someone says it is not fair that Mexican oranges are cheaper than Florida oranges. Well, since NAFTA, the Americans should learn to compete with Mexico or find another game to play. If the oranges from Mexico are as good and cheaper, that is life in the fast lane, so Florida growers not willing to compete must find a new crop to grow on their lands. They prefer to bitch and moan about enacting laws or getting rid of NAFTA. What they don't see is that those selling Mexican oranges are able to buy American products like Tide, Coke, and Hershey Kisses. Many moan about losing their jobs to the Chinese because they can make an iPod cheaper or a Blackberry more efficiently at a lower cost. Those people should come to grips that they are living and competing in a shrinking world where this kind of change is not just a warp, but will continue over time. If a worker's expertise is no longer viable, they must find a new one that is. As mentioned earlier, open a business repairing PC's in the evening or weekends when there is no such service. You will have found a market void that needs filling. So fill it and you will be working for a long time with lots of cash.

Gender Differences

Women are more prone than men to exult in life's journeys with men more inclined to chase life's destinations. This is valid on vacation or in bed. Feminists moan about not being able to compete with men. It is a fact that women are superior to men in many arenas. Women are better at networking, thus better in most sales positions. They are superior at nurturing jobs like nursing and counseling, as well as those that demand multi-tasking, as they are masters of juggling many things without dropping them. Consequently, they should work in the arenas of their strengths while avoiding the arenas in which they are not most likely to succeed. High-risk positions or those demanding aggressive action are not necessarily the forte of the more submissive female. Genders should be treated equally, but since they are different, it should be okay for them to be positioned where they will not be set up to fail. It is a fact that virtually all women cannot hit a golf ball as far, or a tennis ball as hard, or be as affective as a body guard as most men. Males come equipped with a much larger dose of testosterone and more muscles, and that makes them more effective in some jobs. There is a different perspective on the above, depending on whether you come from a patriarchal or matriarchal society. Women have been proven to excel in communication skills. Are there exceptions? Of course! Napoleon, Hitler, Howard Hughes, and Buckminster Fuller come to mind. These charismatic wizards could motivate and inspire through the power of words. They were more self-serving than their female equivalents, but equal in that talent.

There are always exceptions to all rules. There have been women who made most men look like wimps. Women like Amelia Earhart, Golda Meir, Margaret Thatcher, and Martha Stewart were masters of taking charge when in charge. Amelia once told a reporter, "I want to go where no man has gone." Few men would have gone where she went and wouldn't have had the guts to try it. There are many males with the equivalent nurturing nature such as Martin Luther King. Males with high testosterone have been labeled Big T's by psychologist Frank Farley. He used Amelia Earhart as an example of a Big T personality. It turns out that the Big T personality has certain strengths such as creativity, spatially acuity, aggression, and high libidinal energy. Louann Brizendine in *The Female Brain* (2006) offered prescient insight into the brains of the female writing:

> **"The female brain is wired to nurture. Women excel at knowing what people are feeling, men have difficulty spotting emotion. Connecting through talking activates the pleasure centers in a girl's brain. It's a major dopamine and oxytocin rush – the biggest neurological reward outside orgasm."**

Due to their uniqueness, a female is prone to fight with words while a male is prone to fight with their fists. In *Female Genius,* I made a strong argument for America to elect a female president. The reason? In a confrontational world, it is far better to have the leaders talking rather than shooting. Studies show that women are superior at grace, networking, sense of smell, feeling, intuition, episodic memory, and nurturing. Since the genders are not the same, they should not be treated the same. This is a delicate subject, so it needs explaining. If a lady is better at networking, she would be best suited to handle a difficult client in a sales position. Such skills are crucial in education, marketing, or as an ambassador to another nation. In contrast, males, on average, are better suited in those arenas that fit their innate strengths. Those positions fit the innate qualities generally found in men such as: taking high-risks, aggression, physical strength, spatial acuity, and self-esteem. Are there exceptions? Of course! But in general we should accept the fact that we are different, and those differences should dictate where we place ourselves to be most effective.

Those with experience doing business in Asia know that those cultures are far more discriminating than in America. Many have centuries old caste systems that are not to be violated. In France, there is an undercurrent of discrimination in virtually any organization. Frenchmen without the proper breeding or education are seldom found in the boardroom. Watch the news in Hong Kong or Tokyo and you will detect a cultural difference. In those areas, they spend little air time on illegal immigration, same-sex marriages, welfare programs, or bombing of abortion clinics. Those cultures have other issues, but they are radically different than what is found in America. All cultures have what I have labeled a "bitch disorder." People will find something wrong with any system. If it isn't a massive wreck on the Interstate, then it will be moaning about the dirty park. If it isn't about a major recession, it is about a street person denied food at the welfare station. America has become such an affluent society the *bitch disorder* has become a raging malady. At the pinnacle of the Great Depression, headlines near the breadlines romanticized the attractive bank robbers Bonnie and Clyde. These two killers were so disgruntled by the banking failures and government ineptitude they took matters into their own hands. It provided some entertainment value and unconscious admiration for two little people defying the system that had bled the populace of money and jobs.

Educate Metaphorically – Not Too Rationally

The Innovative Mind (2008) was written to force a reader to use both brain hemispheres while reading a book. It was written to spite the American university systems that outlaw the use of illustrations to validate the words in research papers. Today's academics hide behind the old-fashioned APA style. It was good at first, but like all control systems, has become biblical and part of the problem. The psychologist Robert Aunger saw this happening and wrote, "The only way of directly communicating an idea is by means of an icon, and every indirect method of communicating an idea depends upon the use of an icon." (*The Electric Meme* p. 232) A scientist that was not lost in the data was one of the greatest minds that ever lived. Nikola Tesla's approach to life and inventing was to use an internal mind-picture approach to inventing that he described so well in his memoirs:

> "I needed no models, drawings or experiments. I
> could picture hem all in my mind. The inventions
> I have conceived in this way have always worked.
> When I get an idea, I start at once building it up in
> my imagination. It is absolutely immaterial whether I
> run my turbine in my thought or test it in my shop."
> (Landrum 1995 p. 261)

Futurist Ray Kurzweil validated the above saying, "Those learning by rote don't really understand since they are not connected to it through sensory metaphors. Understanding something in one way means you don't really understand it at all." Those in power know this well, as they use their edge to keep those below them in line. *The Scientific American Mind* (May 2005) said, "Schools place an overwhelming emphasis on solving problems correctly, not creatively." When rules become more important than creativity, then something is amiss. Rules to control tend to cause the reverse to occur. Those having to live by them suddenly stop respecting them. Stupid work policies achieve the same disdain. When personnel are forced to draw within the lines, they will never become innovative. In *A Whole New Mind*, Daniel Pink wrote, "Many left-brain workers in this country face career extinction." The blame is directly due to the schools where they were forced to regurgitate data, a left-brain quality, instead of being allowed to dream and attempt new creative things.

China is producing around half a million new engineers annually. America is graduating 1/5th or around 100,000, and one-third of them are foreign born. The opposite is seen in the law schools and in math. In 1999, Singapore 8th grade students were ranked #1 in an international study on math. The United States ranked 19th. A *Wall Street Journal* article said, "Singapore students routinely score among the highest in international math tests. Why? Singapore books teach kids to draw bar models to visualize a math problem before they start solving it." I have repeatedly told my students that if you can't see the problem and the potential solutions, you will struggle solving it. The article offered an answer to envisioning when they wrote, "Kids in Singapore learn to use visual tools to understand abstract concepts – to draw bars and other diagrams to visualize problems – a technique called bar-modeling." This is using graphics, a right-brain phenomenon to find left-brain solutions.

One of the problems in American schools is that less than half of the teachers ever majored in math. Internationally, 70% of math teachers majored in math. In a 2004 study by the *Organization of Economic*

Cooperation & Development, the United States ranks 24th out of 29 nations in the application of math skills to real world problems. Street smarts are inherently crucial to learning the way to fix, create, or build new things. Those more inclined to take textbook theories and give them a practical applications have a far better chance of communicating esoteric ideas to younger students. That is why many gifted departments use practical, on-the-street concepts to teach math and science. It is easier for the children to grasp and retain, rather than forcing them to memorize esoteric concepts that they will forget in three days. It appears in some cases we become too smart and sophisticated to be practical. Most educational systems honor teachers who spoon-feed their students. They're the ones who get the good grades. However, success on the streets and in the trenches is not about regurgitating data. On the street you will not have a person standing beside you telling you the answers are multiple choice, you should do X or Y. You are forced to look at the situation, compare the inputs, and come up with the answers. If the student doesn't learn to risk in the classroom, it is unlikely they will be found risking on the street.

Neurogenesis & Brain Plasticity

More and more information proves that nurture, not nature is the panacea of power. It is now known that nurturing actually begins in the womb and continues through life. Sharon Begley, writing in *The Wall Street Journal* (Jan. 13, 2006) said, "A gene contributes zero (0%) % of what you become. If you don't grow up in an environment that turns the gene on an environment contributes nothing of the individual's behavior." She went on to say, "Different environments can produce different traits from the same genotype." Think about what you want and you are emitting an inner electronic frequency, which will cause the energy of what you want to vibrate. Focus on what you want, and you are changing the vibrations of the atoms and causing it to vibrate to you! Want to change the brain? It is possible, but not easy or possible without a great deal of dedicated effort. *The Scientific American Mind* discussed the fact that music and exercise can contribute to the brain's growth and healthiness. They said, "The brain is surprisingly malleable. It can rewire itself and even grow new cells. Behavior and environment can cause substantial rewiring - especially learning and long-term memory" (*Scientific American Mind* March 2009 pg. 63).

Introspection, that ability to look within before pontificating, is crucial to becoming more innovative. Turn your mind inward and you will be amazed at how much better you can be at self-evaluation. No behavior can be managed, controlled, or motivated, including your own, if you don't get it. Many studies show that even IQ is as much as 15% dependent on environmental influences. In *Intelligence Reframed* (1998) Howard Gardner wrote:

> **"I reject the nature-nurture dichotomy. I stress the constant and dynamic interaction from the moment of conception. It takes about a decade to master a domain and up to an additional decade to fashion work that is creative enough to alter that domain."**

This is a common finding in most entrepreneurial geniuses. It took about ten years for Thomas Edison, Henry Ford, Richard Branson, and Michael Dell to make their marks in the world. It then took them about another ten years to earn the epithet of superstars. An example is Tiger Woods in golf. Tiger began early, competing in his very first golf tournament when he was just five years old. By 15, he had won the U.S. Amateur Championship. By 24, he was the very best in the world, a 19-year genesis to greatness. Had Tiger began later would he have been good? Yes! But he would never have won the U.S. Amateurs younger than anyone in history. The bottom line is success takes time and eminence even more time. There is no such thing as instant success. A University of California study on brains and nurturing found,

"Bright rats placed in *impoverished environments* lose their brightness and dull rats placed in *enriched environments* lose their dullness; bright rats placed in *enriched environments* double their brightness edge over dull rats and vice versa." (*Eight Keys to Greatness* 1999)

M.D. Robert Burton told us in *On Being Certain* (2008), "The gene's most crucial for survival are the ones most likely to have a direct effect on behavior." He spoke about not being able to discern ugly; you don't know beautiful. If you haven't been in the presence of a cacophony, you can't perceive harmonious. This is so true. Despite this knowledge, politicians continue to babble on about things that they have not one clue about. They have not ever made a deal in Japan, China, or India and most have never walked through a plant in Shanghai or Hong Kong. Yet they tell the media what China or India can and cannot do. They even suggest how the Chinese should operate their businesses. Ignorance sure is bliss. If one is going to flagellate another nation or industry, they should at least know something of which they speak. That is seldom the case with politicians.

The Wall Street Journal published an editorial on *Mind & Brain* (Begley 2007) in which they spoke of the nature versus nurture argument. They wrote, "What determines the activity of the gene is the environment. Rats born to attentive, conscientious mothers but reared by neglectful, low-licking adoptive mothers, grew into neurotic, stressed-out adults." The mind is the conscious trying to protect us from what the unconscious knows is best. That makes the mind the enemy of creativity. "Enriched environments spur neuro-genesis in the young and old," wrote polio maven Jonas Salk. He went on to say, "Stimulating environments grow brain cells three times larger. Carl Jung spent his life ferreting out the meaning of different personalities on behavior. He would discover, "The uncon-scious of an autonomous, creative being, is in continuous motion between sets of opposites." It was from this start that he would develop what has since become the largest-used personality test in the world—known today as the Myers-Briggs Temperament Inventory. One of his protégés in this field was Mihaly Csikszentmihalyi. He published a classic work titled *Flow*. It explored the zone-like state of being that helps one transcend what is to find what might be. In *Creativity* he wrote:

> **"Creative people escape rigid gender role stereotyping. Creative and talented girls are more dominant and tough than other girls, and creative boys are more sensitive and less aggressive than their male peers. Creative individuals have not only the strengths of their own gender but that of the other. They escape rigid gender role stereotyping tending to androgyny."**

Testing people prior to hiring them is not necessarily the best way to discern if they are *organized, dependable, emotionally stable, or willing to deal with change.* Those are valued qualities in a manager, but discovering if they fit the profile has found some interesting facts. One study used testing to see if they fit the qualifications, and then they interviewed the subjects extensively. Then the study found a way to look into the candidate's closets, offices, medicine cabinets, car trunks, and home closets. What worked best? The latter, hands down. Researchers found a strong correlation between a person's ability to be structured at home and at play with their ability to do so on the job. If their closets had each rack meticulously arranged by dress shirts, casual attire, and suits and their medicine cabinets were orderly, they would be that way at work. If structured at home, it seems you are structured at work. If dependable in your personal life, you will be dependable at work, and vice versa.

Is Creativity Innate or Learned?

Daniel Pine of the National Institute of Mental Health wrote, "Knowing a DNA sequence is not enough to predict behavior. You need to know the environment in which the organism was reared. It's enough to retire the very notion of innate." (WSJ Jan. 13, 2006) It is amazing how the brain can be programmed by experience. Margaret Mead was reared by two parents that were pretty progressive educators since both were PhD's. Mead lived in sixty homes prior to becoming a teenager. What did that do to her mentally and emotionally? She learned to cope with the unknown and loved to travel the world in her quest to understand the anthropological machinations of mankind. Most surprising is that they refused to permit her to enter a traditional classroom environment until her teens. Why? They intuitively knew that a classroom teaches a child what they "can" and what they "cannot" do. It molds children into a mediocrity state of following, not leading. Meade would become the very first female PhD Anthropologist and a world-renowned writer. When psychologist Jean Houston wired her brain to see what might be different about her, it turned out she had the most brain hemisphere connections of anyone ever tested. Many examples validate that androgynous behavior works. Meade, herself, was bi-sexual as was Napoleon, Isadora Duncan, Howard Hughes, Hemingway, and Hitler. They were often seen as radical and out of touch with reality. Mahatma Gandhi was such a man as was Hitler. Contrary to popular opinion, it was the wives of German industrialists who financed the Nazi party. Hitler had a kind of mesmerizing power over women. Women with a similar propensity were Joan of Arc, Catherine the Great, and Margaret Thatcher. Had Joan of Arc showed up in a dress, no male soldier would have followed her into battle. Had Catherine the Great been a submissive wife, she would have become a nun, not the Empress of Russia. Had Margaret Thatcher capitulated to the male elite and paternalistic system in Great Britain, she would never have become their first female Prime Minister.

Nurture/Nature Dichotomy

"IQ is far more influenced by environment" says a University of Michigan psychologist. For him it is nurture over nature. In the 1980s, political scientist James Flynn noticed that IQ was increasing in all countries all the time, at an average rate of about 3 IQ points per decade. The average IQ across the world had risen over 1 standard deviation (15 points) since WWII. Flynn found that this was primarily due to environmental effects. As a result, new norms continue to be used to rescale IQ tests to "'100." One of those was food and nutrition. Could diet be a factor in higher IQ scores? It is not likely since IQ's kept rising in both well-nourished western countries and undernourished nations. Could it be education? Interruptions to schooling only have temporary effects on IQ. Importantly, it appears that abstract reasoning ability shows the steepest improvements. One researcher, Ulric Neisser suggests that the Flynn effect is based on the incredible electronic visual images such as ads, posters, videogames, and TV graphics that are now pervasive on a daily basis. He suggests that children experience a much richer visual environment than in the past, and that this assists them with visual puzzles of the kind that dominate IQ tests.

Conflict & Creativity

There are various ways to deal with conflict—both personal and professional. We can avoid it, accept it as a natural event, or attack it head on. The fearful tend to take the first position and play the CYA game and just avoid any conflict – personally and professionally. The positive and more optimistic types tend to see is a part of everyday life and deal with it. The entrepreneurial spirits or innovators tend to be of the renegade school and see an obstacle and attack it aggressively. Developing a Creative Mindset is about integrating the following:

✗ **Wonderment:** Tap into your inner spirit of discovery; that childlike curiosity like Einstein or Dr. Seuss works wonders. Question and be inquisitive to a fault.

✔ **Intrinsic Motivation**: Pursue your wild urges and 3am insights; those that introspect find incredible insights floating aimlessly within.

✔ **Intellectual Audacity**: Jump aggressively out of the box of mediocrity since it is what keeps you from daring what others fear Inhibition is the enemy; divergent thinking underlies all creativity, as does curiosity and metaphors.

✔ **Relaxed Concentration Works**: Daydream and wander down the beach while pondering life's wonders and possibilities—you can't create while uptight so loosen up.

Synthesizing to Success & Androgyny

Synthesizing to success is the panacea of greatness. This was validated by *Fortune* (Aug. 8, 1994) when they wrote, "Women are more like men entrepreneurs than they are like other women." Then *Psychology Today* (July 1996) offered further insight saying, "Creative and talented girls are more dominant and tough than other girls." It is akin to what Carl Jung labeled. Jung used the word to describe that feminine side of a man that has been repressed. It is where he can go when needing to be more sensitive. Jung said very feminine women do the same, by repressing their macho urges. Women often become submissive in the presence of men. Not women like Margaret Thatcher and Madonna. They were feminine, but when needing to take the reigns, they did. What is the moral? Integrate the masculine and feminine to excel. This talent has been labeled androgyny by psychologists. An example is Jung's term "introversion." To be introverted is to be internally energized. When an introvert wants to become more extraverted, they must force themselves to find other people more interesting and listen and interact. It takes time, but it will work. It took millions of experiential imprints to make one an introvert, so it will take some time to change them. This tends to be an oversimplification. Extroverts are not necessarily people who talk a lot. They are those energized by other people. They do not receive their energy from within as is the case of an introvert. An introvert doesn't need others to feel good about them. Most extroverts do. This makes it exceedingly difficult for an extrovert to go it alone or to hibernate in a corner with a book. It is just as difficult for a shy introvert to work as a concierge in a hotel. Having to interface all day every day with a parade of people will take its toll and stress or ulcers will result if they are not fired quickly. Transformation only occurs by someone willing to work very hard on becoming what they are not.

Why is becoming synthesized so crucial to becoming great? Studies have shown that that people capable of flip-flopping within are more successful than those that are single-dimensional--George Bernard Shaw was pathologically shy. When his first eight books were never published, he took his show on the road. What did he do? He became an extroverted promoter of his work and made over 1,000 speeches to promote himself and his work. That is pretty awesome for a man who had sat in the British Museum for eight years reading books alone. His ability to attack his weakness head on led to *Man & Superman* getting published. Another example was the highly extraverted Joseph Campbell. One of the most erudite Americans to ever live once spent four years as a recluse in a remote cabin in order to read the Greek Classics without distraction. There is a plethora of examples of superstars that could flip-flop between different dimensions of personality, gender, and even ideologies. This was never said more eloquently than the following by Mihaly Csikszentmihalyi:

> *"Perhaps the most important duality that the creative persons are able to integrate is being open and receptive on one hand and hard driving on the other. When an extravert learns to experience the world as an introvert it is as if he or she discovered a whole new missing dimension. Keep exploring what it takes to be the opposite of who you are."*
> *Creativity* (1996 pg 360-362)

Sophocles described the need to be what we are and what we are not with great insight when he wrote in *The Iliad*, "When woman becomes the equal of man she becomes his superior." What was he saying? That a woman already has certain strengths, like nurturing, and if she could tap into her male side, she would become invincible. Carl Jung offered insight into the above concept. Jung said that the unconscious arena in a woman was an *Animus*--"woman's unconscious self." It was where "all of woman's ancestral experiences of man exist." Jung labeled the male equivalent the *Anima* - where "all man's ancestral experiences of woman could be found." Exceptional people seem to be better able to tap into what they are not more than the also-rans. An example of this principle at work can be found in the world's great visionaries. Balzac's mistress described him as "more female than male." Joseph Campbell, Freud, Martin Luther King, and Howard Hughes all possessed strong masculine and feminine qualities. They could switch roles on command.

Carl Jung labeled inner repressions as syzygy. "In the unconscious of every woman, Jung wrote, "there is a hidden male personality." Such androgyny was apparent in the very essence of British Prime Minister Margaret Thatcher. She would be labeled the "Iron Lady" by the Russian press. Her friend, President, Ronald Reagan, told the media, "Margaret Thatcher is the best man in England." Later, a London newspaper said, "Thatcher does not have one feminine cell in her body." Golda Meir was also a lady in the kitchen but a fighter in the cabinet. Israel's David Ben Gurion told the press, "Golda is the only man in my cabinet." The truth is that she was the only woman, but the only person with the guts and risk-taking propensity to fight for Israel's survival. Howard Hughes is another example of inner duality. Hughes was pathologically shy, yet mesmerized audiences when necessary. At a time when he had not been seen in public for years, Senator Ralph Owen Brewster tried to use Hughes as a foil for his own growth. It was November 1947, when Brewster called for a congressional hearing, fully expecting Hughes to be a no-show, the Senator told the press, "The Hughes Flying Boat cannot fly," implying that Hughes had cheated the government. The normally reticent Hughes refused to be intimidated, called a press conference, and said, "If the plane is judged a failure I will probably leave the country and never come back." Then he brazenly showed up before Congress and wowed the media. This was a man who held Board meetings in Las Vegas by talking through the hotel room doors rather than be seen. When a fake biography hit the streets by a man named Clifford Irving, Hughes went on air live from his Bahamas home to say it was a forgery.

When you hear someone say, "It's just in my genes. It's the way I am," they are often lost in their own reverie. Genes are an important factor but without the experience the genes of little import. Just attend a Mensa meeting of the highest IQ's and you'll find validation. In *We the Living* (1936) Ayn Rand wrote, "No one is born with any kind of talent. Writers are made, not born. To be exact, writers are self-made." Very accurate assessment! Lewis Terman tracked 1470 very high IQ types in his study on what was labeled Termites – brilliant students with genius IQ's. No Termites ever won a Noble or Pulitzer Prize although some that had been turned down as not being bright enough did. They had very nice careers as judges, attorneys and upper middle-class winners but no were eminent.

Chapter 8
The ATTITUDE Game – A Self-Fulfilling Prophecy

We are as good as we think we are or bad as we fear we are.

"The death rates of optimistic men are 63% lower than pessimists. Optimism prolongs life. Laughing makes you stronger, friendlier and sexier." - *Scientific American Mind* (May 2009)

"Seeing the bright side of life strengthens the psyche, eases pain and tightens social bonds." – *Laughing Matters* by Steve Ayan

Attitudes have the power to make us and the power to break us. Ever worked for a know-it-all that is so arrogant individual they are going to do it there way not matter what anyone says? We all have. Fortunately, they are a minority. We are all prone to believing our own shit at times. Remember, no matter how big we get or how many trophies we collect in any discipline there is always someone bigger, smarter, quicker and more skilled on any given subject. Those leaders that become too smart for their own good never understand that their *Achilles Heal* can often be found in the head. Those leaders that get too pompous to come down out of their ivory tower are the most dangerous. When that happens they become the most vulnerable. Start believing you are invincible and ironically you become them most vulnerable.

There are a myriad of examples of those on top losing it all due to a bad attitude. Kodak thought they were invincible and protected their film profits rather than go into new markets like digital photography. They were not in the film business but in the memories business. They lost the war of providing memories when the digital revolution hit. The same was true of Big Blue who owned the computer mainframe business for so many years. The leaders became complacent just as those at AT&T had done since they owned the telephone communications industry. When it gets too easy, it imprints a dangerous malady in the minds of those in charge. They don't want to change what is working, but what they overlook is that there are adversaries looking to knock them off their pinnacle. If they don't the changes, the way the world works, their competition will achieve the same thing. This makes attitude the most fundamental quality for anyone, whether on top or trying to get there.

Attitude is not only important for success, it's imperative. Good attitudes keep people going long after the weak have left for the bars. Those with a strong, positive attitude refuse to participate in the media mania of recession or the Sky is Falling mantra of the media naysayers. In contrast, those with a poor attitude buy in and go down with the ship. Attitudes make us and they can break us. Where do we get these attitudinal perspectives? From programmed mindsets. When an uncle tells the kid at eight, "You are a real worker kid," that is programmed in what I have labeled a "Success Imprint." It is a positively wired mental model that will have that kid outworking his or her peers at age 35. That is why it is important to be very careful what you buy into at all ages. When the aunt says, "You are on your way to becoming a gang leader," at age 10, that is also hard-wired in the mind of the child. It is what I labeled "Failure Imprints" since it is there and becomes part and parcel of one's attitude from then on. Be very careful what attitude you bring to the party, as the party might not fit that particular attitude. Are you the right horse for their course? It is key to most successes and failures in life. One aphorism that attacks negativity is, "I had the blues because I had no shoes until upon the street, where I met a man who had no feet." It proves that all things are relative.

Self-esteem is an inner game. The mind is what makes us walk around smiling or frowning. We have all run into the pessimists with black clouds perpetually draped over their heads. They can find something wrong with a new baby, baseball, or apple pie. Everything is a problem for such types. Babies cry, our baseball teams lose, and apple pie has too much sugar. So what! We know optimists—-those dudes walking the streets with a positive attitude are the ones that get ill far less than the norm, execute above average in any endeavor, and are described as lucky by those pessimists with black-clouds perpetually dealing them a bad hand.

Einstein was correct. It is all relative. When things are bad in a down market, some people opt out while others use the calamity to make their mark in the world. An example comes from a man with a penchant for life, despite humble beginnings. Israel Baline came to America as a child. He had virtually no formal education, but was infatuated with music. Despite his yearning, he never learned to read or write a note of music. How could a Jew write such American religious classics as *White Christmas* and *Easter Parade*? Israel left home at eleven and learned to survive on the streets of Tin Pan Alley and changed his name to a more American sounding Berlin. One-finger piano playing earned him a living during his life on the street. It would lead to such classics as *God Bless America, Blue Skies,* and *Let Me Entertain You.* Attitudinal lyrics emanated from within a seething psyche such as, "I Got the Sun in the Morning and the moon at night." Berlin could identify with such words as "Got no checkbooks, got no banks." A positive attitude emerged from deep within a man who cared about his adopted country. But it wasn't easy. When Berlin wrote the incomparable *White Christmas,* critics panned it saying, "It's a loser." Within a year of its release, it was the #2 song in American on its way to becoming the most played song in history. What if this man who could not read or write a note of music had listened to those who could?

Attitude – A Self-Fulfilling Prophecy

In Chinese, the word "crisis" is composed of two characters--danger and opportunity. This shows the dichotomy of thinking that underlies even strong words. The fact that crisis can make us and it can break us is inherent in the rhetoric. Attitude is often measured by the lengths people will go to achieve or avoid adversity. This was never more apparent than an American high-tech executive who grew up to be a tennis pro. Steve Appleton got into the volatile world of memory chips as CEO of Micron, a $5 billion dollar firm headquartered in Idaho. In tennis, Steve learned that to compete effectively one must look closely at an opponent's strengths and weaknesses and to avoid letting them beat you with the strengths, by picking on their weaknesses. That led to a similar strategy in the highly competitive game of digital memories. In an interview, Steve told the media "Analyze the competition. Study strengths and weaknesses to the point of exhaustion. I learned to speak Japanese so I could study their companies – what they were good at and what they weren't just as I did in tennis." He went on to say, "What displays itself in sports displays itself in business."

The inscrutable Japanese have a simplistic sense of dealing with problems. Once while sitting in a nightclub in the Ginza district of Tokyo, I asked a Japanese executive about how they dealt with lifetime employment if an employee was caught with their hand in the proverbial cookie jar. The executive looked at me and with as close to a smile as you could ever see and said, "We transfer him." With a quizzical look on my face, I asked, "Not sure I understand." And with a grin he said, "We send him to a remote office, like Siberia, without family." And the message hit me between the eyes as a very understated, but effective, manner of forcing the individual to quit.

Studies repeatedly show that happy people are less likely to die as soon as unhappy people. It all boils down to a positive attitude versus a negative one. Attitude has a strong cultural side with studies showing that the reason 85% of people get jobs and do well in that job is their positive *Attitude*. Only 15% of an individual's success is due to some technical or specific skill set. This was never validated more than when Honda opened its first American automobile manufacturing plant in Marysville, Ohio in 1982. Honda became the first Japanese company to build a car in the United States, and like the Honda Accord, the Marysville Auto Plant has evolved into a wonder of technology. The first Accord produced in America--a silver-gray sedan with the license plate "USA 001" came off the line on Nov. 1, 1982. It was enshrined in a museum to mark the incredible achievement of Honda in opening a successful U.S. auto plant. The production of that first U.S. car is recognized as a turning point in American manufacturing. The Ohio plant has built over 10 million vehicles and has had a history of continuous innovation. The Hondo Motto in Marysville is, "Maintaining a global viewpoint, we are dedicated to supplying products of the highest quality, yet at a reasonable price, for worldwide customer satisfaction."

Sitting at lunch one day with the head of OD–Organizational Development--I asked him, "Do you employ the Japanese philosophy of lifetime employment?" The American executive dressed in a Honda logo'd golf shirt told me, "No, we don't." So I continued to dig, "Then what is your turnover rate, if you don't mind my asking?" Smiling, he replied, "Very low." It was apparent that he was being cautious, knowing that I wrote books and wasn't sure if I would be quoting him, but I continued the interrogation. "How about your layoffs since you've been open here in America?" On this subject, he was unable to resist, and said, "We've not had any. We lose people by attrition, but we've actually never had a layoff." We talked more, but it reminded me of the newspaper article that appeared when the plant had first opened. American reporters were sent in to find some human interest story of a

Japanese firm with a whole different culture entering U.S. soil to produce cars to compete with Detroit.

Marysville, Ohio for those that never visited there is a vast divide from Japan. Those that live and work there, prior to Honda arriving, wouldn't buy a foreign car if they had to ride a bicycle to work. Xenophobia is alive and well in the rust belt. Ohio is very conservative and non-accepting of foreign ideas. A reporter had come to that grand opening and was wandering around finding grist for an article. One day he was standing outside the plant as a shirt changed. Watching the people exit, he saw a young Japanese supervisor leave the assembly area and heading to his car. The quiet, unassuming Japanese worker walked slowly, and passing through the new car lot, he stopped before every single car in that lot and rearranged the windshield wipers so they were all exactly aligned the same. This so intrigued the journalist he walked up to the man and asked, "Aren't you off work?" The worker replied, "Yes." "Why are you straightening these windshield wipers then?" The worker looked at the journalist with pad open and said in broken English, "They were not set right. It is my job to make sure all things are right." The reporter stated, "But you aren't being paid to do that. You can go home and have dinner and leave that to someone else, a person getting paid." The Japanese man, with a puzzled look on his face said, "But that would not be right. I am part of the company and the company must do well for me to do well or I won't have a job." That says it all. The sad commentary is that if the reporter had asked a hundred American workers the same question, they would not have cared, or even if they did, they would not have taken their personal time to fix someone else's error. In there lies the underlying difference in the two cultures. In Japan, it is called an "egalitarian attitude."

Firms like Honda have a strong customer service mindset that arms their personnel with an indomitable spirit that permeates their work.

The knowledge that you will be there no matter what transpires removes the C.Y.A. mentality from the game. A problem not in one's job description has little or no bearing on working on it. You are there to solve problems, not for some specific job. With such a long-term perspective, the ego is removed from the mind, as is self-serving agendas. How many times have you called a firm to find a fix for a new product problem and the clerk on the phone responds, "That is not my area of responsibility," and hangs up to get rid of you quick. That is what I have often labeled a "clerk mentality" —the individual that will never leave that desk as they are too micro-minded to grow. They will always be a clerk. Clerks seldom get the message that their self-serving attitude is the basis of their inability to grow.

Positive Energy & Can-Do Attitudes

Beware the energy vampire lurking within. Vampires rob us of vital energy. Just as in the movies, they suck your blood and make you barren. Those that hang with energy leeches wonder why they feel tired so much of the time. Take a close look at who you are hanging with and you will find the answer. Energy vampires zap you without you even knowing it, so I tell students "Tell the energy vampires in your world that you have used up this week's quota for pessimism. See me next week when I may have another opening for your negativity." They smile and look at me strangely.

Norman Lear wrote, "You have to expend energy to get energy." Touché! Most people spend as much energy being average as it would take to be great. Take charge of your energy tank, and it will take care of you. This is never more poignant than when suffering some problem or illness. Psychiatrist John Diamond in his work *Life Energy* (1990) said, "Your thoughts have the power to alter the physiological response in your muscles. By learning your negative emotional states, you can transform or transmute them into positive ones," and then said:

**"By getting in touch with your mind and body, you
will find new freedom. Drugs relieve symptoms of
a disease, but it does not cure. The true cure always
involves a major change in the person's attitude
toward himself and life…it is the spirit pervading the
mind and body which is the healing force within us."**
(John Diamond pg. 15)

Diamond found that hanging with losers can drain the life blood from
a person. One study had positive and negative people socially interface
to see what would happen. Sure enough, the positive person became
more negative and the negative person became more positive. In his
work on kinesiology, Diamond found that frowns drain us of vital energy and smiles imbue us with more energy. In *The Law of Attraction*,
Joe Vitale said, "We attract who we are. The more positive energy we
give off the more will magnetize to us." Jazz master Quincy Jones offered profound insight into what had made him a success saying, "I live
by goose bumps." Is that right on or what? It turns out that the best
antidotes are never in the medicine cabinet. They are lying dormant
in our minds. Laughter is the best pain killer in the universe. Why? It
attacks that part of the brain that makes us emotional basket-cases. It
is why ballet instructors tell their students "Don't think." This same
advice comes from martial arts where the Master informs his students
to never attack until the adversary stops. Why? That is when they think
and will be most vulnerable. The inner energy is inextricably tied to the
head that is tied to the heart.

Believe You Can & You Can

Achieving demands that a person believes they can achieve. It is not
far removed from the mental attitude existing at any given moment. If
they question that they can, it has been found they cannot. This is what
textbooks label as "having a strong Comfort with Ambiguity or Self-

Efficacy." When a person is uncomfortable with their environment, they often are stymied due to their inner anxieties. The unknown scares such people while it inspires those with a positive self-efficacy. An unquenchable belief that you are capable of performing no matter the environment or adversary is what fuels superstars. No matter how much talent an individual possesses, they are unlikely to succeed if their minds and hearts are not positively programmed to do so. Most people become mired in their own internal insecurities. After his defeat at Waterloo, Napoleon sat in St. Helena, and writing his memoirs said, "I had supreme confidence in my power; I felt I could divine everything in the future." That is self-efficacy. It was also the thing that made Frank Lloyd Wright so successful. He was being cross-examined and justified an act saying, "Ordinary men follow rules. I am not an ordinary man. I am the world's greatest architect." That is confidence bordering on arrogance.

A quintessential example of positive attitudes comes from the Irish wit Oscar Wilde who explained why one of his plays had been panned by the critics, "The play was a great success. The audience was a failure." Is that a positive attitude in the face of adversity? Applied Kinesiology tells us that a smile releases *endorphins* into the body with a tonic effect on the immune system. High energy flow and physiological strengthening of muscles is a by-product of smiling. The converse is also true. A frown releases *adrenalin* into the body with a deleterious affect on the immune system. This suggests that it is not only important to smile and be happy to stay healthy but it is dangerous not to. Those spending their lives with a perpetual scowl are making themselves and those around them ill. An example of this can be found in those that do well in the world. Those that walk around with a messianic sense of self like Napoleon, Hitler, and Carl Jung believe, and their belief becomes a self-fulfilling prophecy.

David Hawkins, psychiatrist and Behavioral Kinesiologist, wrote "Muscles strengthen and weaken from positive or negative stimuli." Hawkins was a fan of John Diamond's work and had tested thousands of patients and found that when people became negative, they also became weaker with lower energy flow through their systems. Martin Seligman also studied attitude extensively and found that optimistic thoughts are 100 times more powerful than pessimistic thoughts. Studies have shown that our health is directed related to how we think. Pessimistic students assigned to an optimist workshop turned out to have fewer visits to their school's health clinic. They also experienced lower rates of depression and anxiety. Lynn Grabhorn in *Excuse Me, Your Life is Waiting* wrote, "Every time we think of anything, we're flowing positive or negative energy. The litany never changes; as we think, we feel, as we feel, we vibrate; as we vibrate, we attract. Then we get to live the results." Psychologist Erik Erickson wrote, "Study and after study has shown that children with superior intelligence but low self-esteem do poorly in school while children of average intelligence but high self-esteem can be unusually successful."

"Flow" is a mental state of deep concentration. It takes only about 15 minutes to put oneself into a state of "flow." The constant interruptions and distractions of a typical office environment will force most people out of the "flow state." In other words, placing a person in a happier environment will often lead to a more positive result. Many studies have shown that one's mood affects their attitude, and of course, the attitude affects everything that happens to them. A good mood enhances their ability to think outside the box, and conversely, a tunnel vision can be associated with fear and anxiety. Unquestionably, a good mood enhances creativity. It also affects the way we process information. *Scientific American Mind* wrote in 2006, "Research has shown that a positive attitude helps the unconscious brain look at a problem from a different angle, improving the chance of solving it."

Mental Magic Can Be Mysterious & Metaphysical

One of the most metaphorical stories in our nation comes from a Notre Dame All-American running back by the name of Mario Tonelli. Mario destroyed USC in the 1937 Rose Bowl. In the stands that day was a young Japanese student watching the game. As fate would have it, the physical specimen, Tonelli, ended up in the Philippines Death March where 10,000 GI's perished. Mario was using every ounce of courage to survive that horrid experience. One day while marching through the horrendous heat of the Philippine jungles, Mario was accosted by a Japanese soldier who took his Notre Dame Class ring. It was exasperating, but Mario was too ill with malaria and too weak to fight. Tonelli had dropped from 200 lbs to 125 and knew he was close to the end. And a day later a Japanese officer came to him, that same guy who was in the stands that day long ago in the Rose Bowl, and said, "Here is your ring. I was there that day. You deserve to keep it." Tonelli told the media years later, "It left me with a new will to live."

But his travails were not over. When General Douglas MacArthur returned to liberate the Philippines, the prisoners, including an emaciated Mario, were moved to a Japanese prison in Nagoya. By now, Mario was but a skeleton of his former self, weighing less than 100 pounds, and beginning to wonder if he would ever leave Japan alive. That is when he experienced an epiphany. The guard in Nagoya threw him a uniform to don while there. As he removed the wrappings, Tonelli looked down at the number on the shirt he had been assigned and was shocked to see the number was the identical number of his Notre Dame jersey--#58. In 2005, Tonelli was featured in an article and told the journalist, "A surge of energy surged through me that day and I knew I was going to make it." What a mystical story of a number and a life that makes us keep on trekking.

The ability to think positively is crucial in all facets of life. Eddie Arcaro--the legendary jockey--lost an incredible 250 races before he ever won just one. Most people would have quit long before and certainly would not have gone on to become one of the greatest jockeys to ever mount a horse. Joseph Lister was ridiculed by virtually every surgeon in Britain when he suggested they wash their hands prior to surgery. His innovative concept of antiseptics was denigrated be many hospitals. They thought he was a kook. Sixteen years after being denigrated, the British Medical Congress eulogized him for his work in the field that had saved so many lives.

No better example exists in the lore of tenacity and a positive attitude than the one of an aging Thomas Edison losing his life's work. At age 67, long past his life expectancy, he stood outside his Menlo Park lab and watched it burn to the ground with all of his work going up in flames. A reporter walked up and asked Edison what he was thinking. The intrepid inventor with the positive attitude looked at reporter and said, "Thank goodness all our mistakes were burned up. Now we can start over fresh." That is the epitome of optimism in the face of disaster, coming from a man at the very end of his career. It brings to mind the words of Abraham Lincoln who said, "Most folks are about as happy as they make up their minds to be." Attitude has never been more important than in athletics. Coaches have learned that if they walk to the mound in the bottom of the 9th inning with the bases full, they need to say nothing negative. They have learned to say, "Throw the next pitch high and inside," and not, "Throw it low and outside." Whichever you say is recorded in the brain and will be the most likely to happen. Never, ever say the negative, or the bases will be empty in your world as well.

Happy Minds Lead to Creative Minds
A large part of one's attitude is unconscious. Those of us who grew up fretting over making the mortgage payment each month have a built-in anxiety alarm. It is an inner alarm mechanism put there to deal with anxiety and fear. That is why anxiety has been found to be the enemy of positive thinking. Children are not yet programmed with a lot of worry, and consequently, test as being happy far more than adults. Einstein and Dr. Seuss refused to grow up as they knew intuitively that maintaining a child-like mentality made them far more creative. Einstein often said that he learned little after his teen years. Dr. Seuss

writes, "My books do not insult children's intelligence because I'm on their level. When I dropped out of Oxford, I decided to be a child." It is a fact that kindergarten kids laugh 300 times each day while adults laugh but 17 times. Better to be a child with a positive attitude than a frowning adult. On arriving in New York City, the customs agent asked Oscar Wilde what he had to declare. The cynic responded, "Nothing, but my genius." That is a positive attitude.

Hospital cardiac care units have long known that the death rates of their patients are highly correlated to the mood of their nurses. In one study, the death rate was four times higher for units with nurses with a foul attitude compared to those with a positive attitude. In retail, the stores with the happiest sales clerks have the strongest sales results. Jim Clark, the founder of Netscape, offered insight into all this when he said, "By not planning for failure, you don't leave yourself room for failure. I never think about failing. I just look for ways to win and forget there's any alternative." Robert Noyce, the Silicon Valley maven that invented the first integrated circuit and started Intel was a card-carrying optimist. Noyce had developed the first integrated circuits and then introduced the microprocessor chip saying:

"Optimism is an essential ingredient for innovation. How else can the individual welcome change over security, adventure over staying in safe places? Innovation cannot be mandated any more than a baseball coach can demand the next batter to hit a home run." (*Investors Business Daily* Jan. 12, 2001 A4)

Howard Head was a mechanical engineer who invented the first metal ski. What led him to do something totally outside his area of expertise? Head refused to believe that he was the problem on a ski slope. Head had a strong ego that refused to admit that it was him that was not good at flying down a mountain on wooden skis, so he built metal ones. In doing so, Head wrote "I was humiliated and disgusted at how badly I skied. I blamed it on the wooden skis, saying to myself, 'If wood were the best material they would still be making airplanes out of wood." With $5,000 in poker winnings, the Big T personality quit his job and launched Head Ski. His attitude had made him rich. Then he bought a new home with a tennis court and decided to take up tennis. The tennis pro soon gave up on him as totally inept. What happened? Sure enough, Head blamed his incompetence on the small tennis racket. Once again, the man with the positive mindset went into his garage and built a tennis racket with twice the sweet spot for striking a high speed tennis ball. It became the first oversized tennis racket with the name Prince. Head's racket had 57% more speed than other rackets. Head began beating friends and patented his invention. Four years later he sold out for a $75 million profit. This success story was all attributed to a man with the right attitude.

Attitude is often associated with what academics label "Locus of Control." Those with a strong Internal Locus of Control believe that they are in control of their destinies. They are better able to deal with adversity, and if it occurs, they are able to recover much faster than those not so inclined. University of California psychologist Charles Garfield trained the first astronauts for going into space. In his book, *Peak Performance* (1986) Garfield wrote of his findings, "Peak performers have a high Internal Locus of Control." Garfield had discovered his subjects were "less anxious, conform less to authority, set higher goals, and tend to be overachievers." No better example of this is the story of the Bambino, Babe Ruth. A reporter outside Wrigley Field stopped him and asked about the chance that he might have struck out after pointing to the center field seats in the famous "called shot." The Babe looked at the reporter and said, "I never thought of that possibility." That winter Ruth was given the highest salary in the history of baseball at $80,000. *The NY Times* reporter asked how he could justify making more that the United States President, Herbert Hoover. The effervescent Babe said, "Well, I had a better year than he had." Hoover had just led America into the Great Depression. Such competitive zeal is immersed in the attitude of a seething soul. Studies show that "uncertainty" is the key. Those that don't believe over 50% that they can succeed are preconditioned to fail. In his SCAT Test (1990 pg. 222), Rainier Martens wrote, "Uncertainty about winning or losing in competition can be determined by the person's perceived probability of success or probability of failure." It is all in the head after all.

Rushing Sickness & Eminence

We live in an instant-gratification society. I want it now trumps I'll wait until later. Pay me now is pervasive in the offices of organizations from leaders who refuse to go fast for fear of failure or worse, losing their job. In such a world *Time is King, Speed is Queen, and Money is often the Prince*. We often forget that time is money, assuming a person is a diligent worker. There is always an implicit cost built into each endeavor. Relationships are often lost due to forgetting the implicit costs of our decisions. It takes time to buy the raw materials to cook a dinner and time to prepare it and to serve it. That is often lost in the cost of the raw materials. This is a fundamental economic precept often lost in the vagaries of making our bargains in life. Deferring our personal wants and desires to those of our boss or mate; trading off a weekend of golf for that retirement seminar; shopping all day Saturday in lieu of a leisure beach afternoon with a loved one. Sometimes the implicit price we pay is tougher to extract like the implicit stress we get from trying too hard to move up the social ladder. Do you think at age eighty you will care whether you missed a day at the office in lieu of a day walking the beach? Don't think so. And the couch potato syndrome comes to fore here. Why not get off that couch as that is your implicit cost of seeing the doctor for blood pressure meds or diabetes problems.

When analyzing the inner costs of those that make a difference, you find that they were infused with a kind of rushing sickness, hyper and driven. This was as true for many male visionaries as well as female. More recently, we have found a similar propensity in Margaret Thatcher, Donald Trump, and Martha Stewart. Techie marvel Michael Dell wrote, "In managing innovation, you are either quick or you are dead." The reason for this section is to note the wide difference between the Asians and Americans who have left their footprints on new technological breakthroughs in comparison to the corporate hired-hands and politicians that don't get them and don't get what is transpiring with and because of them. When normal, it is very difficult to relate to those that are not so inclined. Politicians often call such people sociopaths. Well, the sociopaths are making things happen in the world while the politicians are merely trying to reap the rewards of public office. The corporate hired-hands are even more of a problem in America since they keep asking for the government to bail them out due to those low offshore labor rates that are keeping them from maintaining their market share.

The movers and shakers are often perpetual motion machines. Most have been labeled ADD in school. A disproportionate number of superstars such as: Napoleon, Mark Twain, Walt Disney, and Howard Hughes were afflicted with bipolar or OCD problems. It was their problem that would make them rich and famous. Teachers were guilty of wanting to drug them to slow them down to make them normal. Kay Jamison of Johns-Hopkins found that about 1% of the normal population is afflicted with bipolar disease compared to about 33% of entrepreneurs. Jamison wrote, "Who would not want an illness that has among its symptoms, elevated and expansive mood, inflated self-esteem, and an abundance of energy, less need for sleep, intensified sexuality, and sharpened and unusually creative thinking." Larry Ellison of Oracle fame is one of the world's richest men. He is a primal example of a man that does not drink decaf. An Oracle board member said, "He has the attention span of three seconds. I mean it's infectious. When he's into something, man there's energy around it and he drags people around in his wake." Such emotional commitment and drive causes such types to be up when others sleep and to go where others fear. They are often unable to restrain themselves like a Richard Branson of Virgin fame. What drives such people is an inner mania that is hard to quell. John Gartner, in *The Entrepreneur Gene* said, "One hundred percent of the entrepreneurs I interviewed were hypomanic. They tend to be energetic, driven, zealous, optimistic and innovative." The items he characterized about entrepreneurs were:

✓ Feelings of euphoric brilliance

✓ Easily irritated with quick trigger response

✓ Big T risk-taker overspending personally & professionally

✓ Sexually active with impulsive judgments

✓ Fast talking, witty, and gregarious

✓ Prone to making enemies, feels prosecuted due to vision that few people see

The hypo-manic sleeps sparingly. For them, sleep is an irritant and waste of valuable time. Many sleep as little as two or three hours a night and many never make it to bed. Nikola Tesla and Bucky Fuller would take catnaps during the day. They were in such a hurry they had very short attention spans. These types tend to drive their mates and family nuts as they are on a perpetual high. Napoleon, Hitler, and Stalin were manic-depressive as was Walt Disney, Ernest Hemingway and Howard Hughes. Napoleon showed this side when he saidr, "I will lose a man but never a moment." Both he and Catherine the Great had six secretaries trying to take notes due to their maniacal delivery style. The Little General once killed 5 horses in a 5-day dash across Europe. His valet, Constant, told the media, "He is perpetual motion. I never comprehended how his body could endure such fatigue. He never even stopped to change clothes." (Landrum 1996. pg. 129) Such people walk, talk, think, eat, work, and drive faster than most. In America, Speed Dating is in vogue and 24/7 lifestyles are rampant.

Today's newspaper headlines scream, "New record of 10% unemployment." What about the fact that 90% are gainfully employed? For some reason the negative trumps the positive. No matter what we think, good or bad, our minds tend to make it so. Jung told us that there are few accidents. He labeled it *synchronicities.* The concept is about us being the driver in charge of your destiny. Both Harvard and Stanford Universities authenticated this principle finding that the reason 85% of people get jobs and do well in them is directly linked to their ATTITUDE. Only 15% of success is attributable to some technical or specific skill. Get your mind in synch and everything else follows suit. I lecture on this precept and love to tell audiences, "People make 'em, sell 'em, service 'em, and buy 'em, not companies. So take care of the people and they take care of you." As we've discussed, 95% of all decisions both personally and professionally take a very personal spin. This makes attitude so important to being able to transform oneself and for leaving a legacy of meaning.

Chapter 9

The PITCH Game – Make it Easy for 'em to say Yes!

"I don't care if you're an engineer, a marketing guy or a reporter, there's somebody you've got to sell to."
Martin Cooper, Inventor of Cellular Phone Technology

"There is hardly anything that someone cannot make a little worse and sell a little cheaper, and the people who consider price alone are this man's prey." – John Ruskin

It is the entrepreneurs that are often the most incredible sales mavens. They must sell their mates, their followers, the banks, customers and distributers that their dreams are viable. The media forget that the majority of new job creations come from the start-up sector. It is also the place where new market segments are formed and new distribution arenas are created. It is not the Fortune 500 firms like GM and Bank of America that lead in new markets but the firms like Amazon, Dell and Facebook that makes the world go around. No matter what the political pundits say entrepreneurs are on the hot seat every hour of every day as they must sell to make payroll. That is not the case with Hired-Hand types in their board rooms wondering how they can keep their posh quarters and plane flight to Vegas for the next convention.

The top dogs are not selling even though they should be. The self-employed are often looked by these CEO's as mavericks on a maniacal mission to succeed. They are! This was never truer than with Thomas Edison, a man with no formal education other than the books he read voraciously. Edison wrote with cynicism, "I can hire mathematicians but they can't hire me." He told the press, "Do you think I would have amounted to anything if I went to school? University trained scientists only see that which they were taught to look for and thus miss the great secrets of nature."

In business the bottom line is being able to get your clients or customers to say "Yes!" This sounds silly, but it is a fundamental law of business. Contrary to what most people think, we must all sell to somebody, sometime, no matter our calling. Picasso had to sell his paintings, and Mozart had to sell his compositions. In life's Pitch Game, a person should begin by asking a question and then shutting up. Why? The one listening will tell you his needs and wants and how to sell him, assuming the question is posed properly. That can't happen when talking, only by listening. Professors are the worst offenders. They often assume those who talk a lot make good sales people. The fact is they tend to be the worst. Extroverts talk too much to learn anything and that is precisely why the world's great pitch artists have always been slightly introverted. Hitler was pathologically shy, but took over a nation through his power of persuasion. He knew the people feared inflation and Communism and he promised to cure their ills if they would put him in office. They did. Mahatma Gandhi was equally shy and brought down the British Empire through simplistic rhetoric. Studies show that extroverts will chatter endlessly on some topic, but when queried, the introvert goes inward and thinks about what they should say, and when they talk, they have a tendency to be far more profound than an extrovert.

Studies show that when someone nods their head in agreement at least six times, they are prone to nod it positively the 7th time, even if it is to some inane comment. Powerbrokers are masters at this kind of ploy. Since over 80% of all sales are made to people that like you, then it is incumbent on sales people to keep clients smiling. That makes it imperative to show up with a happy face and complement the buyer, even when it is challenging. Everyone has some redeeming quality, so find it so you can complement them. Nothing shows this more incisively than the Willy Loman-like sales story. The VP of Sales walks into the President's office and says, "Big problem boss." And the President asks, "What is it?" The VP says, "I told Joe Rogue that he couldn't do a deal because it wasn't budgeted. Then he tells me to go F... myself." The President smiles and responds, "So what did you do?" The VP says, "I told him I would be telling you about this insubordination." The President says, "And how did he respond to that threat?" The VP, looking all the worse for the wear says, "He told me to tell you to go 'Shit in your hat.'" The President asks, "And where is Joe in the sales standings?" The VP looks at his pad and says, "He's still #1 with 300% of his quota this year." The President sits back in his chair with a grin on his face and says, "I think I'll find a new hat. You have a bigger problem."

"Selling is an inner game," Brian Tracy said, "with the difference between top performers and average ones are not as great as you might think. Top performers just do certain things a little bit better each day." Research shows that about 80% of sales success is about attitude. Just 20% comes from some innate aptitude. Ever meet a super sales person? They believe unequivocally. I have often been accused of believing in the Easter Bunny. But such belief is the fuel of those that must convince others of some esoteric concept. For such people, rejection is but one more hurdle to leap to reach the goal. Super sales types come armed with a positive and enthusiastic outlook. They smile a lot and agree with most things. And they are more adept at getting clients to agree. What differentiates them from the pack is a winning mental mind-set. Since sales performance is 80% mental, this winning edge is far more psychological than rational. To gain such a psychological edge, it is imperative to program the mind with the right messages and to eliminate the wrong ones. Change the way you think and you will be treated differently. Self-concept is inextricably wrapped in those inner messages that become hard-wired in the brain. They affect everything you do, think, or feel.

Keep Doing What You're Doing – You'll Keep Getting What your Getting

People tend to do what they know as they are in a comfort zone. They become transfixed with certain patterns and tend to repeat those actions–even when they are not working. Different cultures see selling differently. That doesn't make one right or the other wrong, only different. That is often lost on many people. American Politian's can be the worst. They take the Judeo-Christian stance that say it is not nice to take or give bribes. What is wrong with this is the word "bribe." Other nations see getting monies for opening doors as seed monies and a very natural way of doing business. Asia, the Middle East, and Latin America operate this way as standard business practice. The poor American sales agent who gets assigned these territories and told to never give or take a bribe has been set up to fail. In a shrinking world with a growing trade economy, it is imperative that Americans become more global-oriented. Cross-Border alliances are antithetic to American individualism, but as mentioned earlier, they could learn a great deal from the Japanese in their *keiretsu* approach. A recent flat-panel plasma television deal offers a primal example of such as multi-national mentality. A 42-inch LCD Plasma TV found at Best Buy contains a panel from Korea, electronics from China, processors from America, and it was finally assembled in Mexico.

Launching a new idea or product without promoting it is akin to winking at a girl in the dark. You know what you are up to, but she doesn't have a clue. That elevates promotion to position of power in all new launches. Often, an inventor or top dog becomes so enamored of their creation they think everyone else gets it too. Not true! Those that think everyone else has the same interest and passion for their cause are setting themselves up to fail. They will have a rude awakening, but often don't discover their dilemma until too late. Most people are unaware that when someone must make a deal, they are far less able to make it. Donald Trump said this best, "The worst thing you can possibly do in a deal is seem desperate to make it. That makes the other guy smell blood and then you're dead." The moral here is that one must be willing to go where the pack fears and do it with unmitigated gall and guts.

Subliminal Sales Solutions

In much of the world, food and meals are a way of socializing. Americans do lunch as a business meeting, but would find it annoying or impossible to have a three-hour lunch as they do in many European nations. In Asia they often eat four times daily when entertaining business associates. For most of the world, eating is a socialized method of getting to know new friends. It is a socializing necessity to do business. Not so much the same in America. In the Far East can be a ritualistic way of getting to know their new friends. Americans are far more prone to use food to vanquish hunger. In France three and four hour lunches are more the norm than the exception. In Kuala Lumpur, it is not uncommon to eat four times a day, where socialized networking is the name of the game. Those societies eat far more logically and frugally than Americans. British researchers found that playing French accordion music in a supermarket wine section led to higher sales of French wine – 77% of their customers opted for French wine. To test this, they then played tapes of a German brass band in the wine section. Sure enough, the vast majority of customers purchased German wines. It showed them the power of the unconscious is sales environments. Other studies have found that people cannot, or will not provide accurate information about their mind relative to their decision-making. Bakeries have found that the smell from their baking entices customers to enter the store, with certain smells a strong sales motivator. In Europe, some bakeries use a national anthem to sell German or Spanish pastries or wines. Studies have found that placing a lime wedge in a Corona beer increases the demand for that beer. A brand added cachet causes customers to identify with the brand as if they are thinking, "I'm a Macho guy, give me one of those machismo beers."

American marketers are far more functional than necessary. When sales go down due to a recession, the first thing they do is cut marketing. In most cases, it should be the very last thing cut. As mentioned earlier, in the 2008 automobile sales drop due to exorbitant gas prices, the very first act GM did was to cut the Tiger Woods advertising campaign. Buick had never been a dominant force in American car sales, but it was the #1 American car sales in China. Why? Because of Tiger who was seen as a national hero. General Motors would have been far better served to cut the white-collar million dollar bonuses or the CEO's salary of $32 million. For GM, it was a short-term expediency to a larger problem that was union based. They couldn't do much about that, so they took the easier path. A few months later they cut their brand offerings from eight to four with SAAB, Hummer, Pontiac, and Saturn eliminated. GM had lost their dominant position to Toyota in 2008 and might just fall further due to their limited entries, Chevrolet, Buick, Cadillac, and GMC.

When market demand is way down, it is imperative to become more, not less aggressive. But there seems to be a latent undercurrent of cut, cut, cut when it should be go, go, go. That axiom was never more cogent than in the middle of the 2009 recession. During such times, it is important to look within and become irrationally exuberant. That is what visionaries do in tough times. Don't sit in the office conjugating over your dilemma. That only makes it worse. Think about the new possibilities since the old ways are now history. In tough times, it is imperative to get tough with yourself and those in your organization. In work situations in business, it is best to bring in new people with fresh ideas since those with the old baggage tend to remain with that baggage. In the 2009 recession, many high-priced restaurants like Ruth

Chris Steak House offered $25 cash-off gift certificates or free hors d'oeuvres to attract new customers with a champagne taste and a beer pocketbook. Nieman Marcus, a firm accused of being Needless Mark-Up, took an opposite path of lower pricing. Upscale eateries opted for promotions they had never tried before. McCormick & Schmick started selling food online in the down market and reported an increase in average unit sales. They offered bar cheeseburgers for $1.50. This is at cost or below. Why? In the bar, you are not interfering with the fine dining crowd in the dining room, but some of those inebriated end up in the dining room opting for a $50 filet mignon to sate their troubles. Besides, liquor has a far higher margin than food.

Super Sales & Charismatic Flair

The charismatic are able to walk in doors the less flamboyant find difficult. They are able to attract attention merely by being up and vibrant as people are energized by their animal magnetism. Such individuals come armed with a seductive power. "Charismatic leaders have always personified the forces of change, unconventionality, vision, and entrepreneurial spirit" wrote Jay Conger. But no one ever offered a better explanation a woman dining with the two English statesmen Benjamin Disraeli and William Gladstone. She offered this insightful interchange, "When I left the dining room after sitting next to Mr. Gladstone, I thought he was the cleverest man in England, after sitting next to Mr. Disraeli, I thought I was the cleverest woman in England.." How do you tap into such inner power? The following qualities are considered one path to charismatic power:

Secrets of Charisma - Personal & Professional

1. **BE OFF-THE-WALL:** Differentiate yourself – Get out of the clutter.

2. **HAVE SWAGGER:** Depict an arrogant style with panache – look deserving and sometimes you are and are treated as special.

3. **EMPATHIZE WITH OTHERS:** Identify with the target customer in order to deal with them.

4. **BE PASSIONATE:** Passion with purpose is a super ploy. Get excited and those in your sphere of influence will also get turned on.

5. **BE PERSISTENT:** Tenacity works in all communications. The last one standing often leaves with the order.

6. **BE VERY GOOD:** Excellence leaves a strong message to those listening.

7. **LIVE ON-THE-VERY-EDGE:** Push the limits especially in any new venture.

8. **BE ORIGINAL:** Creatively destroy what "is" to get what you want. Be different to be so.

Harley-Davidson has known for a long time that their sales have a closer tie to a machismo image than to motorcycle features or benefits. In one annual report, they stated, "Other bike companies sell transportation. We sell dreams and lifestyle." In a 105th anniversary promotion in 2008, they wrote, "For over 100 years, we've unleashed a lot of souls. We've made men bolder, women stronger and shrinks poorer… so screw it, let's ride." The CEO of Harley-Davidson told the media:

> *"What we sell is the ability for a 43-year old accountant to dress in black leather, ride through small towns, and have people be afraid of him. Creating that experience is what distinguishes Harley from the pack and is worth billions in market capitalization."*

How does a firm achieve such powerful brand recognition as Harley? By not conforming and getting so lost in the benefits that you forget what your ideas or products really bring to the party. Personal packaging is so crucial to pitching your wares. Show up not in the attire for the position you have. but that of the one you want. Clothes are your packaging. Walk into the place looking as if you are deserving of success and you will be. Are you seen by friends as a green Dodge or a red Ferrari? The first gets you treated as normal, the other as special. Neither may be correct or deserving, but that is the nature of life. Despite the propensity for altruism, in public sectors, some people are just more equal than others. Who are they? The dude with the best brand! The lady with the most flare! No matter the laws passed, everyone is not equal and never will be. Show up in a red Ferrari and you will be treated more special and will be seated in the window seat at the restaurant. Show up in Chevy, and you'll find yourself looking into the kitchen. You might argue that such treatment isn't fair. You're right. It isn't. But that doesn't change the facts.

Be a Publicity Maven

Thomas Edison has a legacy as an inventor. But the truth is that he was a master of hype. Edison had little formal education. Books had been his means of knowledge. One of his aphorisms was, "I didn't read books. I read the library." This man with little formal education played the press like a puppet, a kind of Pied Piper. When he had a new idea for a product, he would call a press conference to announce his new invention, despite the fact he had no idea how to make it. This was what he did when he awoke one morning with the idea to make an incandescent light bulb. The Wizard of Menlo Park conceived the idea for perpetual light in the days of candlelight dinners. Despite having no clue how to do it, he used publicity to get money to finance his work and to self-motivate. It would prove to be one reason he never left his lab for days at a time since he was motivated within to prove that what he had said was true. Similar publicity stunts worked for Adolph Hitler and Howard Hughes. Few PR campaigns worked as well as the Spruce Goose airplane by Hughes. It would make him the master of hype, dwarfing the glitz of P.T. Barnum and others. No hired-hand would have even suggested pouring $75 million on publicity for a product that would never make it to the market. Even Hughes's most faithful disciples and the head of TWA thought he had lost his mind. Despite the knowledge that his pet plane would never fly anywhere, he kept it in Long Beach Harbor as testimonial to his ability to create what mere mortals only dreamed about. Congress tried to get their $25 million back, since it was an obvious boondoggle, and the media labeled him an eccentric madman. Hughes was mad like a fox. The masterful image of him as a man able to build the world's largest plane got him preferential treatment for the emerging satellite business. Hughes Tool would be the major beneficiary, as they received well over half of the satellite contracts granted in America. They were worth billions.

More recently, Richard Branson of Virgin Records and Virgin Air fame admittedly used publicity to offset his inability to finance his new ventures. Without ad monies, the press is a convenient method to get ink. Few people ever used the press like Branson. An example is when he decided to launch Virgin Cola. Branson had a devious mind and decided to put on the can that his new cola had aphrodisiac qualities. The lawyers went berserk and said, "Absolutely not!" What did Branson do? He reversed the logic and put on his can, "Any rumors to the effect that this cola has aphrodisiac qualities are unfounded." Wow! Such is the flamboyant personality is what made this 9th grade dropout a billionaire by age 39. In his memoir, Branson wrote, "Editors have to put pictures in their publications. We try to make their job easier." When he launched Virgin Cola in America, the brash one hired a tank and drove it down 42nd Street crushing cans of Coke and Pepsi as the TV cameras recorded his bravado.

Do You Know the Business You are In? – Few Really Know!

Most have what is called market myopia. They can't see the forest for the trees blocking their vision. The vast majority of bosses have no clue why customers walk in the door or choose their products. Wall Street analysts are often the worst. They insisted on saying that Ray Kroc's McDonald's sensation was about being in the burger business. When they asked Ray Kroc about his business he told them, "I'm in the real estate business." Kroc was right, not Wall Street, in the same way a restaurant is not in the food business. Food is available way cheaper in grocery stores, far more convenient in a 7-11, and far more efficient in a fast food joint. Restaurants are really in the entertainment and socialization business. Most aren't aware of this simple fact, and that is why there is such an incredible turnover in that industry. Coffee shops are not in the coffee business. They are in the meet and greet business with upscale coffees conducive to that kind of atmosphere. Colleges are really not in the education business. They are in the "teach me to think" business and "pedigree" business for moving onward and upward.

Sales mavens don't sell organic food. They pitch a long, healthy life. Gym manufacturers don't sell exercise equipment. They sell a strong and sexy bodies and sense of self. Sell underling benefits and the product will fly off the shelves. Most businesses write a Mission Statement that defines their products. Wrong! A mission statement is a philosophy or credo. I've heard executives say, "Let's measure our mission to the results." It has been known for decades that it is impossible to measure a mission just as it is impossible to measure a philosophy or credo. Amazon.com's mission is, "Work hard, have fun, make history." It says nothing about selling books on the Internet. Another correct mission can be seen on the business cards of the Ritz Carlton Hotel chain. It says nothing about rooms, pools, food, or the bar. It says, "Ladies & Gentlemen, serving Ladies & Gentlemen." Right on, especially when you are paying $500 bucks a night for the privilege. Jay Morton wrote the first *Superman* movie. In that work, he didn't say The Man of Steel was "fast, strong, and powerful," but that the hero was, "faster than a speeding bullet, more powerful than a locomotive, and able to leap tall buildings." That is selling your ideas through powerful and evocative words.

In the 2009 book *War in the Boardroom*, the authors make a dramatic point that "Management deals in reality; marketing in perception." They spoke of the fact that Motorola launched the cell phone business in 1983, but led with a left-brain management strategy of diversification while Nokia came in later with a marketing-oriented or right-brain strategy of cell-phone supremacy. Nokia, despite being the second in, came out on top. This is typical with management types focusing on the product and marketing on the brand and message. Marketers tend to be masters of seduction. Such people walk in believing they can make a deal, and they walk out with a contract. Branson was like this as was Donald Trump. Those worrying about making a deal and show up with detailed data and all kinds of charts seldom score. Too much detail is contra to pitching eminence. Much of our successes and failures originate in the head. This was validated in a Harvard study that found women who believed that they were prone to heart disease were nearly four times as likely to die as women with similar risk factors who didn't hold such fatalistic views. Studies show that 80% of all sales are made by the 20% that make the 5th call. The 80% that stop after the 3rd call get but 20% of all the sales. Tenacity is crucial for those making their living selling, and everyone is, but most are unaware they are.

Sales Mavens Use Stories - Not Words

Visionaries pitch with stories, traditionalist just offer the facts. That makes one more successful due to a more fine-tuned sales pitch that has a fantasy flavor. "Transcendence from mediocrity to eminence," wrote David Hawkins "occurs at a point just beyond the apparent limit of one's ability." This is never truer than in down markets. When down, it is too easy to buy into bad, and then the actions we take become a self-fulfilling prophecy and we end up experiencing bad. Negative press leads to negative actions and thus becomes a catalyst for our problems. The Manhattan Hot Dog vendor story validates this all too well. Joe, the Manhattan hotdog vendor, had survived many ups and downs for many decades by a tenacious work ethic. The profits paid for his son Billy to attend college. That is where Billy learned about economics and recessions. Billy read about the impending recession and at dinner told his dad, "Bad times are coming, better cut back on promotions starting next week." His dad, with little formal education and no idea about economics, listened to Billy's sage advice. The next week he pulled his flyers from the subways, cut his hours, and stopped promoting daily specials. Sure enough, sales dropped the very next week, and he told his wife, "Billy is sure smart on that economic stuff." Pessimism is a self-fulfilling prophecy. Be leery of most of what you hear, and some of what you see.

Image & Branding are Everything

Image pervades everything we do and say. FDR understood this fundamental truth more than most. He was conscious of being a cripple that could not walk and new that many voters would hold that against him. A man in a wheelchair is not the kind to run a dynamic country in trouble, so FDR refused to ever be photographed or shown as an invalid. It worked like a charm. Every time he appeared in front of the American press he was standing with his crippled legs hidden or sitting behind a desk. From that position, he would mesmerize the masses with rhetoric of a powerful man in a normal venue.

It is not an accident that bankers wear white button-down shirts, conservative ties, and drive middle class cars to show they are just like their customers. For the same reason, it is not a mystery that Madonna walks on stage wearing a bustier. Want to date Paris Hilton? Then better not show up in the station wagon. Arrive in a limo with a driver or a rental Rolls. Want to get hired by a conservative investment banking firm? Then show up like you fit the role as someone able to interface effectively with their personnel and clientele. Pick the role needed for the situation, and that is the consummate pitch ploy. Estee Lauder understood this very well. In her autobiography, the Grande Dame of cosmetics lied about her lineage and upbringing. The last of a big brood born and reared in Queens spread the word that she was from the German Hapsburgs in a horse country setting. It is quite telling that the quintessential entrepreneur with a fantasy for reality actually became her fantasy majestic estates in Southern France and Palm Beach. Lauder was so obsessed with becoming a Grande Dame of the landed gentry, she became one. There are numerous traits that correlate well with being a Pitch Paragon. Most of them are intrinsic to a driven and passionate person. If people aren't enamored of your style and program, they will not give you the time of day. Below are Dr. Gene's Traits for being an eminent sale producer:

Dr. Gene's Traits for Eminent Sales Performance

✓ <u>Listen Well</u> – Superstars talk 20% of the time and listen 80%

✓ <u>Be Optimistic</u> – Believe you can and your customers will–positive works

✓ <u>Enthusiasm Sells</u> – Get excited and so will your audience will get jacked also

✓ <u>Be Nice</u>–83% of customers only buy from those they like – make em like you

✓ <u>Be Empathetic</u> – Emotionally connect and they'll like and work with you

✓ <u>Be Tenacious</u> – Never give up and you seldom lose – perseverance works

✓ <u>Be Willing to Walk</u> – Or you'll never make the best deal – too needy scares

✓ <u>The Answer in Sales is Always Yes</u> – Agree and you'll figure out if you can

Pitch Mavens Find Someone's Hot Button & Push it

Most people buy products based on the hyped benefits. We all do it as we buy into the spin and become enamored with the benefits of those ads we see on television. The ads aim at the hot buttons of their target customers. That elevates the magical power of inner motives more crucial to making sales than product benefits. No one epitomized this better than Coco Chanel. An orphan from the wrong side of the tracks – a real no-no in Paris - became the vivant of Parisian couture. She understood the game, living lavishly beyond her means in the Ritz-Carlton Hotel near the Opera House in Paris. Just after launch of her couture house she purchased a Rolls-Royce, hired a driver to pick her up at the front door, drive her block to her store and in ostentatious fashion she elegantly emerged as the queen of the arena. It took place in style and grace and led to a billion-dollar empire.

Those that learn to play the pitch game like Coco end up being the winners in life's sweepstakes. The way to success is the ability your clients, personnel, or mates to say "Yes." Pitch Mavens never ask a question that can be answered, "No." Why? Because that sets a dangerous precedent for when you ask for an order and the answer had better be, "Yes." This is never possible until the Pitch Person knows the hot buttons of the conquest. Never forget. You pitch a benefit that lies deeply hidden in most people. You don't have to have the best product or service, just the best pitch to make it appear to be the best choice by a surety-driven buyer. My Florida business buddy, Scott Robertson says, "The market has changed dramatically. Your customers face new challenges that require different solutions. Selling product and 'needs-based' selling will no longer work. Partner with your customer to help them solve these challenges." He's got it right. For a fantasy win, pitch a fantasy win for your prospects.

Chapter 10

Superstars Begin at the End
& work back to the Beginning

> *If you don't know where you are going, any road will take you!*

"The sense of certainty and revelation comes before any definite belief," Bertrand Russell

"The only way of directly communicating an idea is by means of an icon, and every indirect method of communicating an idea depends upon the use of an icon,"- Aunger 2002 *The Electric Meme* p. 232

Always, and I mean always, start a new venture, book or creative endeavor at the very end. Then go back to the beginning and you'll have a clear view on where you are headed. When you begin at the end you are not leaving your fates in the hands of lady luck. You know where the journey ends thus you have a map to the destination. Sounds trite, but the end should always be the beginning. Begin at the end, and you will know where you are headed, and thus will not get sidetracked in some inane place along the way. This sounds counter-intuitive, but it is axiomatic when exploring new fields of endeavor or attempting to deal with a bum market. Remember, when you write the last line of a book, you then know where you are going and the rest is a piece of cake because you see a clear path to the end. When you predict what sales will be in year five in year one you are starting with the answer which is golden. If not you are leaving yourself open to the fates and if you suddenly see that the answer isn't possible you need to stop immediately. This is never the style of those with a CYA mindset. They want to just plug along and not rock the boat with things they are unsure of to begin with. For them, predicting where they are headed is antithetic to the reality. They are way too grounded for such a path and is why they never become rich and famous.

Michelangelo wrote, "I saw the angel in the marble and carved until I set him free." Such insight is incredible as in that block of marble was David and it was his job of releasing him. Why was he special? Because he saw what most of the world cannot see with profound insight such as:

"In every block of marble I see a statue as plain as though it stood before me, shaped and perfect in attitude and action. I have only to hew away the rough walls that imprison the lovely apparition to reveal it to the other eyes as mine see it."

George Bernard Shaw wrote, "Any fool can start a love affair; it takes a genius to finish one." Well it is tough to even begin if you don't know where you want to finish. An example of getting lost in the stuff comes from a study using psychologists and medical scientists. They were shown a 30-second video showing guys with black jerseys and white jerseys passing a ball. They were asked to record the # of passes by jersey color. When asked they responded 11 passes. Correct! When asked, "What about the gorilla?" None knew what the question was about. Of the 30-seconds, 9 were devoted to a gorilla walking on the floor and pumping his chest. Not one scientist saw it.

Simple trumps complexity, even with the erudite. This became apparent in a Sarasota, Florida speech which I ended with a Joseph Campbell quote –"Just Follow Your Bliss." Upon leaving the stage, an attractive and sharply dressed 40-something blonde walked up and said, "Dr. Gene, I was impressed. I want to buy a couple of your books, but that bliss thing intrigues me. I have a doctorate in psychology. Can you help me find mine?" I was stunned. A PhD in psychology asking me what turned her on. I had assumed that most people, especially the well-read, had some idea of what made their heart skip a beat or what they would do without being paid since they loved it so much. Was I wrong? In my inimitable style, I told the lady, "What gives you goose bumps?" She looked at me in amazement. I continued, "If you had your choice in life to do what you love the most, to chase your most ardent bliss or fantasy, like lecturing on an around-the-world cruise, would you go?" I told her to do whatever she would do if she wasn't even being paid. She thanked me and went on her way, after I explained that life is way too short to be chasing the bliss of parents, teachers, preachers or mates.

Answers Should Anticipate Questions

Want to write your memoirs? Write the last sentence in the last chapter. Now go back to Chapter One and you have a clear picture of the ending. When you don't know the end it is difficult to find the right path to that amorphous destination. Does that last line remain intact? Never! It will be modified on the trek back. That is part and parcel of how we should plan new products and our life. What market void are we attempting to fill? If there isn't a void, we are probably on the wrong road. Why are we doing it and what is the win at the end? People never bought instant cameras from Polaroid because they were special. They wanted to record for history an instant memory. When that benefit was filled by digitals, Polaroid was gone. Whenever there is a better way, it obsoletes many of those in lost in their past sense of values. The cell phone led to the demise of the copper cable guys. The iPod relegated the Walkman to the trash-can of the electronic age. When the magnificent Sony Walkman came to market, it sold 25 million in a few years, and no one thought it would ever become obsolete. It did when the iPod hit the market in 2001. And that will be gone when a better long-term solution to listening to music while running, on our bikes, or while we ski hits the market. This makes it imperative to see the future and make it happen in the present. That is so difficult for most people to fathom.

Peter Drucker, the father of modern management and wrote, "To displace an old technology, the challenge must be 10X better." That tells us that just copying an existing model such as opening a coffee shop, pizza parlor, or Hallmark type card shop is not the correct manner in which to make one's mark in the world. If your idea is not dramatically different, then don't do it. Following the herd is a strategy for schizophrenia, or minimally, business disaster. Find the herd and go somewhere they don't have the guts to go. Don't ever forget, people make them, sell them, service them, buy them, and distribute them, not some large corporation. We are all in the people business and that says that we should place the people who will be our target first, products second, and profits last. Think that happens in most firms? No chance! In the Fifth Discipline, Senge told us, "Rigid authoritarian hierarchies thwart learning." That is lost on so many short-term thinkers in today's world.

Management Styles Differ Dramatically – What is Yours?
Let's take a stroll on the wild side of management organizations. Most people still insist all people are the same or at least similar. No chance! Everyone sees the world through a different filter, one that is conservative, liberal, grounded, or sometimes on the wild side. This is never more evident than in the way the East and West think and operate. The West is steeped in *Objectivity*, the East in *Subjectivity*. One has a short-term rational perspective. The other a long-term more gut perspective. In Japan, the management style most prevalent is one that differs dramatically from the West. As discussed earlier, they have a strong egalitarian culture, or what William Ouchi labeled a Theory Z

management system. This contrasts dramatically with the West's style concocted by Douglas McGregor, known as "Theory X" and "Theory Y." In America, the X types feel that people are lazy, not highly motivated, and should be managed in a control and command style. In his Theory Y system, the leaders see the personnel as self-starters and responsible and imaginative. This is more of a carrot kind of motivational system of management. Theory Z is what was discussed earlier as the way the Japanese manage from the bottom up. They don't want anyone to lose face since it is a lifetime employment system there so no one does from bottom up. Ironically, Theory Z had its genesis in the Deming method as discussed earlier. It is far more end-oriented than beginning-oriented. Dr. Deming wrote:

> *"You cannot measure performance. Appraisal of people is ruinous. You cause humiliation, crush out joy of learning, innovation, joy on the job. You are not measuring him, you are evaluating the interaction with him and the system."*

Deming's rule #12 from his 14 points offered prescient insight on the essence of this work, "Eliminate management by the numbers and numerical goals as they are a substitute for leadership." That is not seen in America very often. The executives hide behind a fear of failing and budgets. Deming showed the Japanese how to use numbers and Quality Control systems, but they were tools, never bibles. Their Theory Z is a combination of Deming's rules and their cultural heritage. It placed a large amount of freedom and trust with workers, assuming workers have strong loyalty, long-term commitment to the firm's goals, and operate with a kind of esprit de corps.

Gestalt-type management styles are where eminence lives. This was shown vividly in *The Web of Life* (1996) by Berkley futurist Fritjov Capra. "A new paradigm of deep ecology is upon us," he wrote, "It is a holistic world view." This holistic management style is about seeing an integrated whole rather than a disassociated collection of parts. Few leaders in the Western World seem to have a handle on this fundamental precept. Capra had 20-20 foresight when he said, "The striking emergence of new structures and new forms of behavior—the hallmark of self-organization—occurs *only* when the system is far from equilibrium." If it isn't out of synch with the pack, it is not about to be innovative or original. An example of this at work occurred many years ago when I was having dinner with the head of the Hitachi Corporation, at the time the largest Japanese corporation in America. After dinner in a fancy Japanese restaurant on San Francisco's Russian Hill, I went into the parking garage with the two men dressed in button-down Ivy League attire. I accompanied them to their car since we were close to signing a $25 million contract. The grey haired man was the elder statesman and the head of U.S. for Hitachi. The operations Vice President was a man in his 40's, well spoken with a Harvard MBA and very cordial. I was shocked when walking to their regal Mercedes-Benz, and the Harvard underling walked to the back door, opened it as if he were a limo driver and put the elder statesman in. He took the driver's seat and they drove off waving. The next day I was unable to contain myself and called the younger man. I asked about his role. I explained how in America two business associates would have sat together in the front seat. It was my youth questioning them on their cultural roles. But he responded to the question honestly, "Mr. Miyota is the head man. I'm the underling. I must treat him with the utmost respect. If I do, someday I will have his job and some younger man will open the door for me and drive me to and from meetings." It left me with a lasting image of the Japanese culture.

The Japanese use what has been labeled a Ringi system of operating— a bottom-up approach to ensure that no one loses face and everyone becomes totally steeped in what is transpiring. This is very frustrating to Americans not used to such a long and tedious route to a solution. Ringi fits the gestalt model, or whole, if you will, in the sense everyone knows everything. Everyone in the organization knows exactly where you are headed before you even begin. All strategies are aimed at the destination from the start. It is why the Japanese begin with a market share analysis prior to pricing a product. As discussed, the direct opposite approach is the Western way. For the East, dominating the market comes first, followed by the methodology and strategy to ensure it happens. Since cost is an illusive target, it is not as important in the East as in the West. Numbers-crunchers insist that the receptionist is a fixed cost in the West. Not so in the East where the person is a function of the volume being done. This is precisely how the East came to dominate so many mass market industries in the West.

Right-Brain Solutions Trump Left-Brain Logic

Instinct is the mother of originality whereas the grounded logic of the CYA personality is a path to mediocrity. The biggest publishing phenomenon in history was the Harry Potter books by J. K. Rowling. Nine publishers turned down the manuscript saying, "Potter will never sell." When he did sell, the magnitude of sales was such that it made Rowling worth more than the Queen of England. What wonderful insight those publishers had. It cost them a chance at making history. I wonder if they think back about their stupid decision. Even more frightening, what if Rowling had believed them? Fortunately, this visionary writer didn't listen as is the case for most intuitive types. Even more interesting in this story is that she started with the answer and then went back to the beginning to start the seven-book series. That is an intuitive, not rational, approach to the creative writing process. Rowling was being interviewed by Larry King on *CNN* after her second book hit the bookstores and she reached down for an envelope and told him, "Here is the last chapter of the last book on Harry." Wow! She wrote these profound words after the second book was published:

"My magical characters were not thought up in any methodical way. They normally come fully formed. Harry came very fully formed. I knew he was a wizard, and then it was a process of working backwards to find out how that could be, and forwards to find out what happened next."

No more profound observation was ever made than the one by Victor Frankl, a survivor of Auschwitz and author of *In Search of Meaning*, "Don't aim for success. The more you aim for it and make it a target the more you are going to miss it. For success like happiness, cannot be pursued, it must ensue." The British contrarian Bertrand Russell offered sage advice on the subject of starting with answers when he wrote, "The sense of certainty and revelation comes before any definite belief." The gut is quicker and more correct, but few ever come to this conclusion until too late. The head is wired to keep us safe. It has all those imprints that are there to keep us out of trouble. But what keeps us out of trouble keeps us from being creative. Those poor souls lost in minutia and head-surety are destined to be buried by it. No matter what happens--even losing a loved one, losing all of your money, or breaking your leg--is but a fleeting part of the whole. Those caught up in that will suffer. Those seeing it as but a passing roadblock or hurdle to get past it and will live a far better life.

The creative have an ability to see what the pack only imagines. Valerie Hunt in her book *Infinite Mind* told us, "Ultimate reality is contacted, not through the physical sense of the material world, but through deep intuition." That is what differentiates the innovative from those that call them lucky. As we have discussed in this work, the herd is lost in the trees while the innovative icons spend their time conjuring up the mysteries of he forest, but also have an ability to deal with the trees. Often, intuitive types have their feet firmly planted in outer space, but have an ability to rationalize where they are. While lost in the forest of opportunity, such people can rationally deal with the details of making their dreams come true. In his book *A Whole New Mind* (2005), Daniel Pink said, "Many left-brain workers in this country face career extinction. Future leaders will need to master right-brain creativity." What he was saying is that the right-hemisphere types reside in the forest of the mind while the left-brain types live in the trees. The left brain thinks in words, the right in pictures. So if you can't see an idea visually, it is often difficult to make it happen. When I was researching the idea for opening the Chuck E. Cheese prototype, I actually saw the store in a completed form, with a sign, people milling around, and kids playing games and sliding down into a bawl crawl prior to ever designing it. What I had envisioned made it far easier to pull off since I saw the vision in my head and then it was a matter of drawing the plans to make it happen.

Those capable of differentiating the essence of things from the trash are special. Most people get lost in the stuff to the degree it makes it impossible for them to see beyond it. Most have been caught up in the CYA syndrome. If they can't see it, touch it or feel it, it isn't viable. Psychologists classify such people as "Concrete-Sequential." Those inclined to follow a ritualistic path, no matter where it leads. Their opposites are "Abstract Learners." They are the type that is not so steeped in what is but what might be – a kind of free-floating mystique. A Concrete-Sequential hears the clock strike noon and they have to eat. They see the time to go to bed and that is where they head whether tired or not. This is not true of abstract types. They eat when hungry and sleep when tired.

Studies show that abstract types are better at tapping into their unconscious and are far more creative. Nancy Andersen wrote in *The Creating Brain (2006)*, "Creative people often slip into a zone in which ideas and thoughts come up freely in a disorganized way." Peter Senge wrote in *The Fifth Discipline*, "To be a catalyst for change, think in systems, never pieces." We know that chess masters store as many as 50,000 patterns of play in their brains for recall, and they can play "blitz chess" with little need to study the board of play. The 50,000 patterns are the forest. Their moves are the trees. And we know from brain studies that Eureka moments occur only when the right-hemisphere of the brain sends signals to the left making those individuals more adept at flip-flopping between the two hemispheres.

Zen-Types & Locus of Control

Everyone has the potential to control their destiny, but many are pro-grammed to believe they are not in charge. These types are known in academia as External Locus of Control types. They believe some higher power or the Big Boys at the top are in power. Not true! The Internals believe they are in control and often prove it beyond any reasonable doubt. Power is in the mind of the beholder. Mike Murphy in his book *In the Zone* (1995), wrote, "Out-of-this-world experiences are really out-of-mind experiences." Murphy quoted Arnold Palmer on his golf prowess, "My game is not merely mechanical, it is not only spiritual, it is something of both, on a different plane and a more remote one." Murphy went on to speak to this phenomenon writing:

> **"Moments of illumination alter the perception of time and space. Stepping into the terra incognita by deed seems to trigger openings into the terra incognita of metanormal experience."**

This was captured so well by Zen Master Phil Jackson, coach of the Chicago Bulls. When asked about the essence of the Michael Jordan mystique he said, "Michael is like a Zen student – relaxed and intensely focused in the midst of chaos." Those special people capable of being like a Michael Jordan or Mother Teresa are the ones capable of adopt-ing a Zen-like mystique. In that state, they easily transcend the prob-lems plaguing them at the moment as they have lift themselves above it all. Such Zen Masters are holistic beings. They becomes *empowered and enlightened* by an unquenchable inner fire emanating from within a seething psyche. When stable, most people do not see a need to escape into an ethereal place. It is when things turn sour that most people look for a way out of their dilemma. This is when they are best served by removing themselves from the calamity and going into another place where all things work. That is the fundamental basis of meditation. It is a Zen state of inner wisdom. While the masses crawl into the proverbial bottle or worse, Zen-Men have risen above it all. They are steeped in an imaginative moment on a trek to find Shangri La. This demands a larger perspective than most people have. It is about giving power to the right hemisphere of the brain and relegating the left to more reality-based needs. Such early insight came down to us from the story of the Greek Archimedes. When emerging from a tub of water, he had a Eureka moment realizing that he had displaced water in the tub, and now it was left in a whole different state.

Many Eureka moments occur while in a state of relaxed concentration, such as happened to Archimedes. In such a time, we go into a kind of focused tranquility, where all things are seen clearly in absence of turmoil. They tend to be states of harmonic intensity such as happen often with visionaries. They are Zen-like states of reverie when all cylinders are clicking at optimum. Everyone has been there and wants to find the path back. Think of where you were when in that *zone*-state of unconscious reverie. It often occurs in a shower or while walking on the beach. Your right-brain or *zen-state* is operating efficiently because you inhibition is asleep. It was where Einstein was when he first saw the idea for relativity. As a teenager, Albert was awestruck by the contradictory theories of space and time, and one day with thoughts racing through his head while on a street car, it came to him out of the blue. He had been looking at Bern's famous clock tower and wondering how in the world the conductor was ahead of him in time and space but seeing the identical time on the clock. At first it was a bit paradoxical, but it haunted him until he came up with the solution. He discerned that time can beat at different rates throughout the universe; depending on how fast the mass was moving forward.

An example of such metaphysical insight comes from one of the most visionary minds that ever walked the earth. Nikola Tesla was one of those men who were out of tune with the rest of man, but in tune with the world around them. Tesla had always claimed that ideas sprung from his head fully formed and then it was a matter of structuring them to fit the universe. From such revelations came the first electric clock, remote controlled cars, and fluorescent lighting along with an incredible array of electronic concepts like alternating current and induction motors. One day Tesla was out for a walk and in a delusionary state of mental breakdown. In his memoirs, he spoke of quoting Faust when the theory of alternating current came to him in a flash. Tesla then used his walking stick to draw a picture explaining how alternating current would work to his walking partner. Later he wrote:

"I could visualize with such facility. I needed no models, drawings, or experiments. When I get an idea, I start at once building it up in my imagination. It is absolutely immaterial whether I run my turbine in my thought or test it in my shop. Before I put a sketch on paper, the whole idea is worked out mentally."

Similar revelations are found in many fields. The mother of modern dance, Isadora Duncan, wrote of waking in the middle of the night with revelations of grandeur on modern dance. In her memoir she wrote, "I feel the presence of a mighty power within me which listens to the music and reaches out through all my body, trying to find an outlet, this power grows furious, sometimes it raged and shook me until my heart nearly burst from passion." (Landrum 1999 pg. 224) A similar sensational insight struck the inventor of television. The 14-year-old Philo Farnsworth was plowing an Idaho potato field one day when an incredible insight hit him like a lightning bolt. Philo saw the plowed rows on his dad's farm as rows of electrical current that could flow through space and be captured in the form of pictures. The teenager saw an electron beam scanning images line by line, which would become the underlying premise of transmitting TV signals. He went on to demonstrate the first operational, all-electronic television system in his San Francisco lab in 1927.

Eureka moments need not be technical. One of the incredible success stories of our age comes from the creation of the Clif Energy Bar in Northern California. Gary Erikson was a biker, and one day in a race he hit the wall. It struck him that the Power Bars he had been consuming in volume to maintain his energy were not the ideal answer for jocks like him. It was 1990 and Gary listened to his gut and started a firm to solve the problem. He had been competing in a175 mile bike race and towards the end had devoured six Power Bars, but was slowly losing it and he told himself, "I can make a better energy bar." The next day he went to his mother's house and in her kitchen formulated what would come to be branded as the Clif Bar–after his dad. But the story doesn't end there. The bar became a staple for competitive athletes in many disciplines. Gary told the media, "I ride my bike for hours. I hit the wall and it forces me to listen to my gut." Eight years later he and his partner were offered $120 million for the company that need had formed. During the final negotiations on a contract that would have made him very rich, he had another epiphany. Why sell out when he was having so much fun? That day he went into the office and turned down the offer and would later admit to the media, "My investment bankers said the company would go under within six months. My partner thought Clif Bar couldn't compete against the big companies and demanded I buy her out. I listened to my gut and said no to the huge offer." We should all be so insightful on a bike.

Tunnel Vision Types Get Mired in Life's Trees

One marketing guru states that 85% of all firms suffer from a Tunnel Vision Syndrome. Too often the media in America focuses on sensationalism rather than what is actually occurring. In the 2008 Kentucky Derby, the filly *Eight Belles* had a horrid accident breaking both front legs. The poor horse was euthanized on the spot. An adversary Big Brown won the Derby by a staggering 4+ lengths. What did the next day's *USA Today* feature as the headline? Right! It was a ghastly picture of Eight Belles lying on the turf about to die. Golfers often become lost in their tunnel vision when encountering a win or lose golf shot. They permit their heads to get in the way of insight. They start thinking about how far they must drive the ball in order not to look bad or worse, to end up losing. Those thoughts are burned into brain neurons that send signals to the body, and sure enough they take a mighty swing at the ball and blow it. What happens? They hit the shortest drive of the day.

Millions of well-meaning leaders are guilty of tunnel vision. Many reside in the U.S. and many can be found in Congress making and enforcing our laws. Such people become so lost in the details of a problem they are incapable of finding an elegant solution. That is why every firm and organization needs to hire at least one individual with a strong visionary bent – right-brain dominant thinking. Most leaders are not interested in having underlings offer a new way, but if they can't see the new, they need someone on the team who is not locked into a CYA mindset or lost in that box of mediocrity. The world needs more people capable of stepping outside traditional ways to find new ways-- individuals that have relegated tunnel vision to the archives of history. Those locked into tunnel vision are part of the problem, not the solution and at best become mediocre leaders. If you keep switching the on and off a switch that is not working you are lost in your frustration. Stop switching and start looking within for the problem. Remember, the obvious is seldom obvious. Stop confusing the map with the territory or the metaphor with the story. They are both used to find the way through new lands and new ideas. To do so effectively, it is imperative to plan quantitatively (rationally) and operate qualitatively (globally). That is just the opposite of what most executives do. Why? It is the way they were trained in school. Most leaders would be better served if they would Zap the *Yes Men* in their heads and become more the entrepreneurial spirit.

Chapter 11

Never, Ever Listen to an Expert –
They're lost in their own reverie

Arrogance interferes with reasoned analysis & questioning.

"Experts can be self-interested to the point of deceit. Experts depend on the fact you don't have the information they have or that you are befuddled by the complexity of it." Freakonomics (2005)

"An expert knows all the reasons an idea will not work." - Henry Ford

The editor in charge of business book publications at Prentice-Hall in 1957 had great insight into America's future when he said, "I have traveled the length and breadth of this country and talked with the best people, and I can assure you that data processing is a fad that won't last out the year." How could a man in such a powerful position be so lost his in his own reverie? So-call experts are often arrogant know-it-alls and pontificate endlessly on their expertise. It stifles innovation and is why so many jobs are lost to those nations and firms not so lost in their own reverie. Experts are often found on a self-serving mission to validate their own view of the world. Such was the case when 28 publishers turned down Dr. Seuss's first book. It happened when nine turned down Harry Potter and the first eight books of the incredible George

Bernard Shaw were never published. It is why Boston experts banned Twain's Tom Sawyer and Huckleberry Finn.

Such arrogant myopia is not nearly as wide-spread in Asia as in America since they are not so lost in give it to me know. One example of pragmatism at work is that in Japan an aging CEO does not go to the beach or country club as in America. They often become the head of Human Resources. Why? They are the most astute, seasoned, and know the organization best. In this job, they don't have all the pressure as they once had, but they are responsible and dedicated. In other words, in that culture, the top dog gets out as they got in, slowly. That would never happen in America where a CEO would never take a staff position, even if they were forced to. They would quit. That is a huge difference between America and Japan. That is why the Japanese model is so confusing to Americans. In Japan the people are more important than the products or even the profits. Is that unique? After all a job in Asia is a lifetime employment deal, not so in America. One culture abides by a short-term mentality with people a factor in the process of what is truly important. In Japan, with a long-term mentality, people are of great importance, protected, and nurtured. When that happens, they ensure there are good products produced and profits happen.

Time in Asia can be a real eye-opener for Americans. Meals are a kind of ritualized encounter. The Japanese show up bearing gifts. They opt for lunch and a Geisha Club experience to calm the waters. I once arrived in Tokyo and was met by a top Hitachi executive. I had never met the man. At the airport the very first thing he did was hand me a gift. Stupid me, I opened it–you're not supposed to do that until later-- and to my shock, it was a set of pure pearl cufflinks and tie clasp. They owned me, psychologically, right then. What happens in our heads and hearts is that we feel a sense of wanting to be nice and to work together. Sometimes, such cordiality is lost on many Americans. After each day's work, the first stop for the traditional Japanese executive is the local pub. I asked my new friend, "Everyone knows you here and some quite intimately, do you spend a lot of time here?" I was told that it was part of his job. That confused me. It turns out that every executive of a firm is given half their salary in an expense account that is supposed to be used. Of course their salaries are lower than in the West. In 2005, one study showed that in Japan the average top executive earns about 11 times what the average beginning wage is in that nation. That appears to be a huge gap, but pales in comparison to America–75X less--where the top CEO's average 820X the lowest worker. The message here is that the Japanese executive is expected to entertain. The Geisha House is one of their haunts, as well as a myriad of pubs in virtually every section of Tokyo with the Ginza the Mecca. Walk in and the Japanese executive is greeted cordially by a momma-san with drinks on the way.

The Bane of Expert Opinion

"Men that are most sure and arrogant are the most mistaken," wrote David Hume. "Their passion without deliberation leads them to the grossest absurdities." No greater validation at the time came when Europe's most prestigious University–the Sorbonne--told the media that Diderot's encyclopedia idea was totally without merit. That gives credence to experts being so psychologically invested in what "is" they are unable to ever see "what might be." If you ever start a new viable venture that is out of tune with the industry, everyone will tell you it is insane and senseless. Louis B. Mayer of MGM told the Hollywood press that Disney's first full-length animated film, the classic *Snow White*, was Disney's Folly. Industry experts often make fun of your venture. The CEO of Holiday Inn told me, "Gene, we kill rats in restaurants. You're having one deliver a pizza to birthday parties. You can't do that man." I looked at him and said, "I didn't know that I couldn't, and I did, and he is doing pretty well." Prior to opening the first prototype, an owner of a 250 store pizza chain welcomed me in, but I could tell he didn't get it, but being nice he told me, "Why don't you go by my

CFO's office and I'll tell him to share the food costs and other data with you." That is where I learned the nuances of food cost, labor cost, occupancy cost, and other key items. The info helped, but it wouldn't have materialized had he had any idea that Chuck would pass his chain in revenues within three years.

Sam Walton of Wal-Mart fame had a visionary mindset. This inveterate workaholic constantly searched for new ways to cuts costs and find what others were doing that he could proselyte. Store managers were a faithful flock and therefore were given total autonomy, as if they owned the store. Think that happened at Sears or K-Mart? No chance! Wal-Mart store managers were permitted to try any kind of store promotion such as Shopping Cart Bingo. That had worked so well Sam borrowed it for other stores to perk up sales. Each cart had a number on it and if that number was called while customers were shopping, the individual with the lucky number got everything in the cart for free. In some organizations, such an enterprising manager would have been ostracized or fired. Not at Wal-Mart. Sam wrote in his memoir about the value of his employees saying, "The more they know, the more they'll understand. The more they understand, the more they'll care. Once they care, there's no stopping them." And the thorn in Walt's side was the non-believing experts who constantly badgered him and told him what he was doing made no sense. Sam's entrepreneurial style led to the largest retailing empire in the world, leading his memoir comment, "In all my years, what I heard more often than anything was, a town of less than 50,000 population would not support a discount store for very long. My rule #1 was, if it ain't broke, break it!" Sam left us with the sage advice, "Ignore the conventional wisdom. If everybody else is doing it one way, there's a good chance you can find your niche by going in exactly the opposite direction."

Expert opinion can be a thorn in the side for innovators. "What is a cynic?" asked Oscar Wilde, "A man who knows the price of everything and the value of nothing." Such individuals are often so arrogantly steeped in what is they cannot cope with new ideas or strange environs. If you are out on the edge of the establishment, even your family and closest friends will demean your ideas. Science fiction writer Robert Heinlein saw this most of his life and wrote, "Always listen to the experts. They'll tell you what can't be done and why. Then do it anyway." His *Stranger in a Strange Land* was his way of demeaning the experts who had demeaned his work. Resistance to the new has a long and sad history. Alexander Fleming's revolutionary discoveries on antibiotics were met with apathy; Niels Bohr's doctoral thesis on the structure of the atom was turned down. It later won him a Nobel Prize. Joseph Lister's advocacy of antisepsis was resisted by surgeons.

When things hit bottom, it is difficult to see the sun through the clouds. "The more connected we are to a belief," wrote Stanford's Leon Festinger, "the harder it is to relinquish, even in the face of overwhelming contradictory evidence." That is why many people in trouble don't rebound as quickly as they should since they become immersed in what "is" to the detriment of "what can be."

That is why I like using the term "innovation" to skirt such problems, since it is means to *creatively destroy*, and if the problem in internal, we must destroy those internal programs that keep un in harm's way. Festinger went on to say, "Certainty is contrary to basic biological principles. Experts depend on the fact you don't have the information they have or that you are befuddled by the complexity of it." In his book, *On Being Certain* (2008), Robert Burton spoke to this saying, "Certainty is a mental sensation, rather than evidence of fact." Studies validate this. Thomas Edison was an expert on power distribution systems, and that is why he denigrated alternating current distribution systems that had been created by Nikola Tesla. Edison went so far as to develop the Electric Chair for New Jersey's penal system to strike fear in those in favor of A/C.

Market Research – Beware Focus Groups

So many firms have bitten the dust due to the CYA need to get expert opinions to insure they don't personally look bad. This was never truer than when IBM and other heavyweights in the office products industry retained Arthur D. Little - the largest market research firm in the world – to tell them the viability of the first plain paper copier. This magical product would come to be branded the Xeros 914. It was 1959 and IBM, Remington, and Bell & Howell were looking at the possibility of buying the patents developed by Richard Carlson. The wise R&D experts from Arthur D. Little predicted a market potential of about 5,000 Xerox 914 plain paper copiers, commenting, "It has little commercial future." They were only off by a few hundred million. A few years earlier the second largest market research firm in the world–Stanford Research Institute--told the Board of Directors of Disney not to invest one cent into Disneyland. Why? "It's a fantasy and won't work," they told Disney's Board. Why? Walt, in his enthusiasm, had violated all of the old traditions of the amusement park industry. His sketches had the park with but one entrance, not many, free parades that earned no money, entertainment shows with costume characters, and on and on. Each of the problems they featured would ultimately be the very things that made it such a huge success. During the battle over Disneyland, Walt's brother, Roy, told him, "An amusement park with pirates and Indians is the stupidest idea you have ever had." When Roy and the board refused to finance the project, Walt hocked his personal insurance policy to buy the land in Anaheim and went ahead with his dream to build Disneyland. When the Board of Directors rejected it once more, Walt refused to capitulate and sold his soul to ABC for $15 million in seed monies to build the park. For those not familiar with the era, TV had been predicted to destroy Hollywood since a family could now sit at home and watch a movie rather than buy a ticket at a local theater.

The above are not isolated cases of myopia. The market research department of Hewlett-Packard told Bill Hewlett that the HP-35--the very first hand-held calculator with transcendental functions--"has no market value." Why such a comment? Slide rules, they said, were too cheap at $19.95. Fortunately, Hewlett was the boss and ignored the sage advice and said, "I don't give a damn if no one else wants one. I do. Build it." For the next three years, it was the hottest electronic product in the world. Good thing the boss didn't listen to the hired-hands. A few years later the head of Sony, Akio Morita had a prototype of the first Walkman. It permitted the avid biker to listen to his favorite music while riding through the park. Sony's market research department told Akio it would never sell. This is a big problem in Japan where everyone must agree or a new idea or product is never implemented. What did this entrepreneurial wizard do? He bet his job on the new product telling the underlings, "I will quit as Chairman if we don't sell 25,000 units." It sold 25 million in the first few years. When Ted Turner launched *CNN*, his CPA quit for fear that the intrepid Turner would destroy the company with his insistence on being the first 24-hour TV news operation known as *CNN*. The networks – ABC, CBS and NBC told the media Turner was nuts. *The Washington Post* wrote of Ted's early demise saying bitterly, "The industry experts doubt that Ted Turner knows his ass from a hole in the ground. It just can't be done." Ted bet everything he had at the time--$100 million--on his brainchild. At the time, he owned *WTBS* and other stations and gold bullion. Ted bet everything he had all on his dream and the bet paid off as he is now worth about $10 billion. History has a plethora of such stories. The Catholic Church put Galileo in jail for daring to say that the earth circled the sun--that was in direct opposition to church dogma. It only took the church about 400 years to admit that he was correct.

Paradigm Shifts & Innovation Mindsets

Older individuals steeped in the good old days tend to be experts. Belief has its genesis in our minds. Stanford's Leon Festinger says, "The more committed we are to a belief, the harder it is to relinquish, even in the face of overwhelming contradictory evidence." There is much evidence to corroborate this. With the advent of talkies, Harry Warner said, "Who the hell wants to hear actors talk." Such industry mavens get so wrapped up in their own sense of what makes sense they cannot see an innovative approach. They become arrogant to a fault. In *The Aquarian Conspiracy*, Marilyn Ferguson put her finger on the pulse of this when she wrote, "New paradigms are nearly always received with coolness, even mockery and hostility." The fact that the new is seldom accepted until the older generations die off came from Thomas Kuhn in his landmark work *The Structures of Scientific Revolutions* (1962). Kuhn concocted the term "paradigm shifts" by looking at the early works of science such as Copernicus's *De Revolutionibus* or Newton's *Principia*. These works he said had *become paradigms* because they were "sufficiently unprecedented to attract an enduring group of adherents away from competing modes of scientific activity," Kuhn spoke of the raging arrogance of those in charge that was to the detriment of the radically new saying, "Successive transition from one paradigm to another via revolution is the usual developmental pattern of mature science." Kuhn went on to argue that science is not a steady, cumulative acquisition of knowledge. Instead, science is "a series of peaceful interludes punctuated by intellectually violent revolutions." He described these as "the tradition-shattering complements to the tradition-bound activity of normal science." After such revolutions, "one conceptual world view is replaced by another." One conclusion was that until the old gentry dies off it is difficult for a new idea to gain a foothold. Validation can be seen in many different arenas. Kuhn's dissertation work at Harvard on paradigm shifts spoke of the lack of such shifts unless there was a world crisis. When that happened, it would open doors of wider acceptance. He wrote:

"Probably the single most prevalent claim advanced by the proponents of a new paradigm is that they can solve the problems that have led the old one to a crisis. ... Copernicus thus claimed that he had solved the long-vexing problem of the length of the calendar year, Newton that he had reconciled terrestrial and celestial mechanics, Lavoisier that he had solved the problems of gas-identity and of weight relations, and Einstein that he had make electrodynamics compatible with a revised science of motion." (Kuhn pp.153-54)

A Paradigm Shift is a change from one way of thinking to another way of thinking. Studies show that small changes are resisted more than large changes. That makes paradigm shifts difficult at best. Today the world is integrally involved in an Internet revolution. It has materially altered the way we think, communicate, and even write. It has relegated snail-mail to the past. Today, a small percentage of people grow the food necessary for survival. That wasn't true one hundred years ago. Johann Gutenberg's invention of movable type in the 1440's was an agent of change that materially altered the way information was disseminated all over the world. Books became readily available, smaller, easier to handle, and cheap to purchase. Masses of people acquired direct access to the scriptures. Attitudes began to change as people were relieved from church domination. When we look back at the Millennium period, we will see change so fast that it obliterates those of past centuries. Studies show that the knowledge in the world is doubling every few years.

It takes a unique individual, an iconoclast if you will, to alter paradigms. Studies show that traditionalists fight change rather than lead it. Visionaries like Bill Gates and Jeff Bezos have led in the transformation mechanical to electronic business. The Keynesian Revolution is typically viewed as a major shift in macroeconomics. Joel Arthur Barker in Paradigms (1992) wrote, "Those who choose to change their paradigms early do it not as an act of the head, but as an act of the heart" Barker categorized Paradigm Shift types as:

> **Young Tigers:** Einstein, Bill Gates, and Michael Dell were young an exuberant

> **Older Change Masters:** Edward Deming, Henry Ford, and Bill Lear used their experience

> **Mavericks:** Wild Ducks and eccentrics like Tesla, Coco Chanel, and Hugh Hefner

> **Tinkerers:** Kinesthetic types using Trial & Error like Edison, Honda, Howard Head

Paradigm Shifts Take Time

Think about the time lapse in accepting new ideas and products. When TV was first offered for sale, it took twenty-six years for just 25% of Americans to own one. Then, almost overnight, the home saturation for TV's was 97% with the average home owning 2.5 TV's. What happened? A shift had taken place and those fearing the new bought in at warp speed. TV's are still in the maturity stage of their development, but may soon be replaced by hand computers where a person can watch their shows in any environment rather than being constrained to the living room or den. Traditional leaders tend to resist all change. Why? It threatens their power. Traditionalists prefer to maintain the status-quo as that is their comfort zone. Barker spoke of this saying:

> **"New paradigms put everyone practicing the old paradigm at risk. The higher one's position, the greater the risk. The better you are at your paradigm the more you have invested in it, the more you have to lose by changing paradigms."**

Einstein concocted the theory of relativity, but no scientists of his era bought in until it was proven. That is the problem when you have a radical creative idea. Einstein, himself, was tainted by the expert illness, going to his grave in denial of quantum physics. This happened with Edison after he had invented the first phonograph. A couple years later he told the press, "The phonograph is not of any commercial value," and the prolific inventor went to his grave denying the viability of Tesla's alternating current. Highly educated scholars tend to be the worst at demeaning others in their fields. Such men detested Edison, since he was an uneducated and thus unworthy inventor. Dr. Henry Morton of Stevens Institute told *The New York Times*, "The Edison incandescent bulb is an absurd claim attributed by sheer ignorance and charlatan." Jumping on the heresy bandwagon Professor Silvanus P. Thompson told the media, "The Edison bulb is doomed to failure and shows the most airy ignorance of the fundamental principles of electricity and dynamics." Not to be outdone, Lord Kelvin in Britain told the press, "Such plans are good enough for our transatlantic friends but are unworthy of the attention of practical or scientific men." They were not believers, even when the light lit up rooms and offices. In trying to implement change in your business, office, home, or even when trying to hit a tennis or golf ball, Dr. Gene suggests you follow these simple rules for changing your world:

↗ **Be Simple:** If your teenager does not understand your pitch, neither will your mate, client, investor or personnel. Use the KISS principle and you have some chance of success.

↗ **Be Positive:** Smiles release endorphins and frowns adrenalin. The troops will be more inclined to follow a positive direction than one employing force or hesitation

↗ **Be Excited:** Use emotion to titillate and to motivate. If you are not getting excited about your new idea or direction, no one else will either – let em see your eyes dilate.

✔ **Be Inspirational:** Motivate with a reason to change others; give them an incentive beyond the norm and offer them a role in the implementation process; excite them with the possibilities.

The moral here is to listen to your gut, not some arrogant expert. Those wanting to remain in the Dark Ages are destined to remain there so let them stay. Arrogance reigns supreme at the very top. It is where people become so enamored of their title or position they become steeped in what I label the "Not-Invented-Here Syndrome." If it isn't their idea, it will not be implemented. As Sam Walton told us, "If everybody else is doing it one way, there's a good chance you can find your niche by going in exactly the opposite direction." This idea is hardly new. Socrates was poisoned for daring to teach the youth of Athens to *Know Thyself.* We should have learned from that.

Chapter 12
The Bottom Fuel's the Trek to the Top

Superstars excel when everyone else is running for cover.

"Many systems of breakdown are actually harbingers of breakthrough." - Ilya Prigogine, Nobel Prize 1984

The Law of Increasing Entropy: The order of life takes place amid great chaos." – Ray Kurzweil, 1999

Lord Byron wrote so eloquently, "Adversity is the first path to truth." Individuals like Byron who have grown up with an infirmity have a prescient insight what it takes to push the window of opportunity. It was no accident that the inventor of the microphone, phonograph and first talking movie could not hear. Edison and those like him are able to look beyond the obvious and find elegant solutions to difficult problems. When lame, you become tougher and more resilient than your adversaries. Lance Armstrong would write in his memoir on why he had won an unprecedented seven consecutive Tour de France races, "The torture of the hills on the Tour paled in comparison to the torture of chemo therapy." Armstrong would become introspective on his bad hand and wrote, "There's a point in every race when a rider encounters his real opponent and understands that it's himself." A similar factor intervened with Beethoven's 8th symphony. The maestro was deaf when writing it. Crisis is the true mother of creativity. When a person stares at their mortality in the mirror most other bumps in the road are pretty trivial. Getting fired can be the catalyst to a great new life. Few see this positive aspect of adversity. Why? They become too immersed in surviving to be looking at new opportunities.

Tragedy is not something to smile at, but from a deeper perspective, it is what makes a person more resilient. The adage is true, "What doesn't kill you, makes you." If your job suddenly disappears as your industry is replaced by a new one, then make your career in that new industry. Don't worry about the CYA crowd as they will be too busy predicting your demise to be a challenge – just don't hire any. Losing your job or life savings is a bitter pill to swallow, but once it is digested, a whole new vista of opportunity opens up. No longer do you have to make that same trek to the same old job. You can suddenly accept some wild opportunity such as opening a Chickee Bar on the Florida Keys or accepting a position with a new start-up venture that pushes your buttons. Hitting bottom is the catalyst to the very top if we can only envision it happening. When an individual stares mortality in the mirror, they become reprogrammed. I saw this in the first 25 superstars I researched, and it blew me away how many had a near-death experience or lost a loved one at a very early age. An example later in life came from Frank Lloyd Wright who had terminated from his first architectural job in Chicago. That forced him to open his own architectural firm and it led to him becoming a titan in the industry. Had Walt Disney not lost his prized character Oswald to a charlatan, Mickey Mouse would never have been created. Had Lance Armstrong not contracted cancer, he would never have become the biking icon he did. Disaster becomes the catalyst for dominance.

Those that have been laid off can become caught up in the poor me mindset and jump into a bottle or just hang at the unemployment office with others in a similar situation. They tend to internalize it and take it personally. That is a program for self-destruction. *The Wall Street Journal* during the 2009 debacle wrote, "Anxiety grew as the economy sunk." The chaos of not having money often is the catalyst for personal depression. They wrote, "Life stressors like losing a job can really lead to emotional states such as depression." But there are also studies that show those with the right mind set are able to take the negative and turn it into chasing new opportunities that they would never had the guts or bucks to chase had things stayed the same. Visionaries often use their time in muck land to go where they would not have gone. Frank Lloyd Wright, Bucky Fuller, Walt Disney, Sol Price, Oprah Winfrey, and Steve Jobs were all fired but used the problem to self-motivate. Did they feel bad? Of course they did. That is a natural phenomenon. But had they not been fired they would not have done what they did and many be-came billionaires. They all relegated the trauma to the trash bins of the past. A similar thing occurred when Matisse told Picasso that his portrait *Les Demoiselles d'Avignon* – the painting that launched Cubism -- was "grotesque and nihilistic," Pablo responded, "Art exists to use against the established order." Gertrude Stein exclaimed, "It's a virtual cataclysm," and when Braque saw it, Picasso finally pulled the painting from a closet where it had been stashed for ten years. European sculptor Salvador Dali liked to say, "There is only one difference between a madman and me. The madman thinks he is sane. I know I am mad." That is taking the bad and reorganizing it in the mind for a positive outcome.

Failure Can Be the Fuel to the Top

Studies find that even a death sentence can lead to super success. Albert Camus, the French existentialist was told at 15 that he had but 3 years to live due to TB that had no cure at the time. The teen dropped out of school, and began writing nihilistic words to maintain his sanity. Three years later he married a drug addict, and within 10 years the dead man had written a Nobel Prize winner – *The Stranger*. How did Camus, a man without any formal education, accomplish such a fete? Anthony Storr, a British psychiatrist, said it best, "Writers are commonly afflicted by severe, recurrent depression and their work can often be interpreted as a way of relieving their distress." Camus used his trauma to write of a world that had gone nuts. It was an era of Communism, Nazism, the Great Depression, and Surrealism. It all made life cheap. The renowned French existentialist would write such fatalistic, but philosophic words as, "Sleeping is a waste. I have a mad and avid thirst for everything. I'm in a hurry to live a lot, with lots of experiences." (Landrum 2001) Camus had taken the death-threat as the fuel to fire his raging inner need to live. It programmed him into a maniacal writer of nihilism. Had he not been told he was terminal, such words would never have been written. Most people are unaware that President John F. Kennedy had been given the last rites by the Catholic Church three times before he reached age thirty-five. Kennedy was afflicted with Addison's disease, malaria, serious back problems, and had many cases of STD's. Florida Senator George Smather was his party buddy and told Kennedy to slow down. Kennedy replied, "I can't. The drugs are going to finish me off by the time I'm 45. I have to live every day like it's the last day of my life." That helped him win an election he was never supposed to win. When bad stuff happens it often becomes the catalyst for many good things.

Crisis can be inhibiting. It can also be motivating. The difference lies in the mental map of the one experiencing the mishap. It is true that *the path to the top demands a trip to the bottom.* Berkley's Fritjov Capra said it well in *Web of Life* (1996), "Any organism in equilibrium is a dead organism." Chaos is good was a strong theme in the work by Stephen Wolinsky, *The Tao of Chaos* (1994). Wolinsky wrote, "In order to be free one must ride the rapids of chaos." Why? It is through chaos that higher order can be revealed. Order is actually born out of chaos, rather than chaos out of order. A personality is born of chaos. Resistance to chaos can only beget more chaos and resistance. Chaos is no longer the enemy; it is the fuel for a new journey. That is true of the world's movers and shakers. None fit this profile any better than President Abraham Lincoln who was a dismal failure most of his career. One of Lincoln's most insightful aphorisms was, Abraham Lincoln,

"You can please some of the people all of the time and all of the people some of the time, but you can't please all of the people all of the time." The following recap offers insight into a man that lived a life of tragedy and failure until his very last win that evolved into a legacy of merit:

> ➤ **1832 Failed in business – bankruptcy**
> ➤ **1832 Defeated for legislature**
> ➤ **1834 Failed in business - bankruptcy**
> ➤ **1835 Fiancé died**
> ➤ **1838 Defeated in election**
> ➤ **1843 Defeated for U.S. Congress**
> ➤ **1848 Defeated for U.S. Congress**
> ➤ **1855 Defeated for U.S. Senate**
> ➤ **1856 Defeated for Vice President**
> ➤ **1858 Defeated for U.S. Senate**
> ➤ **1860 Elected President of the United States of America**

In 2006, Apple's CEO Steve Jobs was the commencement speaker for Stanford University's graduate school. The one-time orphan and newly anointed guru began with a statement that was pure heresy in any school, let alone Stanford's grad school. The school's leaders were in shock as he told the new graduates, "The best thing that ever happened to me was dropping out of college." That start was a springboard for other aphorisms like, "stay hungry and stay foolish." But his anthem centered on having been fired by a guy he had hired. Steve told them "I had just turned 30. And then I got fired. How can you get fired from a company you started? As Apple grew we hired someone who I thought was very talented to run the company with me, but then our visions of the future began to diverge and eventually we had a falling out. I'm pretty sure none of this would have happened if I hadn't been fired from Apple. It was awful tasting medicine. But I guess the patient needed it."

At the Bottom There is Little Downside & A Large Upside

Martin Seligman of the University of Pennsylvania studied pessimism and optimism and told the media, "Pessimistic people are more likely to blame themselves for bad things that happen. They think that the unfortunate event will have an adverse impact on nearly all aspects of their lives." In contrast, the optimist experiences the same bad event as the pessimist, but they see it through an entirely different filter. Optimists are less likely to blame themselves for bad things that occur. They see it as a specific and momentary event and not as permanent. That is diametrically opposite of those walking around with a dark cloud hovering over their heads. Optimism has been found to make you healthier. In a recession, the optimist tends to look beyond the problems and focus on the future where the pessimist often gets mired in the mud of the present. One goes forward; the other builds a trench of remorse. This scenario was enacted in the mid-70s recession when Soichiro Honda ignored the advice to cut back and doubled production. Honda didn't make a lot of friends, but he grew disproportionally and it grew Honda from a wannabe to a major player in the automobile industry.

In the early years of Virgin, owner Richard Branson was unable to pay his bills. Many firms have been there before, but most cower and cut costs. They certainly don't expand into new markets. Branson's partner from childhood pleaded with him to file for bankruptcy or cut back. Not Branson. "The only way to cope with a cash crisis," Branson wrote in *Losing My Virginity*, "is not to contract but to expand." It led to the end of that relationship. Branson went out and bought a chain of pubs for nothing down. It was a cash business. Such businesses can be drained of their cash without it being noticed at first and the move provided the cash to pay his bills at Virgin Records. On launching Virgin Atlantic Airlines, a business he had no clue how to run or finance. His partner shrieked, "You're crazy. You're mad. You're a megalomaniac," and split. The dude may have been close to being correct, but Branson is now worth a few billion, not the partner.

Nikola Tesla was a renegade who had many bouts of near-dementia. The Serbian turned American was unable to sleep in any hotel room not divisible by three. In school, he had committed the logarithmic tables to memory, and could solve a differential equation in his head. When he started something, he could not stop, such as reading one of Voltaire's works led to reading all 100 volumes, and he broke down. The rebellious OCD had to compute the cubic contents of every meal prior to taking a bite of the food on his plate. He lived for years in the Waldorf-Astoria where he dined in silk ties and black tie and after dinner threw everything away after one wearing. In a state of breakdown, he decided to kill himself at the stroke of midnight on his 30th birthday, but suddenly his life was reborn when he sold his inventions to George Westinghouse. This bizarre but brilliant iconoclast mesmerized the media with his electronic wizardry. It led to his being cast as the mad scientist in the very first *Superman* cartoon published in 1941. Tesla would tell the media that he could bring down the Empire State building in a couple minutes and had a death ray capable of destroying 10,000 planes 250 miles away. Tesla told them if inclined, he could drop the Brooklyn Bridge in minutes. Writers depicted him a as a modern day Prometheus with supernatural powers.

Another woman who hit bottom and used it to make it to the very top was Mary Kay Ash. After being passed over by a man who worked for her due to being female, Mary Kay quit and built a cosmetics empire at age fifty. A parallel story came from Arkansas, where a young black girl who would be known as Maya Angelo was broken many times prior to making it to the very top. Angelo lived with her grandmother as she had parents who had split for California. At age 7 she was raped by her mother's lover and went mute. A caring school teacher named Bertha Flowers took her on as a project and used Shakespeare and Poe to bring her out of a self-imposed silence. Emerging from that internalized hell, Maya Angelou would become a best-selling author and poet speaking at President Bill Clinton's inauguration. She told the media about her transformation saying, "When I read Shakespeare and heard that music, I couldn't believe it."

The following list of poorhouse to penthouse stories shows that crisis can often become the catalyst for creativity. They are not some accident, but providential happenings:

Breakdown is Often the Fuel for Breakthrough

❖ **Mark Twain** was fired as a reporter for the *San Francisco Call*. Devastated, he considered suicide and retreated to a small California mining town where he wrote, *The Jumping Frogs of Calaveras County*. It would catapult him into a whole new career that ended up with him becoming the Father of Americana literature due to Tom Sawyer and Huckleberry Finn.

❖ **Carl Jung** was terminated by Freud as the head of the International Psychological Association and then went into a four year depression that he labeled "psychosis." It led to his most incredible contributions published as *The Symbols of Transformation* (1918) in which he spoke of Personality Types (Archetypes), Syzygy, The Collective Unconscious, Synchronicities.

❖ **Bertrand Russell** was fired from Cambridge for his anti-war demonstrations in the early 20th century. He then spent six months in prison, where he wrote *An Introduction to Mathematical Philosophy* and *An Analysis of the Mind*. As they say, the rest is history.

❖ **Soichiro Honda's** factory was decimated in WWII; with no way to get around, he attached a GI motor to his bicycle. The next week he was asked to put a motor on a friend's bike. Then others asked and soon he was in the motorcycle business and his factory had a reason to exist. Out of his personal chaos emerged a motorcycle empire.

❖ **Bucky Fuller** was fired when he was in his mid-twenties for being too innovative and not into the bottom line. The chaos of being fired on top of his daughter dying led to a death-wish. That didn't transpire and out of the crises and being unemployed emerged a man of the ages, a creative wunderkind that developed the geodesic dome.

❖ **Walt Disney** was fired as a cartoonist at age 19. Within two years, his fledgling firm making *Alice in Wonderland* cartoons had gone bankrupt. Walt broke down, tried suicide and out of the chaos would come Mickey on that train back to Hollywood.

❖ In 1968 **Arthur Jones** had his African film firm confiscated by the Rhodesian government with a contract out on his life. Jones landed in Florida broke, unemployed, and destitute. From that bottom position, came the Nautilus fitness empire.

❖ **Oprah Winfrey** was fired as news anchor in Baltimore. It led to drugs and an attempted suicide. She then took a job as a talk-show hostess and found her niche that has led to her becoming the Queen of daytime TV and a net worth of $2+ billion.

❖ At age 60, **Sol Price** was fired from his job in San Diego. Walking the streets he saw an opportunity for a warehouse industry and opened a suburban warehouse that would ultimately become Costco's; the father of the warehouse industry would be a billionaire by 70.

❖ **Sam Walton** was duped by a nefarious landlord and lost his first retail store in Oklahoma. When he handed the keys to his landlord's son, he moved to Arkansas where he would become the king of discounting; the irony of it all is when a Wal-Mart put his first store out of business.

Dissipative Structures – Crisis & Creativity

The above stories are not some accident of fate as was proven by Russian defector Ilya Prigogine. Ilya was enamored of removing the nihilistic concept of the 2nd Law of Thermodynamics that said "all things end up perishing in heat death." In *Order out of Chaos* (1984), Prigogine concocted a theory of Dissipative Structures to explain away entropy in the light of logic. It would win him the Nobel Prize for Biology. Science shows that when energy is introduced to matter, the disintegration process is bad, but during the transition it can be altered and matter can take on a higher organization. Entropy or a destructive force transpires but out of that breakdown comes breakthrough. An example is when we break a bone in our arm or leg. It will never break in that spot again after it has healed properly. This would become the basis for Prigogine's theory, but he took it to include the mind and emotional system. When they break, they also can re-emerge stronger for having had the experience.

Prigogine showed traumas can be attacked head on and altered to be a kind of fuel to the top. "All dissipative structures," he said, "are teetering perpetually between self-destruction and reorganization." When a person reaches bottom, what he labeled a "Bifurcation Point," it is a place where they will self-destruct or re-emerge better for having had the experience. It is true that many become caught up in the chaos and drink or sometimes die. They are so immersed in the fear and degradation they are unable to see the possibilities for success. That is why people become strange when depressed. They attend more movies, see fortune tellers, and escape in food or booze. In 2009, there was a 25% increase in Fortune Teller revenue in the U.S. The unemployed were found paying $100 per visit to have some mystic tell them hopefully, to hang on, as life will be okay. It has always been true that the fearful turn more to metaphysics than the intrepid warrior. Those that are more resilient are often found launching some new business or learning a new career to take them to a new opportunity. Prigogine found that when in a state of entropy, people either perish or rise above it all like a mythical Phoenix rising out of the ashes. As in the Phoenix myth, Prigogine was quite prophetic in his work. When Prigogine's Phoenix regenerated it would lead to magical healing powers with him saying, "All machines eventually run down and burn out. It is out of this chaos, turmoil and disorder that higher levels of order and wisdom emerge." Prigogine said that all breakdowns are a harbinger of breakthroughs, "Psychological suffering, anxiety and collapse lead to new emotional, intellectual, and spiritual strengths, confusion and death can lead to new scientific ideas." (Dr. Ilya Prigogine 1984 – *Order out of Chaos*)

Dissipative Structures have both a personal and professional dimension. The two nations annihilated in the Second World War–Japan and Germany--both were expected to grovel for many years. It did not happen as economists had predicted. The irony is that Japan and Germany not only recovered from their devastation by American bombs, but re-emerged far stronger than prior to their demoralizing defeat. Within thirty years of these nations hitting bottom, the Yen and the Deutschmark were the strongest currencies in the world. Even more shocking is that their GNP had become #2 and #3 in the world behind the United States. The 2008/2009 banking crises could have a similar heritage. By hitting bottom, it will force the industry to look in the mirror and learn from their debacle. Hopefully, American politicians will go down a similar learning curve path.

A further example of Prigogine's dissipative structure work is evident in the life and work of Russian novelist Fyodor Dostoevsky. Freud called Dostoevsky the greatest psychological novelist ever. He had been sentenced to death for being a radical young man. While standing in front of a Russian firing squad, he expected the bullets to tear him to shreds. Then out of nowhere the Czar showed up and commanded the firing squad to cease and desist. Dostoevsky was then sent to Siberia for ten years of hard labor. On his release, he wrote his brother, saying, "Prison destroyed many things in me and created the new, the escape into myself from bitter reality did bear its fruit." A year later he wrote *Crime & Punishment*, considered the greatest psychological novel ever. Madam Curie had a similar breakdown and breakthrough experience. She had a nervous collapse just prior to both of her Nobel Prizes for Chemistry and radioactivity and she told the media, "Nothing in life is to be feared. It is only to be understood." That is what made her capable of overcoming inner fears to become a legend in her time. A similar thing occurred just prior to Einstein's Nobel Prize for relativity. He had collapsed under the pressure and non-acceptance of this elegant theory. It had always been true, but the traditionalists had to have proof. Within a few years he was eulogized as the genius of the 20th century.

A similar concept of Dissipative Structures has been labeled a "Tipping Point." It later became the title of a book by Malcolm Gladwell in 2000. In contrast to Prigogine's magic place where we re-emerge stronger for having endured a test of our wills and survival, the *Tipping Point* has been described as that magic moment when an idea, trend or social behavior crosses some imaginary threshold and then spreads like wildfire. It is when you think your new idea or product is gone and then it suddenly takes off in a kind of magical transformation. It is when an epidemic hits, or an earthquake or devastating hurricane as Katrina did to New Orleans, and you find yourself at a crossroads, and then everything takes off and becomes even better than prior to the catastrophe. It can be that near-death experience that remakes us in a transformational way.

Lose Your Mind to Make Any Sense

The eminent Swiss psychotherapist Carl Jung broke down for five years in the prime of life. It could have led to the end, but it became the genesis of virtually his entire legacy that we use today in psychology. Jung was the President of the International Psychological Society when his friend, Freud, his mentor and colleague, broke off with him. Jung hit bottom like a rock in a lake and would go into a 5-year state of psychosis. Every single breakthrough that took place could be traced back to that few years when Jung was lost in his own reverie. When you lose your mind, so to speak, you don't have to pay much attention to existing dogmas or rules. It was during the period that Jung concocted his: *Personality Types, Archetypes, Syzygy, Synchronicities* and *The Collective Unconscious.* They all had their genesis while Jung was out of his senses.

In *Tracking a Finer Madness* (*Scientific American Mind* Oct/Nov 2007) Peter Brugger wrote, "Many believers in psychic phenomena," something Jung had done, "are also inventive. They bridge the gap between creative genius and clinical insanity." Brugger makes a strong argument for having a global perspective during such innovative periods. Being a bit mad and losing your mind permits you to challenge the system far more than you might if you were in your right mind. Most people are unaware that Charles Darwin suffered from an almost debilitating illness from the time he stepped off the *Beagle* where he collected the artifacts that led to the *Origin of the Species* and the theory on natural selection. Anxiety and hysteria were rampant in his body and it lasted until his death in 1882. Darwin once wrote, "Ill health has annihilated several years of my life but has save me from the distraction of society." His physicians concluded, "had it not been for this illness, his theory of evolution might not have become the all-consuming passion that produced *On the Origin of the Species.*"

The election of Barack Obama as American President has had a similar parallel that has been likened to FDR's New Deal. It is true that desperate people do desperate things. It was seen in the passing of Obama's $830 billion bailout in early 2009. A Keynesian spending mentality prevailed. Unfortunately, many in congress have little or no understanding of money and banking or the expansion theory of money and mostly no idea of the self-serving nature of all corporate executives. Studies show that 95% of all decisions tend to be self-serving. That was latent in their early decisions on the use of those funds. Studies show that many top officials used two-thirds of the bailout money to cover their own butts. If a troubled bank receives $500 million, they will first cover their assets, so to speak, and pay their debt down and the bad mortgages or loans. The balance will be given out to consumers looking for loans. It is too early to decipher, but the amount loaned out will probably be in the area of 25% - 30% of what they received. Money Supply theories say that the bank's ability to keep money flowing and expanding is crucial for creating new jobs and thus effecting unemployment in a positive way. The problem with the system is that people are making the decisions, and those individuals will absolutely take the path of least resistance. Their jobs trump helping the economy in every case.

Crisis & Creativity is Alive & Well

Most people are unaware that Disney's first great cartoon character was not Mickey Mouse, it was Oswald the Rabbit. Walt being a visionary was not into the fine print found in contracts. That permitted a nefarious New York distributor to take control of his first cartoon character and to hire away all of his animators. Walt was in New York trying to work out a solution with the disreputable distributor and while there, the guy was on the phone hiring away his California personnel. Walt was devastated when told he not only didn't own Oswald, but that his personnel now worked for his mortal enemy. Walt broke down, almost committed suicide, and on the train ride back to California he drew Mickey. The New York cartoon distributor was Jewish. For the rest of Walt's life he refused to hire one Jewish person at Disney Studios, no matter the skill or talent. The moral here is that had Oswald not been stolen, Mickey would never have been born. Walt's crisis would turn out to be his ultimate gain from a creative perspective.

A more recent example of crisis leading to creativity comes from the story of Fred Smith, the father of overnight package delivery. Fred was born with Calve/Perthes disease, a hip joint disease that inhibited his ability to walk. When he finally learned to walk without crutches, young Fred began to run. The cripple would become a high school football hero in his home town of Memphis, Tennessee. Fred's father died when he was age six. Starting out with no dad and not being able to walk without the aid of crutches left an indelible imprint on his mind. By the time he turned 15, he had a pilot's license. By 16 he and some buddies had formed Ardent Record Company. The high school entrepreneurs made money from two hit records, "Big Satin Mama" and "Rock House." After college, Fred became a jet fighter pilot in Nam. On returning home he cut a handshake deal with the Federal Reserve for shipping their money between offices. The ever-diligent Fred formed Federal Express immediately with all of his family's money. Suddenly, his turbulent life would come crashing down around him when they backed out. Fred now had a small fleet of planes with the logo Federal Express painted on their tails. What to do? At Yale he had written a paper on overnight package delivery. The Yale professor gave him a C for his effort saying, "The paper is well written, but makes no sense since if there were a market, the U.S. Postal Service would be doing it or the airlines themselves." Due to Fred's state of despair, he had few options. That is when he took a crisis and turned it into a titan. Federal Express was launched in April 1973, and Fred is now a very successful CEO and billionaire. Breakdown had fueled his breakthrough.

James Michener's story of crisis leading to creativity dwarfs Smith's-- James had yearned to be a writer at age 11. Without parents, he would write, "When you grow up at the bottom of the totem pole, you see things from a different perspective. Survival was my constant companion. I have lived my life as if it were all going to fall apart two weeks from now" (Landrum 2000 p. 65). Michener's dream of writing led him to major in English at Swarthmore College. That landed him a job as a teacher, but not a career in writing. By 30 he was frustrated, stopped teaching and returned to school to get a Masters Degree in Creative Writing. At 40 he still had not published anything. World War II broke out, and due to his education, he became a Navy correspondent stationed in the South Pacific. During one soiree, the pilot yelled back to him saying, "We are not going to make it. We will have to crash-land." It was on that fateful day when his plane crashed on the small island atoll of New Caledonia that Michener was transformed. It was 1944 and a shaken Michener crawled from the wreckage of the plane, went back to his quarters and wrote, "That night I discovered the unimportance of life. I was unimportant. I was set free." That night a transformed Michener sat down and began writing in his journal:

> *"I swear I am going to live the rest of my life as if*
> *I were a great man. I'm going to concentrate my*
> *life on the biggest ideals and ideas I can handle.*
> *I'm going to associate myself with people who know*
> *more than I do."*
> *Landrum, Literary Genius* (2000 p. 64)

The next day, Michener began writing *South Pacific*. It won the Pulitzer Prize for Literature and was made into a hit movie and Broadway play. Michener never worked again except as a writer of cultural heritages. Books like *Hawaii, Caribbean,* and *The Chesapeake* were about the heritage and culture of societies. It would become his life's passion since he had little knowledge of his own heritage. Tragedy had intervened and put Michener on the right track.

Anne Rice suffered a similar personal tragedy that would turn into an epiphany. Writing in her journal at age nine Anne said her life's goal was to become a novelist. This desire led her to an English Degree from Texas Women's College in Dallas. Fate led her to California where she earned a Master's Degree in Creative Writing from San Francisco State University. She and her husband, Stan Rice, lived in the infamous Haight-Ashbury days during the flower-child era and they had a beautiful daughter named Michelle. While Anne was still struggling to get published, Michelle was diagnosed with leukemia when only five years old. Anne was devastated. When Michelle died, Anne hit bottom and drowned her sorrows in six six-packs of beer daily. She ballooned up in weight and was on the verge of becoming an alcoholic. One night lying in bed she had an inspirational dream. In it Michelle was part of the living dead that have been chronicled as vampires. It motivated Anne to portray her dead daughter as Claudia, an immortal child vampire. The next day Anne got up, stopped drinking and started typing. The result would be her masterpiece *Interview with a Vampire* (1976). In this cathartic work, her daughter was cast as Claudia and would become immortalized as a love child. The demons within were suddenly cast aside and she was now a writer. It launched Anne's career after the movie became a hit that would make her rich and famous.

Many crises spawn transformation. No better example exists than the trauma of cyclist Lance Armstrong. When Lance was diagnosed with testicular cancer at 24 it looked as if his life was over. It had spread to his lungs and brain and his best friend's dad was a physician who told him, "Your friend's dead." When Lance was told he would probably die, he was devastated, but attacked the disease as if it was a cycling opponent. The Houston medical center told him they could not make him a cyclist again but could save his life. He asked for a second opinion and flew to Indiana to meet with Dr. Craig Nichols who told him, "They can save your life in Houston. I may not be able to do that due to my radical new approach, but if it works you will walk again and maybe ride again." Lance never even returned to Texas. Later he would write, "Cancer is the best thing that ever happened to me. Without cancer I would not have won one Tour." That is so telling because studies show that about 90 percent of people would have taken the life guarantee in Houston and been a cripple the rest of their lives. Another example comes from being fired and becoming rich and famous. Oracle's Larry Ellison is one of the richest men in the world. It would not have happened had he not been fired, not once but twice, first from Amdahl and then from Ampex. Walking the streets in Silicon Valley he came up with the idea for a main-frame operating system. That would not have occurred had he been gainfully employed. Ellison and his buddy Steve Jobs were both orphans. Both were eccentric wunderkinds who had lived with tragedy. Both became multi-billionaires. The bottom fueled their trek to the top validating that their breakdowns led to their breakthroughs. Most of us are not feeling very good when bad stuff happens. If we dwell on them it becomes a self-fulfilling prophecy, but when we use the ordeal to motivate it can prove to be an incredible fuel to the very top.

Chapter 13
We Always Get What We Expect –
Be careful what you wish for

Mental Mindsets are the Fuel to the Top & the Bottom.

"There is nothing so useless as doing efficiently that which should not be done at all." – **Peter Drucker**

"High Expectations lead to higher performance; low expectations lead to lower performance – the best managers have high confidence and communicate high expectations to others."
Robert Rosenthal and Lenore Jacobson Harvard study in San Francisco

Be careful of your expectations as those thoughts can have a huge bearing on what you become. Expectations fuel the trips to the top and to the bottom. One's expectations can be motivating or debilitating. Nobel-prize winning economist Milton Friedman was famous for saying, "There is no such thing as a free lunch." It is so true. There are always strings attached. When someone is picking up the tab at an elegant restaurant they are looking for favors – personal or professional. When a bar offers free food, they salt it heavily so you drink more. When the girlfriend asks you for dinner with the family after months of dating has an unspoken objective. The free lunch on retirement will lead a myriad of calls and solicitations on elder care or assisted living. To get a "free lunch" is to trade one resource such as "time" for "sales pitch." When we see the word FREE in ads we expect it be true. But it cannot be in the larger sense. This was further validated by Socrates several millenniums ago, "I say that money does not bring virtue, but rather that from being virtuous one can attain money."

We expect to be led and often become faithful followers of those in the lead. Be careful, there is only one view from that position and it isn't always pretty. Hired-hands always have that view and it distorts their perception and unfortunately causes even the most conscientious to become lost in a *Cover Your Ass* survival mode. Those that can tolerate such a life become tainted with a mind-malady that stifles their ability to be innovative. The short-run rituals become sacrosanct, and without knowing it, they become afflicted with the "now" disease of large organizations. In one sense, most firms are afflicted with the Ponzi scheme where they sacrifice tomorrow for today. This is why true visionaries and those with an entrepreneurial spirit cannot last long in a bureaucracy. If you are so inclined, get them to see the light or move on. Mindsets tend to ingrain us with a leader or follower mental map. Learn what you are and make sure that is your expectancy.

America came of age pushing the limits. Change was her ally. As she accumulated many assets and bastions of power she began to protect what she had won. I have written extensively on the zero-sum game of ventures. As we gain more we have a desire to protect what we have. This is true of organizations and people. Young firms would never put an attorney on staff as there is a better use of those funds and there is not a lot for them to protect. Once there is a substantial asset base the prudent ploy – so say most textbooks – is to protect what you have accumulated. The decision-making is altered radically when one has money and things or is older than when young. I have studied the most ardent visionaries and there is a pattern that defies what the herd does. Frank Lloyd Wright, Mark Twain, Thomas Edison, Buckminster Fuller and more recently, Rupert Murdoch and

Ted Turner defy such machinations. These visionaries kept on betting on their future dreams when most men had long since retired and stuffed their assets into some save haven away from harms way.

When on top, we often become complacent and stop dancing with dame innovation that brought us to the dance. America's lowered expectations became her enemy, just as they had been her friend. Expectations become a friend or sometimes the foe. We expect to be safe and we make very safe decisions. We want to keep on chasing our fantasies and ideas and we are not so inclined to sit in a rocking chair and count our beans. Japan had high expectations for mass production and low-cost leadership. America did not. For the affluent American, commodities were desirable. That opened up mass market opportunities for Japan. The land of the rising sun innovated in high labor cost arenas. America was far more interested in chasing creative innovations than in commoditizing original ideas. As a defensive measure, America began educating more lawyers than engineers – like 20:1 Thus she has become a highly litigate society due to placing law above engineering. Japan and China have far more engineers and physicists than lawyers, consequently the shift in the two societies.

An example of the production orientation of the East can be seen by the months of intensive work they put into taking ½ of one cent out of a part that never appealed to America. I have seen Americans work for months trying to figure out how to sell something for a higher price rather than lower the cost. Asians have a propensity to price products for long-term market share. America has no such inclination as the hired-hand mentality looks for quarterly profits and near-term rewards rather than future rewards. Asia would never even consider the term "creaming"--charging more because you can. George Gilder offered sage advice to those wanting to optimize their market share in a highly competitive market with his study of the East and West in this regard:

> **"Efficiency in manufacturing any product increases some 30% with each doubling of accumulated volume. With lower prices come larger market share, increasing economies of scale, rising morale and productivity, competitive breakthroughs, all in a growing spiral of diminishing costs and growing profits."**
> (George Gilder – *Spirit of Enterprise* 1984)

Success Imprints, Failure Imprints & Expectancy

In m dissertation *The Innovator Personality* it was evident that the truly eminent in the world had numerous 'success imprints' that were keys to their rise to the very top. I found things I was not looking for such as virtually all had self-employed dads. What did that have to do with rising to become a superstar? A lot! They looked at their prime role model and saw someone not punching the proverbial time clock, a man in charge of their own destiny. Over ninety percent of my subjects had self-employed parents. Then I found that every single subject in my early work had been the first born of their gender in the family. That surprised me. But I found that when you are #1 at the start there are imprints of leading that are left in your mind and heart. The first born tends to become voracious readers as they escape into books. Another factor popped out of the research. The eminent had traveled or moved extensively at a very young age. Einstein lived in three nations by his teens. Margaret Mead lived in 60 homes prior to starting school. Frank Lloyd Wright lived in ten states prior to age ten. Walt Disney and Amelia Earhart had attended three different high schools in three different states. It turns out that when you are faced with the unknown at a formative age you learn early on how to cope with the new and the foreign and suddenly become enamored of new things. When Margaret Thatcher's dad was told he would never have a son he looked down at her in the crib and said, "You are my son." She worked in his retail store and became his underling when elected mayor in their hometown.

The above findings were outlined in Profiles of Genius (1993). Malcolm Gladwell presented a similar theme in *Outliers,* something he labeled the Mathew Effect in which he argued that success is due to early patterns of learning due to many environmental influences. "There are patterns of achievement and underachievement," he said, "that stretch on and on for years." When an uncle tells an eight-year old "You are a real hard worker," it becomes an important imprint in the mind of that kid that will produce results far beyond the simplistic and kind words. When a cousin tells a 10-year old urbanite "You are going to become a gang leader, dude," that also leaves a impressionable ring in the mind of that kid. Our prisons are full of those with such a heritage. It was not an accident of fate or genetics that Pele was kicking soccer balls before he had shoes or started school, or that Jeff Gordon was competing on a track with his mom prior to entering school. Those enamored with Tiger Woods phenomenal success as the #1 golfer in the world lose site of the fact that it had far more to do with his early 'success imprints' than any other variable. At two years of age Tiger, a name that also had a strong bearing on his ultimate success, spent hours watching his dad Earl hitting golf balls. After a while the two years old started swinging a club himself.

Pygmalion Effect

Some label expectancy theory as "Pygmalion." One such study was conducted in the San Francisco schools when the nation was beginning to launch the Headstart Program. The psychologists were befuddled to find that a teacher's expectations were crucial to increasing the intelligence of the children but also their attitude played a significant role in the degree to which the children learned. Students that had a teacher that thought they were better actually became better and scored higher on IQ tests - an incredible one standard deviation of 14+ IQ points. It proved that a teacher's expectations are transmuted to the students. The same thing has been found with gung-ho sports coaches and with business leaders. Expectations are often a self-fulfilling prophecy. Studies show that a customer expecting designer jeans at $150 a pair to be more comfortable than the $39.95 Wal-Mart jeans are happier when wearing them. This suggests that expectations are far more in the head than in the pants.

Expectancy theory works both personally and professionally. The mind is not always objective, despite what we may think. Brain studies show that the way a person thinks and behaves effects their brain anatomy. We worry about falling off a bike and we are more likely to fall. We worry about getting hurt on a ski slope and it is far more likely to occur. Our thoughts leave indelible imprints in the brain. The cortex "cooks the books," so to speak, by adjusting its own inputs depending on what it expects. A Stanford study found that when "People expect expensive wines to taste better their brains literally make it so." Researchers at Stanford and UCLA told students, very bright ones, that they were taste-testing cabernet sauvignons ranging from $5 - $90. Although the tasters were told that all the wines were different, the scientists were in fact lying to the students since all of the wines were identical except for the bottle and label. What transpired in their rating of the wines? You got it. The students insisted the higher priced wines tasted superior to the cheaper wines.

A math study of elementary school students was labeled, *Bluebirds, Sparrows, and Crows,* detailed in *Empowerment.* (2006 p. 133) The study took place in an elementary school. Those most skilled at reading and writing were labeled "Bluebirds," the middle group was labeled "Sparrows," and those with the least talent labeled "Crows." The Bluebirds with exceptional reading and math skills were given very advanced courses. The Sparrows were given less challenging work and the Crows were expected to achieve less, so were actually given remedial type work. The Journal for Research in Mathematics examined the self-esteem of each group to see if there were any differences. The highest self-esteem was obviously in the Bluebirds. Wrong! It occurred in the top percentiles of each group. What does this tell us? Our self-esteem is dependent on the reference group in which we associate. How we compare ourselves is a function of how we see ourselves. What about low self-esteem? It occurred at the very bottom of each group. In other words, wherever you find yourself, just be the best of that group and your self-esteem will not suffer. But if you are at the bottom of any group, it will suffer greatly. In much of society today, we are labeled by the group in which we associate. That is the plight of our environmental situation. We become labeled by our place in society. That can be good or it can be bad. If you don't like your present label, then start working on altering it. Visionaries are prone to try and alter their environment to fit their needs. The weak and disenfranchised have a propensity to adapt to their environment. Think you are special, and you often are. Think you are not special, and it will become a fact.

An *Expectation Theory* study was conducted at the University of California at Riverside (WSJ Nov. 7, 2003) on scientists testing rats running a maze. The study put 6 scientists in charge of testing the speed of a rat running a maze based on past tests. They grouped the rats by superior - bright rats - and inferior - dumb rats. The scientists trained the rats for five consecutive days on learning tasks. The bright rats did better from day one and kept getting better – averaging 65% better - validating that bright and best is good in practical skills. Wrong! The head of the study had lied to the scientists. All of the rats being tested were identical based on past testing. The only difference was in the minds and expectations of the scientists that had somehow transmuted to the rats! Another study at Harvard studied 84 women that had worked for a long time cleaning rooms in hotels. One group was told they were getting exercise equivalent to having joined a gym. The other group was told nothing. Those told they were getting exercise lost 30% more weight, had lower blood pressures, and 5% less body fat than the control group. The mind was the master of their fates. An example of the mind at work to help or hurt comes from a Florida school system that has 5,000 employees. In 2008, they dispensed 10,000 tranquilizers. The message from here is, fix the problem stop drugging it. Expectations held dear are more likely to become a reality. Studies show those athletes that show up expecting to win most often do and those showing up trying not to lose end up losing. This was validated by John Diamond who wrote, "Your thoughts have the power to alter the physiological responses of your muscles."

There are not a lot of accidents beyond what is in the head of the combatants. Golf kingpin Tiger Woods once told the media, "I will my own destiny. My will moves mountains. I do it all with my heart. My goal is long-term excellence, not short-term gratification." When asked about losing that inner passion he told a reporter, "I believe I can win every tournament. The day I don't is the day I'm going to quit." Such an insatiable drive and mental state is what influences our success and our failures. The mind and heart have an incredible influence on what happens to us in business, life, and sports. In his book *Evolution of Consciousness* (1991 p. 140), Robert Ornstein wrote "We aren't consciously aware of events at the time they occur, but we think we are." He went on to say:

"Virtuosos in all arenas, women and men who produce at the edge of their ability, such as concert maestros, make hand movements much faster than can be controlled consciously…another mind takes over and doesn't ask questions, doesn't require any conscious direction."

Self-Motivation – Can be a Head Trip

"Heightened arousal enhances athletic performance. Even the fastest, strongest, smartest and most skilled," Dr. Alan Goldberg said at the 2006 Olympic games, "will underachieve if they concentrate on the wrong things." Kinesiology's John Diamond wrote on the essence of self-motivation, "If our Life Energy is high others will benefit from close contact with us; if it is low our relationships with others become part of the problem." What this says is that we do not have the luxury of hanging with losers or energy vampires. Studies show that it is why the effervescent Michael Jordan made his teammates better! It is also why losers often are found hanging with other losers. Check out the mindset of gangs. Futurist Ray Kurzweil wrote, "Soon we must look deep within ourselves and decide what we wish to become." That is profound. So few of us ever go within to find out what we are really about. Studies show that only 20% of us are introspective. A sage reminder hangs over the tennis court entrance at Wimbledon. It is part of Kipling's poem IF that tells those entering, "If you can meet with Triumph & Disaster, and treat those two imposters the same, you'll be a man my son!"

Eckhart Tolle validates this precept in *A New Earth* "There is only one perpetrator of evil on the planet: *human consciousness.*" Few leaders truly get the truth of those words. We become as we think and our thinking gets muddled by what is happening to us. Take a moment and think of the very worst thing that ever happened to you in your whole life. Stop! What is happening to you right now? How do you feel? Take your blood pressure. In medicine, they call it the *White Coat Syndrome* since blood pressures come in with a higher recording while in the doctor's office than at home. This is why poets have always tested as emotional and why accountants test as very insensitive. There is no right or wrong in all this except that we are all a by-product of our emotional state of being. When a rat runs through a maze and they get rewarded with some cheese, they run through faster next time. That says that all managers and leaders are in the cheese business. Sounds trite, but it is true. We always get the behavior we pay for. At Enron they paid for looking good at any cost, and their sales people recorded phony sales. Arthur Anderson was paid to check on such things, but was more motivated by huge consulting fees and perks. That led to approving the capitalization of expenses. In the short run, it worked, but in the long run the Enron's and Bernie Madoff's get caught. Most of those motivating such behavior are now inside looking out.

We Do Get What We Pay For

Be very careful what you are paying for since you will probably get it. All messages from the top have a trickle down effect. Few leaders realize how their ideas and policies get interpreted down in the trenches. If your message is to take chances, personnel will try new things. If you have an underlying fear invective of don't err, you'll never have a mistake, and probably never have anything done that is worthwhile. Remember, pay a premium over industry averages and you will get premium work. If you pay miserly wages, you will get miserly work. Pay premium wages and you'll not have much turnover. The beliefs we all hold are the direct result of all the thinking we are having, and a lot about what we have had earlier in life. Belief is a latent force buried deep within our minds. Those messages keep us doing what we are doing even when that may not be the best course. Some aphorisms in this arena are:

Pay for Nice, You Get Friendly workers
Pay for Normal, You Get Mediocre Productivity
Pay for Super work ethic, you get a maniacal output
Pay for Quick Profits, you get 'cooked books' ala Enron

Beliefs create our expectations about results and future outcomes. Expectations are active forces that ultimately determine our attitudes. An attitude once expressed, determines the behavior. As Mark Twain once told us, "Be careful what you want, you may just get it." Harvard scientists found, "High Expectations lead to high performance; low expectations lead to lower performance – the best managers have high confidence and communicate high expectations to others." Abraham Maslow told us half a century ago, "What is necessary to change a person is to change his awareness of himself."

The ending in all things should be the beginning. No one ever offered more prescient insight into the entrepreneurial spirit found in one of America's most insightful founding fathers, Thomas Jefferson. The voracious reader told us, "I cannot live without books. Books constitute capital. A library book lasts as long as a house, for hundreds of years. It is not, then, an article of mere consumption but fairly of capital, and often in the case of professional men, setting out in life, it is their only capital." Jefferson went on to wax eloquently on the philosophy of competing saying, "Fix reason firmly in her seat, and call to her tribunal every fact, every opinion. Question with boldness even the existence of a God; because, if there be one, he must more approve of the homage of reason, than that of blindfolded fear." These words paled into what I adopted as a Philosophical Creed many moons ago:

My Creed – by Thomas Jefferson

I do not choose to be a common man. It is my right to be uncommon – if I can. I seek opportunity – not security. I do not wish to be a kept citizen, humbled and dulled by having the state look after me. I want to take the calculated risk; to dream and to build, to fail and to succeed. I refuse to barter incentive for a dole. I prefer the challenges of life to the guaranteed existence; the thrill of fulfillment to the stale calm of utopia. I will not trade freedom for beneficence nor my dignity for a handout. It is my heritage to think and act for myself, enjoy the benefit of my creations, and to face the world boldly and say, this I have done. All this is what it means to be an American.

Dogma Destroys from Within

Market Myopia is rampant in America. Few leaders really know the nature or true character of their business. It is time to return to those things that made America great. Rockefeller, Carnegie, Ford, Edison, and Wrigley were willing to bet the safe present on a better future. That seems to have gone the way of the goony bird and replaced by quarterly short-term wins and profits. Studies on those that reach the pinnacle show that it does not happen overnight. It takes about *ten* years to gain expertise in any give discipline and another *ten* to master that discipline. Start early since it is a long and arduous journey. And there are no free lunches on the trek to the very top. The media told Sam Walton that his trek to the top had been an "instant success." In his Arkansas draw, the 44-year old said, "Yeah! But it only took me 20 years to learn how to do it." Such a willingness to take the time to make it big, the tenacity to keep on trekkin has been lost in most of the West. The hired-hand mentality has replaced those intrepid spirits. Their pay me now mantra has replaced the need for life's possibilities. The new mantra is "I want it now, and I don't want to take inordinate risks to get it." Well, we can't have it both ways. To gain eminence, we must embark on that Frost road, "Two roads diverged in a wood, and I – took the one less traveled by, and that has made all the difference." It is always destined to make a difference, but raging xenophobia interferes with such decisions for those afraid to take a chance. Machiavelli advised the Prince that, "Change has no constituency." Well it may not have followers, but it is the way of the leader.

What are those things America can do to bring back the fresh entrepreneurial spirit? What can she do to once again have the names of her products displayed prominently on the shelves of stores in New York, Frankfort, Paris, Mexico City, Hong Kong, and Rio? Change what you have been doing or you will keep on getting what you have gotten. Economists bash what is known as the "underground economy" where people are found on street corners selling their wares. Take a close look at India. It is growing with a larger underground than above ground. You'll find vendors peddling everything from beans to brass pots. A lady manicures finger nails next to a man sharpening nails by using a spinning blade on a moving bicycle wheel. It is true in all ports. Pilaporn Jaksurat, 33 lost her job at a Bangkok textile mill in late 2008. Did she wait for welfare? Hardly! She sat up a stand on a busy highway selling shots of medicinal wine and makes more--$10 a day—than she did in the mill. That is the entrepreneurial spirit.

Those with enthusiastic expectations fare better in a recession than those expecting the worst. The weak tend to show up at unemployment asking for help. The strong use the time to find a new arena in which to stake their claim. Positive mindsets get positive results and negative ones get exactly what they expect. The message here is to find a problem and use it to move forward and the world will be your oyster. Such verve is often demeaned by welfare types who remain in power by feeding the voters for free, but the price is votes. Ayn Rand decried such a system in *Atlas Shrugged*. Her classic in 2009 sold more books than in any other year. In her archetypal way, Rand wrote, "If you understand the dominant philosophy of a society you can predict its course." Is that true! Her "rational self-interest" ethic is at the root of all entrepreneurship. But political rhetoric preaches "selfishness as evil." It is not evil, but at the core of success and in Rand's words, "Selfishness rather than evil is a virtue." Here are Dr. Gene's tips for rewiring the head to get out of the Hired-Hand Affliction:

1. Relegate the need for *instant-gratification* to the trash-can of the past. You can't have it now and also have it later. For some reason this seems to be lost on those wanting it both ways.

2. Get *Humbly Assertive* - they are the ones destined to inherit the future so stop being so arrogant and imperial to believe that you are above getting in the trenches as well as the suites. Followers need to know the leader cares enough to go where they are and not above dealing with their dilemmas first hand. That happens in the front.

3. Leaders need to learn to *Sacrifice the Present for a Better Future*. Not many are willing to play in that game. They so fear losing what they have they worship at the altar of the quarterly

earnings and treat budgets as bibles. When sacrificing the future for the present – the consummate Ponzi mentality, there is seldom a viable future in your horizons.

4. Get **Qualitative, not Quantitative** Why? Because the world is not digital, it is analog. Start planning Quantitatively and operating Qualitatively since the opposite is not correlated with success or personal eminence. Plan with the numbers and operate intuitively.

5. Develop an **American Keiretsu** – a non-adversary relationship with banks, governments, suppliers, and distributors--that has been a detriment to America trying to fight Asian clan-like institutions. A group of individuals dancing to the same drummer succeeds far more than those with adversarial relationships hindering them on the way to the goal.

6. **When in Charge, Take Charge** – this simple attribute seems to have become lost on those attempting to make everyone happy. Leaders are paid to discriminate against those that would destroy the organization, losers, boozers, druggies, and the inept. If you don't know where you are headed, any road will take you on a trek to nowhere and leaders are paid to lead, yet so many seem to have forgotten that axiom of business success.

It is true that we almost always get what we expect. Participate in the negative media spin on recession and a bad job market and sure enough your world is likely to hit the skids and you may just begin to believe the world is sinking. Don't buy in to those media muckraking words as they are there to sell papers and magazines. Remember, the mind has the power to lead you to victory or to guarantee you will lose. The mind is the master of our fate. As we learned in an earlier chapter, we do not have the luxury of spending time with losers or whiners. Their mindsets infect ours. It sounds weird, but data now shows we get smarter by hanging in erudite settings with well-read people. One study proved that listening to a professor made you smarter – not because of anything he or she said but just because they mesmerized via a sage on stage mindset. The same thing works in reverse when hanging with the redneck crowd. Remember my aphorism that all truth is false with more awareness and learning. True happiness comes from chasing impossible dreams to improbable destinations. Go where others fear and you will never have a need to worry. Entering that place athletes label the Zone is about optimizing performance based on removing expectations. Those times when you can be without expectations but high focus is when the Zone is possible. Otherwise, it is not, due to our own self-inflicted mental needs and inability to focus intently on the goal. It is a kind of relaxed ferocity that few people ever reach due to unrealistic expectations and the resulting lack of focus.

This makes transformation a head trip, due to the mind interfering with the execution. When we are able to transform, we have altered our minds with few expectations but an indomitable will that removes all other obstacles to our path to optimizing performance. It is that ability to alter our minds to transcend the past ghosts that haunt us. This ability was documented by Dr. Edward Deming in his *Lessons for Management*. In his 14th point he wrote, "Put everybody in the company to work on transformation. It's everybody's job." What he didn't say is that to do so demands much work on their personal transformation. Until we can be a bit more of what we are not, it is more difficult to become what we desire. The transformational invective is, "What would you be if you didn't know what you are?" Most people don't have a clue, but it is true that we are the drivers of our destiny, thus take the wheel and go where you fear, where you have never been, where you would only dream of and you too will be transformed.

Expectancy and eminence are first cousins. Both are deeply rooted in a philosophical attitude that escorts us to the penthouse or the poorhouse. This has been seen from time emporium, from Plato to

Einstein to Warren Buffett. See the world in a larger sense and that becomes the fuel to their success. True visionaries tend to find where the pack is playing and they go play somewhere else. Why? Because they have found that the pack plays all games conservatively. They permit fear to be their master. Robert Frost wrote "Take the path least taken." He was right on the money. The Greek Diogenes is a primal example of this thesis. Diogenes walked the streets of Athens carrying his legendary lantern while watching the actions of men. Most were not good men so he became infatuated with finding just one honest man. Diogenes came to believe that human beings live artificially and hypocritically and therefore it would be best to study the dog. The dog performs natural bodily functions in public without unease, will eat anything, and makes no fuss about where to sleep. Dogs live in the present without anxiety, and have no use for the pretensions of abstract philosophy. The Greek with the lamp learning metaphor said the only "evil" was ignorance and the only "good" was knowledge. Pretty strong message!

George Carlin used wit to offer advice on what to expect saying, "The IQ and the life expectancy of the average American recently passed each other going in the opposite direction." Expectancy, he had discovered, has both an upside and a downside. No greater down was ever apparent than the tragic death of the Great Wallenda. In psychology, it has been labeled the *Wallenda Effect*. This is the story of the greatest high-wire walker in history. It shows so vividly how the mind is really the master in all things. Wallenda's widow told the media that during the months preceding his death, Karl had changed from a devil-may-care lifestyle and attitude of confidence to one of fear and precaution. She told the press, "He even checked the installation and construction of the wire himself, something he had never done previously." Karl's tragedy took place in San Juan Puerto Rico in 1978 while doing a tightrope walk between two buildings. Karl fell to his death and his wife told the media, "It was very strange. For months prior to his performance, he thought about nothing else. But for the first time, he didn't see himself succeeding, he saw himself falling."

Stop being a Hired-Hand and don the cape of a Superman with a dream. Change starts in the **Head,** gets transferred into the **Heart** and then triggers the **Will.** If you can will it, you can do it, and that is not just flowery rhetoric. Transcendence is that day you will take a giant leap from where you are to where you want to be. Dr. Gene's Transformation Credo is a roadmap for success. Remember, life is a cabaret and you are the one in the theater. This book is about sacrificing today for tomorrow so past truths must be thrown out like old garbage. And what breaks you can be the fuel to make you. Often we have to lose our minds to become more lucid with an ability to hang where the herd fears. Chase your bliss with passion and have the guts to chase your most fervent dreams. Cover your _Ass_ets and it is guaranteed you will become your own liability.

Dr. Gene's Transformation Credo

✗ *All truth is false with more knowledge* – to be transformed attack your fears

✗ *What breaks you, Makes you* – smile as you hit bottom; it's the path to the top

✗ *Get Crazy & Get Creative* – it leads you out of the mediocrity box

✗ *Find the pack and go elsewhere* – there are no wins where everyone plays

<u>Epilogue</u>

Personal Transformation – Fame & Fortune are Attributes of Positive Mindsets

Transformation is easy. It is a matter of altering the way we think in order to get what we want. Those suffering from a Hired-Hand affliction are not inclined to transform anything including their existing life. This is especially true in down markets. The media spin on bad leaves many victims in its wake. The message of doom and gloom becomes contagious. This book was written to help people look deep within to find their inner power. That power comes from playing various games that I have labeled, Bucks, Balls, and Brains, Passion and Attitude in order to have a handle on becoming transformed. One of the needs is to cast aside the Hired-Hand mentality lurking within. It appears that only about 2% are able to transcend their inner wiring to make a difference. Cover Your Assets is about tapping into the inner powers that will permit transformation.

Few people are willing to stop being what they are to be what they want. Most say they are but they are not. When the rubber hits the road they cannot bet what they have to get what they want. People talk a good game but play a different one. Few individuals that have made it to the executive suite are willing jeopardize that reality for a better one. Fear is the culprit. They are reticent to put their *money where their mouth.* Some think they are risk-takers. On a Vegas vacation they once put $100 on Red or Black or on #8 on a crap table. That is not the same as changing careers when things are amuck. Those that have chucked the Hired Hand affliction often say to their spouse, "Take this job and shove it" but not to their boss. Many would like to sell their house and split for Bali or the Virgin Islands to open a boutique or deli but can't go there. Joseph Campbell implored us to, "Follow your bliss." Life is far too short to remain in a relationship that is not working, in a job you hate, or in a lifestyle that isn't working. As I wrote in *Sybaritic Genius* (2001), passion is about being special:

> *Success, vitality and passion are one. Get excited over your game or don't play. Get excited over your job or become an entrepreneur. Get excited with your mate or find a new one. Get excited over your religion or start your own. Get excited about your lifestyle or find a new one. Will it be easy? No! But passionate failure is preferable to an indifferent success.*

The message here is that we are the masters of our destiny so take charge. When we don't we are leaving our destiny in the hands of others. When in charge, take charge is the mantra of those that have become transformed. Change or be changed is the ultimate reality. People elect to stay where they are but that is not possible in a web world where you will change whether you like it or not. If you are not moving up you will be moving down – relatively at least. The mind is the only real agent of all progress. Alter it to fit the map you envision. The path to transcendence is surreal. It's very difficult to see, touch, or understand. It is about zapping the inner Cover Your Assets affliction that we all have lurking within. Stop playing the games you have been playing and begin playing a *BUCKS* game with zeal; a *BALLS* game of taking chances; the *BRAINS game of* modifying mind maladies that keep us buying tickets to Safeville. The *ATTITUDE* game that guides us the *PASSION* game that charges our inner engines. The cartoon character had it right. "I've found the enemy. It's me!"

Transformation has everything to do with destroying the inner Tunnel Vision that warps our thinking and ability to overachieve. If we are able to use our Bucks as a tool, our Balls as a catalyst, our Brain as a change agent, and our Attitude to fit the trip then the Passion or libidinal drives will be in tune with the trip. We must come to the realization that we and we alone are the masters of our destiny. It is shocking how few understand this fundamental precept. Do you know what makes you tick? Do you have the courage to change what you are to what you really desire to be? Define it and go for it. The Transformation matrix is the key to altering that internal Oz that is in control.

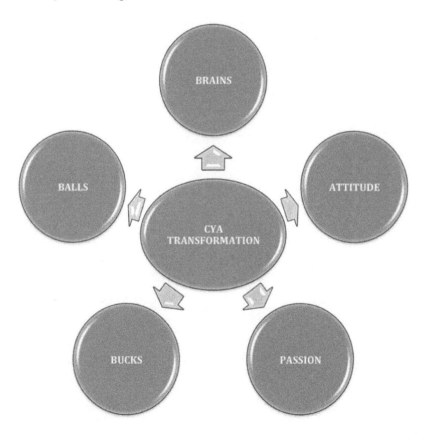

The following self-assessment is about using the above insights to transform a blasé you into a super-you —removing the Cover Your Assets contagion from your mindset. At the same time its cousin; the Hired-Hand Syndrome will be relegated to the scrapheap of antiquated leadership. There is no right or wrong answers in this conundrum. It is about delving into the inner sanctum of the mind to find a viable path for the fantasy trek to Shangri La. Buy a ticket on the transformational train or stop bemoaning the one you are on. Try to answer the following questions quickly and with the proper hat on. Women tend to answer differently depending on their professional or personal perspective. Think about the arena you see yourself in and then answer the question.

Transformation Self-Assessment – What Makes You Tick?

Answer the questions honestly and quickly. Sum up your personal score on each of the dimensions:
Bucks _____ Balls _____ Brains _____ Attitude _____ Passion _____

Total Score: _____

BUCKS ($ Temerity)

1. I'd rather operate my own business than continue working for other people?	1	2	3
2. When I play cards or other games, I enjoy taking chances in order to win?	1	2	3
3. Working on straight commission is okay even if I won't know when the next check will come	1	2	3
4. I would be thrilled for the opportunity to go white water rafting	1	2	3
5. For the chance to make big the real big bucks, I would quit my job in a NY minute	1	2	3
6. I can't wait until I get the chance to take flying lessons	1	2	3
7. I have been told I have a wild side that is often scary	1	2	3
8. I have never written a check before the money is in the bank	1	2	3
9. Trophies tend to be important; when I win one I display it for others to see	1	2	3
10. I have been accused of always trying to win no matter the cost	1	2	3

TOTAL SCORE _____

BALLS (Aggressiveness)

1. Just prior to any competitive game I find my stomach in turmoil and am anxious	1	2	3
2. I only play to win, not just to have fun	1	2	3
3. I prefer individual sports to team sports	1	2	3
4. The night before a big event or travelling I have trouble sleeping	1	2	3
5. Even as a spectator in a close match I can feel my heart racing	1	2	3
6. I hate losing and if I do it bothers me for some time	1	2	3
7. I have a hard time concentrating when I have many things on my mind	1	2	3
8. Friends say that I am highly competitive and can't stand to lose	1	2	3
9. I have been described as ambitious to a fault	1	2	3
10. Difficult challenges are a turn on rather than turn off for me	1	2	3

TOTAL SCORE: _____

BRAINS (Size of Vision)

1. On new projects I am able to see the ending from the very beginning	1	2	3
2. I enjoy imaginative projects that make my mind work overtime	1	2	3
3. I prefer people that are not very grounded with wild visions of the future	1	2	3
4. I've been told that I have my feet firmly planted in outer space	1	2	3
5. I prefer open-ended responsibility to find my own way in difficult terrain	1	2	3
6. I don't often worry about details as I prefer opportunities in my life and work	1	2	3
7. I like books in which I learn something rather than those that just entertain me	1	2	3
8. For me the quality of life is more important that the quantity – my heart trumps my head	1	2	3
9. Many times I have been thinking of a person when they call me, I have a bit of ESP	1	2	3
10. I actually prefer abstract art to portraits or landscapes	1	2	3

TOTAL SCORE _____

ATTITUDE (Esteem)

1. I smile even when things are in the gutter as I know I will persevere in the long run	1	2	3
2. If I screw up, I don't flagellate myself as I will get it right next time	1	2	3
3. When asked a controversial question, I respond without worrying of the consequences	1	2	3
4. I am not afraid of playing devil's advocate when something is incorrect	1	2	3
5. I feel good about myself most of the time and tend to smile a lot	1	2	3
6. I find other people complaints quite irritating	1	2	3
7. I never find it difficult to express my feelings openly and with passion	1	2	3
8. I have been told that I am too optimistic for my own good	1	2	3
9. I take confrontations as a part of life and don't see them as a challenge	1	2	3
10. When someone tells me NO it is a trigger to prove them wrong	1	2	3

TOTAL SCORE: _____

PASSION (Drive)

	1	2	3
1. I am driven to go the very limit in all things I attempt	1	2	3
2. Friends tell me that I am far too caught up in the ardor of the moment	1	2	3
3. I have been described as ambitious to a fault by fellow workers	1	2	3
4. For a new opportunity I am inclined to quit immediately and move to a new city	1	2	3
5. I get turned on easily by visual or sensual pictures or activities	1	2	3
6. My heart races when I see a sensual movie scene	1	2	3
7. I become aroused easily when dancing or touching a stranger	1	2	3
8. I often fantasize about being Shania Twain or James Bond or movie star	1	2	3
9. I have been described as very excitable by mere acquaintances	1	2	3
10. I have been accused of wearing suggestive or provocative clothing sometimes	1	2	3

TOTAL SCORE: _____

Bucks scoring: 24 – 30 = Temerity to burn; willing to bet it all to get it all
                             15 – 23 = Mid-range of willingness to gamble the present for the future
                             10 – 14 = Not a lot of bucks betting going on in this head; need to transform

Balls scoring: 24 – 30 = You've got Balls enough to transform many things
                             15 – 23 = Mid-range of risk-taking in order to get big rewards
                             10 – 14 = Unwilling to live on the edge; transform to get more balls

Brains scoring: 24 – 30 = Mind-Wired to transform the world around you
                             15 – 23 = Mid-Hemisphere oriented with ability to see big and little pictures
                             10 – 14 = Inhibition-laden, thus in need of transformation in this arena

Attitude scoring: 24 – 30 = Strong enough sense of self to be transformational
                             15 – 23 = Mid-range of believing you are invincible and self-sufficient
                             10 – 14 = Need more positive attitude to become transformational

Passion scoring: 24 – 30 = Driven with lots of energy with tumescence to transform things
                             15 – 23 = Mid-range with drive at times but ability to restrain it when needed
                             10 – 14 = Inner energy and drive not big enough to tackle big dogs; transform

Transformational Measure: 130 – 180 score and you are equipped with the attributes of a superstar

About the Author –
Gene Landrum, Emeritus Professor

Website: genelandrum.com

When it comes to geniuses, Gene Landrum wrote the book"
Naples Daily News, May 5, 1996

Dr. Gene Landrum is a Professor Emeritus from Hodges University. This high-tech start-up executive turned educator and writer has a penchant for the big picture and chasing new ideas. It led him to become the first President of the Chuck E. Cheese concept of family entertainment. After many years of interacting with creative and overachieving personalities he began writing about what made them tick. Dr. Gene's doctoral dissertation was titled, *The Innovator Personality.* It has led to many books and lecturing that included such events as U.S. Capital in 1998. Landrum has found a wide demarcation between those that achieve and those that would like to and it is the basis of his many lectures. Robert Toth, a sculptor with a creative flare from North Carolina wrote, "Dr. Landrum, I do sculptures on geniuses. You have been my inspiration from your first book, *Profiles of Genius.* Last night I stayed up all night reading *The Superman Syndrome.* Thank you, thank you, thank you for being my inspiration. My family thought I was weird but you have validated my life's calling."

Dr. Gene's Most Recent Titles:

The Innovative Mind: Stop Thinking, Start Being (2008)

Paranoia & Power: The Fear & Fame of Entertainment Icons (2007)

Empowerment: The Competitive Edge in Sports, Business & Life (2006)

The Superman Syndrome – You become What you Believe (2005)

Entrepreneurial Genius – The Power of Passion (2004)

Eight Keys to Greatness – How to Unlock your hidden Potential (1999)

General References

Anthes, Emily. (March 2009 p. 56-63). "Six Ways to Boost Brainpower", Scientific American Mind

Ariel, Dan. (2008). Predictably Irrational – The Hidden Forces that Shape our Decisions, Harper-Collins, NY, NY.

Ayan, Stever. (May/June 2009 p. 24). "Laughing Matters" Scientific American Mind

Barker, Joel. (1992). Paradigms – The Business of Discovering the Future. Harper, NY

Baumeister, Roy & Smart, Laura. (1996) American Psychological Association, Psychological Review Vol. 103 The Dark Side of High Self-Esteem.

Begley, Sharon. (2007). Train Your Mind, Change Your Brain, Ballantine Books NY, NY.

Boorstin, Daniel. (1992). The Creators. Random House, N.Y., N.Y.

Branden, Nathaniel. (1994). Six Pillars of Self Esteem. Bantam, NY

Buckingham, Marcus & Coffman, Curt. (1999). Rirst, Break All the Rules, Simon Schuster, N Y, NY.

Burton, Robert, MD. (2008). On Being Certain – Believing You are Right Even When You're Not. St. Martin Press, N.Y., N. Y.

Byrne, Rhonda. (2006). The Secret, Atria Books, New York, N. Y.

Campbell, Joseph. (1971). The Portable Jung. Penguin Books, N. Y.

Christensen & Raynor. (2003). The Innovator's Solution. Harvard Press, Boston, MA

Collins, Jim. (2001). Good to Great. Harper Business, New York, N. Y.

Collins, Jim. (1997). Built to Last. Harper Business, New York, N. Y.

Conger, Jay. (1989). The Charismatic Leader, Jossey-Bass San Francisco, CA.

Csikszentmihalyi, Mihaly. (1996). Creativity – Flow and the Psychology of Discovery & Invention. Harper-Collins, NY

Dawkins, Richard. (2006). The God Delusion, Hought-Mifflin, Boston, MA

Diamond, John. (1979). Your Body Doesn't Lie – Unlocking the Power of Your Natural Energy, Warner Books, NY, NY

Diamond, John, MD (1990). Life Energy, Paragon House, St. Paul, MN

Doidge, Norman. (2007). The Brain that Changes Itself, Viking Press, New York, N.Y.

Dweck, Carol. (2006). Mindset – The New Psychology of Success. Balantine Books, NY

Farley, Frank. (May 1986). Psychology Today, "Type T Personality" pg. 46-52

Franzini, Louis & Grossberg, John. (1995). Eccentric & Bizarre Behaviors John Wiley & Sons, NY, NY.

Frankl, Victor. (1959). In Search of Meaning. Pockey Books, N.Y.

Gardner, Howard. (1997). Extraordinary Minds. Basic Books, N.Y.

Gardner, Howard. (1983). Framing Minds - The Theory of Multiple Intelligences. Basic Books - Harper, NY, NY.

Gardner, Howard. (1993) Creating MInds. Basic Books - Harper, N.Y.

Garfield, Charles (1986). Peak Performance, Avon Books, NY, NY

Gelb, Michael. (2002). Discover Your Genius, Harper-Collins, N.Y., N.Y.

Gelb, Michael J. (1998). How to Think Llike Leonardo da Vinci, Dell Trade, New York, N.Y.

Ghislin, Brewster. (1952). The Creative Process. Berkeley Press, Berkeley, Ca.

Gilder, George. (1984). Spirit of Enterprise, Simon & Schuster, N. Y.

Gladwell, Malcolm. (2005). Blink. Little, Brown & Co. N.Y., N. Y.

Gkadwekkm Malcolm. (2008), Outliers – The Story of Success, Little Brown, NY, NY

Goleman, Daniel. (1995). Emotional Intelligence, Bantam, N.Y., N.Y.

Gordon, Jon. (2003). Become an Energy Addict. Lonstreet Press, Atlanta, GA

Grabhorn, Lynn (2000). Excuse me, Your Life is waiting, Hampton Roads Publishing Charlottesville, VA

Greene, Robert. (2001). The Art of Seduction, Viking Press, N.Y., N. Y.

Gross, Ronald. (2002). Socrates Way, Penguin Books, New York, N.Y.

Harris, Sam. (2004). The End of Faith. Norton & Co., New York, N.Y.

Hawkins, David (1999). Power & Force, Veritas Publishing, Sedona, AZ

Hawkins, David (2001). The Eye of The I, Veritas Publishing, Sedona, AZ

Heatherton & Weinberger. (1993). Can Personality Change?. American Psychological Ass., Washington, D.C.

Hirsh, Sandra & Kummerow, Jean. (1989). Life Types. Warner, N.Y.

Hitchens, Christopher. (2007). God is not Great. Twelve, New York, N.Y.

Huckting, Detmar (2006). Mozart, A biographical Kaleidoscope, Earbooks, Vienna, Austria

Hunt, Valerie. (1996). Unfinite Mind – Science of the Human Vibrations of Consciousness, Malibu Publishing Co, Malibu, CA

Iacoboni, Marco. (2008). Mirroring People [Mirror-Neurons], Farrar, Straus & Giroux, NY, NY

Jung, Carl. (1976). The Portable Jung. "The Stages of Life" Penguin, N.Y.

Kanter, Rosabeth. (2004). Confidence – How Winning Streaks & Losing Streaks Begin and end, Crown Business Publishing, NY, NY

Keirsey, David. (1987). Portraits of Temperament. Prometheus, Del Mar, Ca.

Keirsey, D. & Bates, M. (1984). Please Understand Me. Prometheus, Del Mar, Ca.

Hill, Napoleon. (1960). Think & Grow Rich. Fawcett Crest, N. Y.

Homer-Dixon, Thomas. (2000). The Ingenuity Gap, Knopf, N.Y.

Hutchison, Michael. (1990). The Anatomy of Sex & Power. Morrow, N.Y.

Jamison, Kay. (1994). Touched with Fire. The Free Press, N.Y., N.Y.

Kurzweil, Ray. (2005). The Singularity is Near, Viking, New York, N. Y.

Kurzweil, Ray. (1999). The Age of Spiritual Machines, Penguin, N.Y., N. Y.

Landrum, Gene (2008). The Innovative Mind Morgan-James, N.Y, N. Y.

Landrum, Gene (2007). Paranoia & Power, Morgan-James, N.Y. N. Y.

Landrum, Gene N. (2006) Empowerment, Brendan Kelly Publishing, CA

Landrum, Gene N. (2005). The Superman Syndrome, iUniverse, Nebraska

Landrum, Gene (2004). Entrepreneurial Genius, Brendan Kelly Publishing, Canada

Landrum, Gene. (2001) Sybaritic Genius, Genie-Vision Books, Naples, FL

Landrum, Gene. (2000). Literary Genius. Genie-Vision Books, Naples, Fl

Landrum, Gene. (1999). Eight Keys to Greatness, Prometheus Books, Buffalo

Landrum, Gene. (1997). Profiles of Black Success. Prometheus Books,

Landrum, Gene. (1996). Profiles of Power & Success. Prometheus, Buffalo, NY

Landrum, Gene. (1994). Profiles of Female Genius. Prometheus Books, Buffalo

Landrum, Gene. (1993). Profiles of Genius. Prometheus Books, Buffalo, N.Y.

Landrum, Gene. (1991). The Innovator Personality UMI Dissertation Service, Ann Arbor, Michigan

Leman, Kenneth. (1985). The Birth Order Book. Dell Publishing, N.Y.

Levitt. S, & Dubner, S (2005). Freakonomics. William Morrow. NY, NY.

Martens, Rainer, Vealey, Robin, & Burton, Damon. (1990). Competitive Anxiety in Sport. Human Kinetics Books, Champaigne, Ilinois

Maxwell, John C. (2000). Failing Forward. Thomas Nelson Publishers, Nashville, TN

Millman, Dan. (1980). Way of the Peaceful Warrior. New World Library, Novato, CA

Millman, Dan (2006). Wisdom of the Peaceful Warrior. New World Library, Novato, CA

Mills, David. (2006). Athiest Universe. Ulysses Press, Berkeley, CA

Moore, David. (2002). The Dependent Gene – The Fallacy of Nature vs. Nurture Henry Holt & Co., New York, N.Y.

Murphy, Michael & White, Rhea. (1995). In the Zone – Transcendent Experience in Sports Penguin Books, Middlesex, England

Orloff, Judith. (2004). Positive Energy. Harmony Books, New York, N. Y.

Ornstein, Robert. (1972). The Psychology of Consciousness. Penguin. N.Y.

Ornstein, Robert. (1997). The Right Mind. Harcourt/Brace, New York. N.Y.

Parkinson, C. Northcote. (1957). Parkinson's Law. Ballantine Books, N.Y., N. Y.

Peterson, Karen S. (9-14-98 pg. 6D). USA Today "Power, Sex, Risk"

Pickover, Clifford (1998). Strange Brains and Genius, William Morrow, N.Y.

Plimpton, George. (1990) The X Factor – A Quest for Excellence, Whittle Books, N.Y.

Prigogine, Ilya. (1984). Order Out of Chaos, Bantam Books, N.Y.

Richman, Michael. (Feb. 17, 2000 p. A4). Investors Business Daily "Sportswriter Grantland Rice

Rogers, Everett. (1995). Diffusion of Innovations. The Free Press, N.Y., N.Y.

Rosenzweig, Mark. (1971). Biopsychology of Development, Academic Press, NY

Senge, Peter. (1990). The Fifth Discipline. Doubleday, New York, N. Y.

Sheldrake, Rupert. (2003). The Sense of Being Stared At, Crown Publishing, NY, NY

Simonton, Dean Keith. (1994). Greatness. The Guilford Press, N. Y.

Siler, Todd. (1996). Think Like a Genius, Bantum Books, N.Y, N. Y.

Singer, Dorothy & Singer, Jerome. (2005). Imagination and Play in the Electronic Age Harvard University Press, Cambridge, MA

Small, Gary & Vorgan, Gigi. (2008). iBrain. Collins Living, NY, NY.

Stolley, Richard (2003) People Magazine Tribute – Kahterine Hepburn, N.Y., N.Y.

Storr, Anthony. (1996). Feet of Clay – A Study of Gurus. Free Press, N. Y.,

Storr, Anthony. (1993). The Dynamics of Creation. Ballantine, N.Y.

Sulloway, Frank. (1996). Born to Rebel – Birth Order, Family Dynamics, & Creative Lives. Pantheon Books, NY, NY.

Tancer, Bill. (2008). Click, Hyperion, N.Y, N. Y.

Time (1996). "Great People of the 20th Century", New York, N.Y.

Valentine, Tom & Carol. (1987). Applied Kinesiology, Healing Arts Press, Rochester, Vermont

Tolle, Eckhardt. (2007). A New Earth. A Plume Book, NY, NY

Walker, Harris. (2000). The Physics of Consciousness. Perseus Books, NY

Wall Street Journal. (March 19, 2009 p. 38). Wiseman & MacLeod, "Consumerism hasn't caught on yet in China"

Wall Street Journal (March 14, 2009 p. W6). John Newport. "Mastery, Just 10,000 Hours Away"

Wall Street Journal (March 14, 2009 p. W4). Patrick Barta. "The Rise of the Underground"

Wall Street Journal. (Feb. 27, 2009 p. B1). "Slump Sends GM to $30.9 Billion Annual Loss"

Wall Street Journal. (Feb. 26, 2009 p. A13). Samuelson, J & Stout, L. "Are Executive Paid Too Much?"

Wall Street Journal. (Feb. 19, 2009 p. B1). "GM Turns Its Back on Multibrand Strategy" Kate Linebaugh

Wall Street Journal. (Dec. 16, 2006 p. A11). "A Verdict on Sarbanes-Oxley: Unconstitutional," Ken Starr

Wall Street Journal. (Oct. 17, 2005 p.R1). "Living With Sarbanes-Oxley," Diya Gullapalli

Wall Street Journal. Hotz, (June 27, 2008 P A9) Haynes, "The Value of Not Overthinkging"

Weeks, David & James, Jamie. (1995). "Eccentrics: A Study of Sanity & Strangeness," Villards, NY, NY

Wickham, Pete. (Nov. 14, 1994). Naples Daily News – Scripps Howard News "Wilma Rudolph: Watching a friend die" p. C1

Wilson, Anton. (1990). Quantum Psychology, Falcon Press, Phoenix, AR

Wilson, Timothy. (2002). Strangers to Ourselves – Discovering the Adaptive Unconscious. Harvard University Press, Cambridge, MA

Wolinsky, Stephen. (1994). The Tao of Chaos, Bramble Books, CN

Index

A

Addictive personality ADD, 84, 119, 122, 170

Anxiety & fear, 106-107

Arrogance & Narcissism, 7-9

Ash, Mary Kay, 33

Attitude Game, 155-172

B

Balls Game, 89-110

Balzac, Honore, 117

Berlin, Irving, 72, 131, 157

Big T personalities, 90-92, 116-117, 140

Brain Game, 67-86, 153

Brain Fitness, 70-72, 76-77

Brain Plasticity, 72-74. 144-145

Branson, Richard, 55-57, 145, 171, 182, 222

Breakdown & Breakthrough, 12-13, 217-232

Bucks Game, 49-54, 65

C

Campbell, Joseph, 150-152, 190-191

Catherine the Great, 100, 119, 148

Change & Creativity, 215-216

Charisma, 179-180

Churchill, Winston, 22

Clinton, Bill, 105, 108, 118

Coco Chanel, 57, 187

Comparative Advantage, 4-5,

Concrete-Sequential, 197

Creativity, 148-149

Crises & creativity, 217-232

CYA Game, 1-19

CYA Leaders, 112

CYA Preamble, v

D

Darwin, Charles, 228-229

Dell, Michael, 58-59, 82, 113, 170

Deming, Edward, Dr., 65-66, 193, 249

Disney, Walt, 13, 50, 83, 96, 133, 170, 207, 210, 218-219, 225, 230, 238

Dissipative Structures, 225-228

Dr. Gene's Transformation Credo, 251

Dr. Seuss, 61, 205

Dumping, 101-102

Duncan, Isadora, 131-132, 148, 200

E

Earhart, Amelia, 140, 238

Edison, Thomas, 49, 61,99, 105-107, 115, 125, 145, 166, 181-182, 209, 217, 236

Educational divide East v West, 45-46

Einstein, Albert, 105, 114, 133, 157, 166, 199, 215, 228, 238